Michael
OWENS
and the glass industry

Michael Owens, center, with the first Owens Bottle employees. (Owens-Illinois Glass Company Records, MSS-200, the Ward M. Canaday Center for Special Collections, University of Toledo)

Michael
OWENS
and the glass industry

Quentin R. Skrabec, Jr.

PELICAN PUBLISHING COMPANY
Gretna 2007

Library of Congress Cataloging-in-Publication Data

Skrabec, Quentin R.
   Michael Owens and the glass industry / Quentin R. Skrabec, Jr.
      p. cm.
   Includes bibliographical references and index.
   ISBN-13: 978-1-58980-385-5 (hardcover : alk. paper)
   1. Owens, Michael Joseph, 1859-1923. 2. Industrialists—United
States—Biography. 3. Inventors—United States—Biography. 4. Glass
trade—United States—Biography. I. Title.
   HD9623.U45O856 2006
   338.7'6661092—dc22
   [B]

                                                   2006026283

Printed in the United States of America

Published by Pelican Publishing Company, Inc.
1000 Burmaster Street, Gretna, Louisiana 70053

To my grandfather, Finnerty, and Our Lady of Czestochowa

Glassblower with a foot mold, 1908. (Library of Congress)

Contents

Preface and Acknowledgments

When I began this book project, I was advised to spend my energies elsewhere. Several Toledo authors had tried over the years to write a biography of Michael Owens, only to find the paper trail too thin. First- and secondhand business and personal contacts have passed on by now. Michael Owens himself kept no records and used blackboards for his drawings. At Owens' request, no church records were kept of his many donations. Owens wanted no plaques to honor his philanthropy, and some of his many contributions at Rosary Cathedral remain unmarked. Most of his one-on-one cash donations were personal and given with the requirement that they not be revealed. Mike had told the local press that his family was off limits, and in those times such a request would be dutifully honored. In addition, a great deal of the available history related to his business opponents, who outlived him by decades. Some corporate records have been adjusted to support a collection of industrial myths perpetuated in the local press over the years as well. In the last several years, some new manuscripts have become available, such as the Paquette papers at the University of Toledo archives and the Thomas Hallenbeck manuscripts at the Lucas County Library. Kim Brownlee, of the University of Toledo, was critical in researching the corporate archives. The Hallenbeck papers include many handwritten notes of interviews with Owens' chief engineer, Richard LaFrance, previously unavailable to would-be biographers.

9

On the very first day of my research, I was blessed to meet Michael Ryan. He is a librarian at the Toledo Museum, and his friendly help was reassuring. Mike was a biographer's dream. The whole staff at the museum contributed to my research. Another helpful group was the staff at the Lucas County Library's history section. Greg Miller must be noted in particular for introducing me to the Hallenbeck manuscripts. I have worked with many local-history libraries over the years, but the professionals at the Lucas County Library are exceptional. The same customer service and professionalism was demonstrated at the University of Toledo archives. Without such help, this biography would not have been possible.

Being Owens' first biographer led me on many trips to Wheeling, Pittsburgh, and southern Michigan—all haunts of his. Owens left few footprints, but there were always a few pieces of new information. Homer Brickey, of the *Toledo Blade,* was an inspiration in his work to nominate Owens for the Inventors Hall of Fame. Hopefully, these new pieces of information in my book will bring this unique inventor to life for the reader.

Michael
OWENS
and the glass industry

CHAPTER 1

The Glass Age

Glass is an ancient material, but its use as a mass consumer material is attributed to Irish-American glassmaker Michael J. Owens (1859-1923). For almost two thousand years, glass had remained a specialty material of artists and craftsmen. Before Michael Owens, things like milk bottles, pop bottles, beer bottles, whiskey bottles, peanut-butter jars, and fruit jars were costly and uncommon.

To a large degree, Owens revolutionized the American diet as well as the glass industry by allowing for better storage and preservation of foods. Even pasteurization and bottle-feeding had to wait for Owens' commercialization of bottle making. His automatic bottle-making machine produced over twenty-four bottles a minute, compared to a hardworking glassblower, whose rate was one per minute. Such production rates changed forever the beer-making, food, and soft-drink industries.

In 1982, his automatic bottle machine was declared an International Engineering Landmark, achieving the same distinction as Edison's electric light bulb. In fact, without Owens' first invention for automatic glass-bulb production, Edison's electric light bulb might have lost out to the arc lamp. Later in his career, Owens similarly automated the production of flat glass, which also led to the development of automotive safety glass.

In 1913, the Owens Company received a letter from the National Child Labor Committee of New York, commending the Owens machine for its major role in the elimination of child labor. Also, because of the uniformity of bottles produced by the Owens machine, the Pure Food and Drug Administration was able to enforce laws that assured proper amounts for the consumer. The standardized height of bottles in turn allowed for the development of high-speed packing and filling lines.

It was prophesied at the start of the twentieth century that the names of the steel and glass industries would mark the century. The Owens name has been adopted in five corporate names— Owens Bottle Company, Libbey-Owens Sheet Glass, Owens-Illinois, Libbey-Owens-Ford Company, and Owens-Corning.[1] One of the fastest-growing community colleges in the United States carries his name as well.

Owens was bigger than his forty-nine patents and automated glass-making machines. Owens brought automation to all the process industries, years ahead of Henry Ford's pioneering assembly line for manufacturing. His early glass plants were centers of automation. He applied conveyors and moving lines for materials handling on a scale never seen before. He automated all types of glass-making machinery, including grinding and polishing machines. He even worked on inventions for his customers to automate beverage- and beer-filling equipment. He was a pioneer of cam-operated and gear-controlled machinery. Owens was far ahead of the automotive industry of Detroit in automated and process-control production techniques. In addition, his machines were some of the first-ever standardized equipment. His use of standardized gauges and parts was far ahead of most industries. He even pioneered the idea of timely calibration of shop gauges.

The machine shops of Owens' companies were the most advanced in the world. It wasn't just automation and machinery that he piloted, but management techniques as well. Owens took the organization of research and development beyond the earlier model of Edison into the twentieth century by developing project management and matrix management methods to innovate.

Owens looked at mechanical invention as art. He lacked all mechanical skills of inventors like Henry Ford. He rarely used hand tools. He could make few household repairs. He was neither an engineer, mechanic, nor scientist. He could not understand engineering drawings, and he was poor at drawing. He understood little of the chemistry of glass and the raw materials. He was as poor at mathematics as he was at spelling. Yet his designs were more complex than Ford's Model T or the Wright Brothers' airplane. His bottle machine weighed over four tons and had over ten thousand fashioned parts (even today's car has only about two thousand parts). His talents were vision and creativity. He stands with creators such as Thomas Edison, Henry Bessemer, and Steve Jobs. He would mentally design the most complex machines. For him, invention was a craft of its own, and he was a master craftsman. Like a master craftsman, he conceived the invention and put his shop to fashioning it. The best analogy is that of Dale Chihuly, the master glass artist, who no longer physically crafts his pieces but manages a group of apprentice artists. The finished piece is a Dale Chihuly creation but not of his hands.

Owens, like Edison, created one of the earliest research and development centers. Invention to Owens was the combination of art and creative thinking. He believed that the process of invention needed to be managed. Owens, however, modeled his approach on the crafts system. The process of invention was considered a craft in itself. Owens took on the role of master craftsman in his research function. The technicians were specialized and guided by the master inventor. Owens even talked of a "Venetian" research and development approach. Clearly, Owens was the Dale Chihuly of invention. In his later years, Owens was more fascinated by the process of invention than by the invention itself. In this respect, Owens took the study of invention farther than anyone had before, as well as established management techniques for the corporate research and development function. A biography of Owens offers as much to the inventor and manager as it does to the historian. Owens linked the new science of project management to the science of invention. With the help of Edward Libbey, Owens created the concept of a profit-centered engineering company.

Some see masters of glass such as Michael J. Owens as the lords of civilization; yet today few know his story. Alan Macfarlane, an anthropologist at the University of Cambridge, sees glass technology as a measure of civilization. He claims:

Progress in everything from astronomy to medicine to modern genetics would have been impossible without it. . . . Louis Pasteur would not have identified infectious diseases and launched a medical revolution. Biologists could not have observed cell division, understood chromosomes, or unraveled DNA's structure, leaving us bereft of modern genetics. Much of Galileo's work on the solar system would have been restricted to philosophy. . . . It was essential to the barometer, manometer, thermometer and the air pump.[2]

Macfarlane's statement overlooks what might be the greatest symbols of civilization—the electric light bulb and the mass-produced bottle, both of which Michael Owens is responsible for. Edison, at his Menlo Park research center, maintained a glasshouse and a number of master glassblowers, which were key to the invention of the electric light bulb. However, it took Owens to make the light bulb the commercial reality that would support the exponential growth of electrical power.

Macfarlane was not the first to recognize glass as a barometer of the advance of civilization. Samuel Johnson noted the following in an eighteenth-century article:

Who, when he first saw the sand or ashes . . . melted into a metallic form . . . would have imagined that, in this shapeless lump, lay concealed so many conveniences of life? . . . Yet, by some such fortuitous liquefaction was mankind taught to procure a body . . . which might admit the light of sun, and exclude the violence of the wind; which might extend the sight of the philosopher to new ranges of existence, and charm him, at one time, with the unbound extent of material creation, and at another, with the endless subordination of animal life; and, what is of yet more importance, might . . . succor old age with subsidiary sight. Thus was the first artificer in Glass employed, though without his knowledge or expectation. He was facilitating and prolonging the enjoyment of light, enlarging the avenues of science, and conferring the highest and most lasting pleasures; he was enabling the student to contemplate nature, and the beauty to behold herself.

Michael Owens represents one of the glass masters who influenced the very course of civilization. Owens was part alchemist, part artist, and part designer. He rose from the poorest part of American society, breaking many "glass ceilings" as he rose through management. His was a real-life Horatio Alger success story of the time, far more dramatic than those of Carnegie, Edison, or Westinghouse.

Owens was truly a multidimensional visionary. Unable to read or draw engineering prints, he envisioned complex machines and saw them to realization. Owens was able to combine the operational necessities of design with the demands of product marketing. Part showman, part operations manager, he could rival Preston Tucker and Thomas Edison as a marketer.

Owens was a man gifted with superior debating skills but cursed with a legendary temper. He managed with his fists as much as with his brain. His temper caused him as many setbacks as successes. He was a fiery union leader as well as a strict executive. His legendary smile and charm were disarming. He was a natural middle manager who inspired the potential of middle management. He loved the crafts system but changed the roles for both the workers and supervisors, thus transforming the glass industry into a factory system. Though he was no crusader for abolishing child labor, his inventions would do more for that cause than did the politicians.

Owens was a man who answered to no boss. His boss, Edward Libbey, actually had a picture of *Michael* hanging in his office. He could swear with the best of them, yet he was a devout Catholic who prayed daily. Owens was a workaholic who ultimately found escape in golf, car collecting, playing cribbage with the neighbors, and family vacations. He kept his life in two very distinct boxes—business and personal. With the exception of his friend Msgr. A. J. Dean, very few people really understood Michael J. Owens. He left no writings and kept no records. He drew on a blackboard, leaving no sketches of his many inventions. He cleaned his desk of excess material often, keeping no files.

Owens was a very private man, but one whose generosity rivaled that of the better-known philanthropists. He left a legacy of giving, but it is one lacking monuments, plaques, and engraved nametags, by his own design. His generosity can be seen in a beautiful altar in Rosary Cathedral in Ohio and stained-glass windows of a mission church in Michigan. They are all unmarked; in fact, Owens requested that the church keep no records of his giving. His mother had taught him that charity must be its own reward.

Owens' real generosity was invested not in buildings but in people. He supported the education of many priests without receiving any recognition. He handed out tens of thousands of dollars to the poor and needy in Toledo, requesting that they not reveal his giving. When many came forth with these stories after his death, it was clear that he was a one-man community chest. He spoiled his family to a fault as well. Also, to be a friend of Mike was an honor owned for life.

In the end, it was never about money but work. Owens found serenity in work and invention. The money he received belonged to God, and Mike was merely a caretaker of it.

Edward Libbey described Michael J. Owens on the event of his death in 1923:

> Self-educated as he was, a student in the process of inventions with an unusual logical ability, endowed with a keen sense of far-sightedness and vision, Mr. Owens is to be classed as one of the greatest inventors this country has ever known. He has done more to advance the art of glass manufacturing than any other person during the last fifty years. The results of his inventive power alone should win for him a place among those already enrolled in the Hall of Fame. As time goes on, I believe the name of Michael J. Owens will stand out as a pronounced example of what can be accomplished by vision, faith, persistence and confidence in one's creative efforts.

Most important, Michael shared Samuel Johnson's love of glass.

Michael Owens was the apostle and avatar of automated technology, process control, and continuous flow. He built model automated factories years ahead of other industrialists, such as Henry Ford. Owens pioneered the use of automated conveyor belts, electrical power, cam control, and moving lines. Two of the first glassmaking plants were models for integrated process control. Prior to Michael Owens, it would take weeks for a piece of glass to be produced from raw materials. Owens cut that time to hours. This automated, integrated, and fast throughput not only slashed labor costs but reduced inventory and delivery times. His glass factories were examples for all continuous operations, such as steel, oil refining, and even commercial bread making. His concepts of continuous production revolutionized the batch-product industry, just as Ford's assembly line transformed manu-facturing. He even invented automated filling systems for the food and industry, making their processes continuous.

Yet Owens was a true Victorian, who saw romance in science and industry. He viewed them as integrated in the "industrial arts." He saw management as a blend of art and science as well. The crafts model of work fascinated him, and he found in it a purity that automation seemed to take away. He was the ideal of the craftsman, who dignified work and the product of it. Owens found happiness and fulfillment in work. He was self-actualized, and like so many self-actualized people, he had trouble under-standing those who could not find fulfillment in work. Like most Victorian managers, he rose from the worker ranks, but he saw management as a special distinction. His management style was always paternal. Like many great industrialists of his time, Owens followed the leadership style of Napoleon, which he had studied from childhood. Loyalty and chain of command were central to his concept of organization. The "boss" or manager was to be a general. For Owens, managers made decisions, and workers exe-cuted them. The Victorian concept of management, while auto-cratic in philosophy, was paternal in practice. Owens had actually been a union officer early on, but he did not want to share lead-ership with unions in his plants. He believed in hard work to an extreme, expecting others to meet his high standards. Like the later Victorians, he feared and resented the rising class of college-educated managers. Still, he had risen to exclusive financial cir-cles where Irishmen were not normally welcome during that time. In some ways, Owens functioned in two different worlds and was never fully comfortable in either.

To understand Michael Owens requires knowledge of the material he so loved. Glass is mainly silica (silicon dioxide), which is the most abundant molecule in the earth's crust. Silicon dioxide is commonly known as sand or, as a natural glass, obsidian. Actually, volcanic obsidian consists of sand (silicon dioxide), soda (sodium oxide), and lime (calcium oxide) fused with iron and manganese, giving it its dark color. There is an entire mountain of obsidian in Yellowstone Park. Volcanoes are natural glasshouses producing an array of glasses, such as hyalopsite, Iceland agate, and mountain mahogany. Another natural glass is flint. Flint and obsidian became the material for the first human toolmakers. Paleo-Indians cherished their flint mines in places such as Flint Ridge, Ohio, which, interestingly, has become the center of the glass industry. These mines were the hubs of the first known trading routes and networks. One of the most unusual types of natural glass is a "fulgurite." Lightning striking and fusing sand results in fulgurites, and collecting fulgurites is popular in Alabama. Another natural glass is from space, known as a "tektites." While the stellar origin of tektites is questioned, glass is known to be common on the moon.

The History of Glass

The discovery of glassmaking is unknown, other than that it was a result of serendipity. The first written description of glassmaking goes back to Pliny (*Historia Naturalis*) in the first century. Pliny attributes its discovery to the early Phoenicians. The story suggests that a beach campfire formed glass. There, silica (sand) contacted soda ash from the fire and formed a hard material.

The earliest physical proof of manmade glass goes back to 4000 B.C. in Mesopotamia. Like the Mesopotamians, the Egyptians developed and improved the production of glass vases. The Egyptians were master glassmakers. They pioneered colored glass, pressed-glass pieces, and bottle making. The latter involved a much different process than that of Owens' day. The Egyptians cast their bottles and vessels in sand core molds, the way metal parts are sand cast today. They actually cast liquid glass into a sand mold with a sand core. The core created the hollow bottle. The surface of cast bottles was rough, requiring some finishing.

Once the bottle was cast, they might add designs by hot forming or pressing. Mold-cast vessels and pressed-glass pieces were found in the tomb of King Tutankhamon (around 1400 B.C.) in an array of bright colors. The Egyptians' knowledge of using metal oxides to color glass was amazing. Turquoise, cobalt blue, dark green, copper red, manganese violet, uranium yellow, and many other colors were common to the Egyptians in 1300 B.C. They also developed a multicolored, twisted color product known as *millefiori,* which imitated natural agate and onyx. Millefiori was a hot fusion or working process, where "canes" or sticks were fused together in a mold or around a shape. Using different colored "canes" produced the multicolored twist. One of the lasting impacts of the Egyptians was establishment of glassmaking as a "priestly" art. The technology was known by only a handful of clerics.

The Greeks seem to have improved lathe cutting and engraving of glass as early as 200 B.C. The Romans took glass applications a step further with architectural uses such as windows. They discovered the use of manganese oxide (known as glass soap) to clarify glass for superior windows. Excellent examples of Roman windows are found in the villas of Pompeii and Herculaneum.

Bottle casting remained the method of manufacture until the first century A.D. The Syrians appear to have "invented" bottle blowing, but archeology continues the search. These early efforts were extremely thin and more decorative than utilitarian. They also appeared to be free blown without molds, similar to what a carnival glassblower might do with heated glass tubing. The Islamic glassmakers applied hot pressing to increase the thickness. The thick mold-blown wine bottle can be traced to fourth-century France. Color had disappeared during the ninth and fourteenth centuries, allowing the product to have a natural green and bluish transparent color. This early European bottle glass was known as *Waldglas* (forest glass) because of the need to be near the fuel supplied by trees of the forest. From the Syrian and French technology of bottle making in the fourth century, there were no significant advances in bottle making until Michael J. Owens.

The Venetians took glassmaking to a high art with cutting, engraving, coloring, pressing, gilding, and painting. Their craft was in the priestly tradition of the Egyptians. The Venetians recorded their practices to pass on but only to a privileged few. The roots of Venetian glassmaking go back to the production of *Waldglas,* which of course was done in forest communities. Remote, self-contained communities became the centers of glassmaking. In the Middle Ages, the Venetian Council of Ten Doges moved most of the glasshouses to the island of Murano. The Doges created a prisonlike island, except that the craftsmen were well taken care of, even pampered. Venetian glassmakers were smuggled out around the world and interrogated for their knowledge. In other countries, Venetian glassmakers formed a guild known as *façon de Venise,* which means "made in the style or fashion of Venice." These guilds were key in passing on the secrets of the trade to following generations. The glass-mix formulas were particularly guarded. Only the glasshouse owner had them and personally supervised the mixing. None of the workers knew the amounts mixed. This tradition of secret formulas existed well into the twentieth century. The Venetian methods and work positions were the same that existed in Owens' day. Many of the terms and names used today are from the Venetian practice. Glassmakers of the nineteenth century like Michael Owens and Edward Libbey were first trained in the methods of the *façon de Venise.* They found a beauty in this approach to one's work, a beauty that is lost in the unskilled operation of automated machines.

Venetian glassmakers were the earliest to perfect a clear glass known as *cristallo* (meaning crystal). Soda-lime glass was the earliest Venetian composition. The recipe calls for calcined limestone, silica sand, soda ash (sodium carbonate), and potash to be blended or added to wood ashes, which contains both soda and potash. The composition varies, using 60-75 percent silica, 12-18 percent soda, and 5-12 percent lime. The glass produced can have a green tint due to impurities such as iron. The exact additions the Venetians used to clear the glass remain unknown. It is known that they used a much purer form of silica than is found in most sand. The Venetians handpicked silica pebbles from riverbeds for their whiteness. Eventually, glassmakers discovered the use of manganese oxide (glass soap) to decolorize glass. This basic decolorized glass was used in windowpane making and bottle making. Glass melting is facilitated by a much lower melting point than the component oxides; oxides of sodium and calcium that reduce the melting point of silica (silicon dioxide) are known as fluxes. Lime (calcium) glass is the cheapest and easiest to produce and form. The Venetians, however, had an extensive treasury of formulas. They produced all the colors of the Egyptians as well as inventing many themselves. One of these was an opaque white glass produced from the addition of tin oxide.

Even the basic ingredients of soda, potash, and lime varied widely among glassmakers. The English favored more soda than did Americans, which made glass more fusible in the melting process. It also produced a slightly yellow color and less weight. The Irish and Bohemians, like the Venetians earlier, preferred more potash and lime, giving their glass a slightly gray tone and higher hardness for cutting. The early Venetians favored higher lime and potash for clarity and hardness. In fact, they were the first to replace soda with potash. They produced the potash by burning seaweed. In central Europe, burning woods such as oak and beech produced potash. The additional lime also gave the glass hardness, which was necessary for cutting and engraving. The Americans' use of additional lime resulted in a hard glass and a related rise in cut art glass.

In England, George Ravenscroft developed flint glass in 1676. Flint glass derives its name from the use in the early days of glassmaking of calcined (roasted) flint minerals as the source of silica, but these flint materials do not really define flint glass. Lead oxide was added, and the lead content is the distinguishing component of "flint glass." The lead oxide content reached as high as 33 percent, which gave the product a very heavy feel compared to soda-lime glass. The lead addition also imparted a brilliant reflectivity and a unique ringing sound.

The flint glass recipe does, however, require the highest-quality sand to eliminate any green or brown tint from impurities such as iron. Ravenscroft found that a sand of this purity in the Wicklow Mountains of Ireland worked best, which started an Irish tradition in flint glass that remains to this day. Initially, like the Venetians, Ravenscroft used handpicked silica flints to assure purity. Most sand has natural impurities that tend to leave an unacceptable green or brown tint in glass, but the Wicklow sand was of exceptional quality. As a marketing tool, Ravenscroft segmented his market by advertising "flint glass."

Because of its beauty and weight from the lead additions, flint glass was said to approach natural crystal. This comparison led to the use of the term "crystal." This flint-glass process was used in the making of high-quality tableware, large punch bowls, crystal chandeliers, and scientific equipment. Most of these products also had wheel-cut patterns, thus flint or crystal glass became synonymous with cut glass. The cut facets increased the glass's brilliance. Other minor improvements were applied, such as the use of chalk in Bohemia, which produced even more reflectivity.

Ravenscroft discovered the importance of overall formula balance in producing clear "crystal." His early work with crushed flint as a silica source produced a "crizzling," a network of fine, branching cracks. It appears as a surface condition but reflects an inherent instability of the glass, causing decomposition. To fuse the crushed flint, Ravenscroft increased the potash, which improved fusion but caused more crizzling. He found that by substituting lead oxide for potash, he could eliminate this problem of crizzling. Ravenscroft then adjusted his formulas. Amazingly, in 1918, crizzling would be the major problem preventing Michael Owens from producing commercial window glass. The solution would ultimately be the same formula change used by Ravenscroft.

Colored glass has a long and complex history. Glass can be colored by metal oxides of elements, such as chromium, copper, nickel, gold, cobalt, and uranium. Basic soda-lime glass tends to take on a green or brown tint form impurities such as iron. The earliest colored glass goes back to 1600 B.C. in Egypt. A. Sauzay, in his 1871 book, *Wonders of Glass and Bottle Making*, noted, "The priests of Egypt, who were constantly occupied with experiments, made in their laboratory some glass equal to rock crystal; and profiting by the property they had discovered in oxides of metallic substances obtained principally from India, to vitrify under different colors, they conceived and executed the project of imitating every species of precious stone, whether colored, transparent, or opaque, furnished to them by the commerce of the same country." Recent research shows that the Egyptians had a monopoly on colored glass, and they sold colored glass ingots throughout the world. This monopoly would remain unrivaled in size until the arrival of Michael Owens.

Using copper, the Egyptians were able to produce an opaque red glass. Medieval glassmakers, using the Egyptian color technology preserved in the great records of the Benedictine monasteries, started a period of rediscovery. They added ruby red from copper, and by the 1600s, an alchemist used a gold addition to develop a rich ruby red as well. The Venetians invented a crimson-pink.

The first half of the nineteenth century saw an explosion of color in flint glass tableware. Bohemian manufacturers produced a deep yellowish green (called "Anne green") from the addition of uranium oxide. They produced an opaque black from iron and manganese oxides. A deep blue was produced from the use of cobalt. Other shades of blue were produced from nickel and copper oxides. Chromium oxide produced a green color. Opalescent effects could be produced from tin, arsenic, and metal fluorides.

Any biography of such a great glassmaker and technician as Michael Owens requires some knowledge of the production process, since Owens' legacy was to completely change thousands of years of glassmaking. The glassmaking process contains a special language that was incorporated in even the names of the jobs in the industry. The process that Owens started with in Wheeling in 1869 was not much different than that of the Phoenicians of the first century. The glass factory was called a "glasshouse." In Owens' time, glass was made in a "batch" of materials, such as sand, soda ash, potash, lime from calcined limestone, and recycled, broken glass called "cullet." Cullet played the very important role of reducing the melting time of the mix. This dry mix of components might include other oxides such as lead or oxides for color. The mix was done on the floor. In many glasshouses, such as in New England, the person who did the mixing was known as the "metals man." Molten or liquid glass in the furnace is called "metal." In some cases, the mix or metal was preheated to remove moisture, in a process called "fritting" or calcining. Lead mixes were not dried as a mix because lead oxide would cause low temperature fusion.

A furnace or "kiln" was used to melt these "batch" components. A kiln was a beehive-shaped furnace, which was fired by wood, coal, coke, natural gas, or producer gas. The competition of these fuels as we will see had a large impact on the career of Michael Owens. Wood was the earliest fuel and was preferred in the Venetian process. The wood had to be hardwood like oak, hickory, and walnut. Softwoods like pine supplied inconsistent heat and had a lesser caloric value. Generally in the eighteenth and early nineteenth centuries, wood was the preferred fuel until its availability was depleted. Coal replaced wood in Britain in the eighteenth century and in America in the nineteenth century because of a shortage of hardwood. Coal supplied cheaper and higher heat but with the disadvantage of dust and dirt. Gas was efficient and supplied high heat but availability was a problem. Gas and oil replaced coal starting in the 1870s.

The batch or mix was put into a pot and then into the furnace. With wood, the batch could take thirty to thirty-six hours to melt, while the higher heat of coal or gas could cut this time in half. The furnace refractory brick required special clay to withstand the heat. For most of the nineteenth century, this refractory clay was imported from Strourbridge, England, Bavaria, or special deposits in France. Later, excellent clays were found in New Jersey, western Pennsylvania, and Missouri. Refractory clay deposits were often a key factor in selecting a location for a glasshouse.

Inside the furnace or kiln, refractory pots were arranged around arched openings, each of which was known as a "Bocca," siege, castor door, great opening, or working hole. *Bocca* is Italian for "mouth." The floor area around the furnace is often called the siege floor.

The batch mix was added to each pot and represented a unique batch of glass. A typical pot held a ton of melted glass and stood four feet high. Libbey's first Toledo glassmaking plant in 1889 used for its pots German and Missouri clay mixed together by barefoot mashing. Pot makers were craftsmen in their own right. Pot durability was a major factor in glassmaking. A well-made pot could last five to seven months. If the timing was good, all the pots could be changed during the long summer vacation. If a pot had to be removed from a running furnace, the heat complicated the job of removing the pot. Old pots were cemented to the furnace floor by residue glass. It might take as many as twenty-four men, working in three- to four-men crews, a day to remove the pot. The Libbey Glass factory of 1888, which would launch Michael Owens' management career, contained a thirteen-pot furnace.

The "glory hole" was a reheating area to allow the continuous working of glass forms. The glory hole appears to be a nineteenth-century innovation, first mentioned in 1849 in a glassmaking book by Apsely Pellatt.[3] In most glasshouses of Michael Owens' time, the glory hole was actually a separate furnace used for reheating. In fact, one of Michael Owens' first jobs on the crew was to maintain the glory-hole furnace. Sometimes very small openings known as "noses" or "bye holes" (the older Venetian name was *Bocellas*) were used to reheat product in the furnace.

The glory hole was where the crew of workers (known as a "gang," "shop," or, in England, "chair") assembled to work a batch of glass. A gang or shop consisted of five to eight men. When Michael Owens started at Hobbs, Brockunier & Company in Wheeling in 1869, a shop was five men, but this varied by glasshouse and the product being made. The master craftsman and gang leader was known as the master glassblower or "gaffer." Becoming a gaffer was the dream of every young boy like Michael Owens who entered the glasshouse. Gaffers held the social status of artists in the community. They were highly paid and, in Owens' time, generally foreign born, having been heavily recruited by the growing American glass industry. The gaffer sat on a special

Boys at the "glory hole," where glass pieces were reheated before going to a finisher, 1908. (Library of Congress)

bench to supervise the gang. He had full responsibility for the quality and design of the product and reviewed the drawings of the piece before starting. Some glasshouses such as Hobbs, Brockunier, where Michael learned the craft, had assistant gaffers.

If there was no assistant gaffer, the second-highest gang member was the "gatherer." The gatherer represented the start of the blowing process by gathering glass through the Bocca. He used a six-foot-long iron blowpipe to "gather" a ball of molten glass from the furnace pot. The consistency was that of taffy candy—a sticky mass.

The gatherer or another gang member known as "servitor" rolled the mass of molten glass on a metal table ("marver") to form a ball. The gatherer, once the mass was rounded, handed the blowpipe to the gaffer. The gaffer was usually seated in a special chair (hence the origin of the term "chair" for a gang in England) because of the weight of the six-foot iron pipe. The blowpipe goes back to at least 1900 B.C.; pictures of its use can be seen on Pharaoh Usetesen's tomb. For free-blown art pieces, the gaffer would blow and roll the glass into shape. If the glass was mold blown, a "mold-boy" set up a cast-iron mold for the glassblower. Working the glass caused some cooling; when reheating was required, the glass would be handed to a "stick-boy" or "middle-boy." The middle-boy put the partially formed piece into the glory hole or a small side furnace to reheat it. These smaller "glory hole" furnaces began to be common and maintained a very high heat. The high heat caused the piece to be "fire polished," attributing to the smoother appearances of bottles made after 1880.

Near the completion of the forming, the gaffer or assistant attached a "pontil" or "punty" rod on the piece opposite the blowpipe. Tongs known as "pucellas" might aid the forming. Once the piece was near finished, the gaffer took the blowpipe off by touching the contact point with a water-cooled rod of iron, which allowed the gaffer to break it off. The gaffer or assistant might continue to form the piece using the pontil rod. In complicated pieces, handles might be added at this point. A "bit-boy" was responsible for attaching these parts. Wooden tools were often used for additional shaping. Again, several reheats might be required. Finally, the pontil rod was broken off in a similar manner as the blowpipe. The scar left by the pontil rod was known as the "pontil mark." By Michael Owens' time, a slight modification of the pontil-rod practice had evolved in which a molten bit of glass was used to attach the pontil rod and reduce the scar. At the time that Michael had advanced to assistant gaffer, the "snap case" tool was used, completely eliminating the scar. The nature and shape of the pontil marks are used today to help date antiques.

The last step was to put the piece in an annealing furnace known as a "leer" or "lehr." Annealing is required to relieve stress and reduce the possibility of cracking. The lehr was a tunnel-like oven that would slowly cool the glass pieces. A "carry-in boy" or "taker-in boy" carried hot finished pieces to the annealing furnace. After starting at age ten as a fire boy shoveling coal, Michael Owens at age eleven became a carry-in boy. A "carry-out boy" or "snapper-up boy" transferred the cooled, annealed pieces from the lehr to storage or shipping. Another entry-level job was "glasspustere," which entailed cleaning the blowpipes and blower's tools.

Depending on the type of glass, annealing might take days. Prior to 1880, firewood was burned and the lehr was filled with pieces and then sealed for several days. Later, lehrs used gas as the fuel and were sixty feet long. A conveyor moved glass pieces through in about twenty-four hours. Again we see Michael Owens, the apostle and avatar of automated technology, being the first to use conveyor annealing. Annealing was a critical and key step in producing all types of glass. Poor annealing could cause the piece to crack or burst simply if it were placed in sunlight!

Another ancillary job in some glasshouses was that of the "lip-boy," who would grind glass parts that did not meet customer specifications. This was one of the most dangerous jobs, requiring working the part against a water-drenched abrasive wheel. It was a cold and miserable job that the boys hated over all others.

The gang had its hierarchy, but it was not a progressive ladder. Blowing and gathering were distinct crafts, each requiring an apprenticeship and journeyman study. A blower apprenticeship, because it led to the highest-paid position, was difficult to enter. The blower apprentice was usually part of a blower's or manager's family. Sometimes, as with Michael Owens, a hardworking "boy" might be selected as an apprentice. The acceptance, time in learning the trade, and requirements of apprentices were set by a combination of management, union, and masters that varied by company. These guidelines were a constant matter of debate and struggle between the union and management. Once accepted, he might apprentice for five to six years to obtain journeyman status, which might require another five years before he became a blower. An apprentice was paid half as much as a journeyman but after a year was as productive.

Boys at the lehr, 1908. (Library of Congress)

A fifteen-year-old "carry-in boy" at the annealing furnace, 1908. (Library of Congress)

The Rise of American Glass

Surveys of the time showed glass craftsmen to be the highest paid of the period 1870 to 1880.[4] Skilled workers in glass received "at least two, and most often three times the wages of ordinary laborers" and "one-third to two-thirds more than many skilled craftsmen." For centuries labor made up around 40 to 50 percent of the total cost of glassmaking. Glass paid considerably more than the other major industry in the Wheeling, West Virginia, area—steel. One survey reported that in 1896, blowers earned larger incomes than did professors and ministers.[5] The highest-paying segment of the glass industry was the window-glass segment. Glassblowers lived in some of the best homes in Wheeling, which were monuments of hope for boys such as Owens. It is no wonder that jobs in the glass industry were competitive and controlled by lodges. Irish immigrants joined lodges in hopes of entering the glassmaking industry. There was a "glass ceiling" in the 1870s that restricted the Irish from advancing beyond the level of gaffer. Mike Owens would be the first Irish-American to break into the glass executive world of Anglo- and German-Americans.

When Michael Owens began his career, the glass industry had four very distinct branches, which consisted of: plate glass, window glass, glassware (lime and flint), and green glass (bottles and containers). Glassware, where Owens started his career, represented the largest segment of the industry. It was diverse, ranging from household glassware to expensive art and cut glass. New England Glass, Hobbs, Brockunier & Company, and Bakewell were examples of glasshouses in this segment. In 1879, there were seventy-three glasshouses in the segment, with an average of 173 workers per glasshouse. The next-largest segment was window glass. In 1879, there were forty-nine window factories, with an average of 79 workers. The green-glass segment was third, while plate glass was the smallest. The green-glass segment had forty-two plants and plate glass had four in 1879. Plate glass was a thicker, flat product for industrial and architectural applications. Polished plate was also popular in the front windowpanes of larger homes. Plate was a very different product from the others, since it was cast.

In 1941, famous war reporter Ernie Pyle visited Libbey Glass to write a journal of glassmaking. Libbey Glass at the time specialized in art and cut glass. Pyle's journal offers a rare view of glassmaking through the eyes of a writer and reporter. He described a shop as such: "You get the impression in a glasshouse of a real artisan's caste system, and it is simply beneath the nobles of the craft to do minor things. There is actually a sort of heraldry about making a fine piece of glass. In fact I think it would be nice if the 'servitor' were to bow when he hands the pipe to His Lordship, the 'gaffer.'"[6] The "caste system" frustrated early unionization efforts because the blowers, gatherers, and boys each had their own unions. With this system, workers at the glasshouses lacked the solidarity needed to pressure the owners for better wages and conditions.

In cut-glass work, a finished piece was passed to another artisan in the cutting department. Cutting glass actually goes back to the Romans, but the seventeenth-century Germans perfected the technique. Cut glass reached a peak of popularity during what collectors call the Brilliant Period (1880 to 1915). Ernie Pyle wrote: "All of my life up to yesterday, I had thought that cut glass was cut by a man holding a pencil-sized stick in his hand, with a cutting wheel on the end. . . . No, cut glass is cut by emery wheels, spinning rapidly around on a spindle. The cutter holds the glass against the wheel, until it grinds whatever groove he's achieving. So you might say cut glass isn't the right word—it's ground glass!" The cutting process could be done by a single master cutter or split up into three parts—roughing, smoothing, and polishing. The cutting, or roughing, was done using a rotating iron wheel that had water and sand added as an abrasive. In Roman times, sandstone was used for the rough cut. The use of a pressed-in design could reduce or eliminate this roughing step. Smoothing used the less-abrasive pumice powder or the older abrasive of emery, which is the mineral alumina. Polishing was done with a rouge or tin-lead oxide known as putty powder. Some shops used special polishing agents, such as walrus leather.

For more intricate and delicate designs, engraving was applied. Engraving (known as copper-wheel cutting) used a copper wheel with emery and pumice as the abrasive, pumice being a volcanic rock and a mild abrasive. Copper-wheel cutters were considered the highest level of craftsmen employed in the 1880s. These copper-wheel cutters or engravers commanded as much as six dollars a day (the equivalent of blowers at the time), while rough cutters earned three to four dollars a day. The copper-wheel engraver of the 1880s had to work with foot-driven lathes. A piece could take weeks or months to complete. Like blowers, cutters were controlled by an apprentice system, which forced low wages early on as one broke into the trade. The cutter apprenticed for about three years, compared to five to ten for a blower. The cutter apprentice did, however, require a higher degree of artistic aptitude. The popularity of cut glass mushroomed in the Victorian period. In America, the popularity of cut glass goes back to the presidency of James Monroe, who demanded American cut glass for White House tableware.

Flat glass was a much different product, especially in the manufacturing process. Michael Owens not only revolutionized the cut-glass, pressed-glass, and glass-container industries, he also changed the nature of flat-glass production forever. With flat glass, Michael was not the inventor; he was the visionary, project manager, and promoter. Flat glass consisted of two very distinct products—window and plate glass. Window glass was generally thinner and produced in smaller square pieces. Plate glass was more commonly used in large store windows. Flat glass was even more labor intensive than container glass in Michael's time. The earliest colonial flat glass was produced using the crown method (known as "bullions" in Europe). This first required that a spherical bubble be blown. The bubble was attached to a punty rod and broken from the blowpipe. The bubble was spun rapidly using the punty until it collapsed by centrifugal force. Further spinning produced a round sheet of glass with a crown ("bull's-eye") in the middle where the punty rod connected. The glass produced had swirls in it, which distorted light and vision. In addition, the glass surface was uneven. The process also left a distinguishing bull's-eye. Michael saw the first improvement on this method in Wheeling glasshouses of the 1880s.

The new method was known as the cylinder method, which was really a rediscovered Venetian technique. The Venetians had for centuries gone to great lengths to maintain secrecy of the cylinder method. Flat glassmaking operations were among those moved to the island of Murano to maintain better secrecy. Many techniques, such as the cylinder method, became "lost." By the 1700s, it is believed that French spies had cracked the secret. While the cylinder method only started to appear in the Wheeling valley in the 1880s, its first modern description appeared in French science-fiction writer Jules Verne's novel *Mysterious Island* in 1874. Glassmaking was one of the first endeavors of the characters stranded on Verne's island, as described below.

A hundred parts of sand, thirty-five of chalk, forty of sulphate of soda, mixed with two or three parts of powdered coal, composed the substance, which was placed in crucibles. When the temperature of the oven had reduced it to liquid, or rather a pasty state, Cyrus Harding collected with the tube a quantity of the paste: he turned it about on a metal plate, previously arranged, so as to give it a form suitable for blowing, then he passed the tube to Herbert, telling him to blow at the other extremity.

And Herbert, swelling out his cheeks, blew so much and so well into the tube—taking care to twirl it round at the same time—that his breath dilated the glassy mass. Other quantities of the substance in a state of fusion were added to the first, and in a short time the result was a bubble, which measured a foot in diameter. Harding then took the tube out of Herbert's hands, and, giving to it a pendulous motion, he ended by lengthening the malleable bubble so as to give it a cylindro-conic shape.

The blowing operation given a cylinder of glass terminated by two hemispheric caps, which were easily detached by means of a sharp iron dipped in cold water; then, by the same proceeding, this cylinder was cut lengthways, and after having been rendered malleable by a second heating, it was extended on a plate and spread out with a wooden roller. The first pane was thus manufactured, and they had only to perform this operation fifty times to have fifty panes. The windows at Granite House were soon furnished with panes; not very white, perhaps, but still sufficiently transparent. [Verne's formula of coke and sulfate would suggest a yellow tint that plagued French glassmakers of the time.]

Jules Verne gives us a beautifully described process. While the cylinder method represented simple techniques, it was able to reduce costs over the crown method. More importantly, the quality was dramatically improved, with the elimination of the inherent swirls and the bull's-eye. The 1880 industrial view of cylinder plate manufacture is very similar to that of Verne's. The shop or gang consisted of the blower, the gatherer, a snapper (also called a capper), and a flattener. The gatherer first formed a hollow ball of molten glass from the furnace, weighing twenty to forty pounds. In this case the gatherer used a blowpipe and blew the ball into shape. The pipe was then passed to the blower, who reheated the ball. The reheated ball was then blown and swirled with a great expenditure of energy to produce a cylinder ranging from twelve to twenty inches in diameter and approximately seventy inches long. A blower of cylinders could produce 120 in a nine-hour day. In England, the Chance Brothers required a year to produce the glass panes for the Crystal Palace at the Great Exhibition of 1851. The Crystal Palace consisted of a million square feet of 300,000 cylinder-blown panes.

After the glass blower created a cylinder, it needed to be prepared for flattening by removing the ends. The cylinder was passed to a snapper to remove both ends or caps of the cylinder and split the cylinder lengthwise. A February 21, 1889, article from the Tiffin, Ohio, newspaper, the *Seneca Advertiser,* described the operation.

The next thing to be done is to cut off both ends of the cylinder evenly and this is accomplished sometimes with a glass cutter's diamond, but usually this is done by wrapping a string of hot glass around the cylinder where it is desired to cut it off. The hot glass makes a crease in the cylinder and after it is removed a drop of water or a cold iron applied to the spot causes the end to snap off very evenly. The next step is to slit the cylinder, which is done by drawing a hot iron along the inside where the crack is wanted.

The half-cylinders are moved to the flattener, who reheats the glass and flattens it with a hot iron. Finally, the flat pieces are annealed in a furnace before packaging.

The Industry Unionizes

The production of flat glass was extremely hard work, rivaling any industrial labor. Jules Verne compared bottle production to windows in his novel: "As to bottles and tumblers, that was only play." The nature of flat-glass production gave rise to the most powerful labor organization in the history of the United States—Local Assembly 300.[7] The labor movement prior to 1865 consisted of secret local "lodges." In 1865 the blowers of Pittsburgh's Monongahela Valley organized the first glass union. In 1867 the gatherers of the Monongahela Valley formed a union, and by the end of the decade, the snappers and flatteners each did the same. The gatherers were more progressive and joined the national labor movement known as the Knights of Labor. Under the Knights' influence, the gatherers joined up with the blowers' union to form Knights of Labor, Local Assembly 300 in 1875. The major company involved was Pittsburgh's United States Glass. The union consolidation continued as the snappers and flatteners amalgamated with Local Assembly 300 in 1879. This national organization became known as Local Assembly 300 of the Knights of Labor, Window Glass Workers of America. The strength of this new union was that it unionized all the crafts positions—blowers, gatherers, snappers, and flatteners—while preserving their hierarchy. Local Assembly 300 used its organization to formalize the Venetian system.

By 1881, the Window Glass Workers had national control of all the window-glass industry glasshouses. Still, their leader remained Local Assembly 300 of the Monongahela Valley. Local Assembly 300 was the first to set production limits and restrict the grueling schedule. It set limits on the number of cylinders produced in an hour. Snappers and flatteners were protected as well. Furthermore, Local 300 formalized the summer vacation of two months. Traditionally, because of the unbearable temperatures in the glasshouse during summer, the yearly working period was often shortened by a vacation period. Local 300 formalized the production period as September 1 to June 30. Local Assembly 300 members also were neo-Luddites who actively opposed any labor-saving devices. The Assembly's bylaws forbade its members from working in any glasshouses with automatic machines. These internal restrictions on automation would force a split in the union as Michael Owens and others brought automation to plate glass in the 1910s. The split would be between machine producers and cylinder producers. Ultimately, the Owens machine shops won out.

Local 300 also was the first to formalize the apprenticeship system. The entrance into apprenticeship followed the lodge practices of earlier times. Only legitimate brothers and sons were allowed into the window-glass trades after 1882. Wages were also based on the caste system. For every dollar made by the blower in 1879, the gatherer received fifty-seven cents and the snappers and flatteners received twenty-seven cents.

Local Assembly 300 was clearly the most powerful union in any industry. Because of the solidarity of the shop, the union actually strengthened the Venetian crafts system. Local 300 was a fortress against companies trying to reduce wages for the lower crafts positions. The crafts system was its own Achilles heel, because it separated workers according to a type of social class, allowing companies to break the lower positions. Local 300 had resolved the issue and created a powerful model for crafts unionization. This model, adopted by the national organization, the Window Glass Workers, made them too powerful for any single company to take on. This led to the formation of a window-glass manufacturers' association, but even this could not counter the union's power. Eventually, the manufacturers formed an alliance with the Window Glass Workers, which allowed monopolistic-type control of prices and wages. The other locals of the flat-glass industry never fully equaled 300's strength, but they emulated its structure. Had other glass segment unions, such as the bottle makers, adopted the Local 300 model, the structure of the whole glass industry might be far different today.

The non-flat-glass workers actually made some very early efforts to unionize, but success was spotty. The earliest was the Green Bottle Glass Blowers of the 1840s in the East. Bottle glass was the cheapest lime glass. The name "green bottle" referred to the green color of low-quality bottle glass. Common impurities such as iron and manganese caused the light green color. The major area of contention for the Green Bottle Glass Blowers was the use of low-wage boys as "apprentices" for the molder position and higher gang positions. The local Green Bottle Glass Blowers of New Jersey, Pennsylvania, and Maryland did hold a convention in 1857 to form a "Grand Union," but they failed to evolve into a strong national union. Since the blowers lacked full shop integration (the gatherers had their own union), they lacked the power and solidarity seen in Local 300. Management could easily break blower strikes by using gatherers and ambitious lower gang members instead. The national effort of the Green Bottle Glass Blowers fizzled out, but locals remained until 1886, when the Knights of Labor absorbed them. Still, the highly specialized art- and flint-glass workers remained only loosely organized, behaving more as a crafts lodge operating in secrecy.

The flint-glass industry was considered a separate segment from the bottle makers, flint glass being primarily focused on tableware, housewares, and art pieces. The variation in the processes, such as pressing and blowing, and in skill levels created difficulty in achieving a strong union. Unions tended to organize by gang position; that is, the blowers and the gatherers each had their own unions.

The first effort to unionize the flint-glass workers was in Pittsburgh in 1858. The organization was known as the Glass Blowers Benevolent Society. The Benevolent Society continued as a secret organization without much success. Again, as with most blower unions, they lacked the ability to strike successfully against a company who would use gatherers or non-union workers of the gang to fill in.

It wasn't until 1878 that the Knights brought a number of Eastern unions together in the American Flint Glass Workers. This was the first strong union to address the art-glass makers such as Hobbs, Brockunier & Company, where Michael Owens was working at the time. The Flint Glass Workers reorganized in 1881 as an American Federation of Labor (AFL) union. Michael Owens would be involved with the Flint Glass Workers as a young man and would become an officer. The Flint Glass Workers unionized the art and cut glasses factories, such as Hobbs, Brockunier & Company, Libbey Glass, and Corning Glass. The Flints tended to be more focused on the apprentice system and schedules than wage demands. This focus was natural since the flint-glass industry best represented the artisan tradition of Venetian glassmakers. The Flints modeled their union on Venetian glassmaking principles. There was a feeling of superiority and pride in their segment of glassmaking. The Flint Glass Workers also organized in product specialties, such as oil-lamp chimneys, pressed tableware, and bottles, which they called "departments." The chimney workers represented the largest segment when Owens started in the industry. Prior to electric lighting, oil-lamp chimneys comprised a huge growth market in America. The Flint Glass Workers wanted to maintain the crafts model but were open to some automation.

Labor was the critical element of glass manufacture, representing 75 percent of the product cost, when Michael Owens started his career. Even with unionization, the working schedules changed little throughout his time. A glasshouse would have ten to twelve gangs (or shops). The gangs were assigned to one of two shifts (moves). The first shift might have two sets of gangs, one working 1 A.M. to 6 A.M. and the other 7 A.M. to noon. The second shift's gangs were divided between noon to 5 P.M. and 6 P.M. to midnight. Boys such as the fire boy, Michael's first job, worked the full ten-hour shift. Many glasshouses had a " knocker-upper" to walk the streets waking up gang members as needed, knocking on windows. Most glasshouses closed during the summer because of the heat.

The leading local of the Flints was Owens' home district, Local 9 of the Wheeling area, and like Local 300 in the flat glass segment, Local 9 of the Flints was the dominant local in the national union leadership. Local 9 pioneered unionism in a crafts system. The flint factories saw flat-glass workers as factory or production workers versus true craftsmen.

The concept of unions, of course, was inconsistent with the crafts system. Glass workers had always favored secret organizations and guilds, which respected the glassmaking process as a craft or art. The union's success depended on its ability to honor the hierarchy of the glassmaking system while standardizing working hours, wages, and apprentice systems. Wage increases were, of course, important, but the wage structure had to be sensitive to the craftsman's position and apprentice system. One of the abuses of the Wheeling companies had been the insertion of cheaper and poorly trained workers into skilled positions. Companies saw the tradition of the crafts as restrictive and expensive. Glass industry executives preferred the factory system over a crafts apprentice system. The union itself struggled with the crafts concept and its application. Still, it was obvious that the crafts model had to be honored if the industry were to be unionized. For strikes to be successful, all the glasshouse workers had to be united. While the union wanted to preserve the crafts hierarchy, it realized it had to dumb it down to achieve the solidarity needed to deal with management. The model that evolved allowed for the hierarchy of the gang but also allowed one to move up the ladder based on seniority. This prevented the company from putting in "blower apprentices" from outside the union.

The most unusual branch of the glass industry was the plate-glass maker. Generally, plate glass required less skilled labor, but it still remained an art when Michael Owens started his career in 1869. Plate glass was similar to window or crown glass except produced in thicker and larger pieces for shop windows, showcases, and mirrors. The real craftsmen of the "French pot" method of plate glass were the pot makers. The few plate producers imported their clay for the pots from France until 1900. The pots required many pluggings of the clay, to increase density. The plugged clay was then aged for three to six months. The dense, aged clay could then be molded into crucible pots. A pot could hold around a thousand pounds of molten glass.

A pot of molten glass was transferred to a casting table, where it was poured by hand into the shape of a plate. Pulling an iron roller across the plate flattened the glass. A hand-operated winch pulled the iron roller. The rough plate was moved to an annealing furnace (lehr) for three days. The plate was then moved to a twenty-four-foot-diameter grinding table. Moving the table under grinding wheels ground both sides of the plate. Next both sides were polished. Handling of the plates was difficult and labor intensive. Clamps and cranes facilitated the handling. Finally the glass was hand cut into panes.

Plate-glass making was a highly labor intensive process, but the skill level was low. It lent itself to the factory system of heavy supervision with unskilled labor. Flat-glass production was growing along with the population. In 1887, the Chance Brothers of England improved the plate-glass casting method with the help of steel inventor Henry Bessemer. Michael J. Owens would in the 1910s help automate and revolutionize this branch of the industry as well.

The hand-blown or mold-blown bottle market was experiencing growth throughout the period 1860 to 1900 also. This "green bottle" industry was separate from art-glass or flint manufacturing due to the lower quality of glass used for bottles. Generally the inherent colors of green or brown were acceptable for most products.

Bottles were mainly used as alcohol containers in the nineteenth century. The Bininger family grocery store in New York popularized bottles for whiskey in the 1820s. One of the most popular glass bottles was "log cabin bottles" used for alcohol in the 1840s. Whitney Glass of New Jersey produced these souvenir-type bottles for E. B. Booz, a Philadelphia distiller. Booz was an active supporter of William Henry Harrison's presidential campaign, and he made the log cabin bottle an American icon. He is the source of our word "booze" for liquor. Whitney Glass was the oldest bottle company in the United States, tracing its heritage back to Casper Wistar in 1738. Interestingly, Owens would purchase Whitney in 1918 and make it one of the most automated plants of the 1920s.

By the 1860s, whiskey was commonly sold in pocket and picnic flasks. The Revenue Tax Act of 1862 created demand for the "bitters" bottle. It put a higher tax on alcoholic beverages than medicines. Bitters were listed as medicine, being a mix of herbs and alcohol. Actually, bitters were very high proof. These bitters claimed all kinds of cures, but they were mainly purchased for their alcohol. The famous "Dr. Hostetter's stomach bitters" was purchased for Union soldiers in large quantities during the Civil War. Gin "bitters" were also a popular "medicine" in square bottles.

Henry Heinz started to bottle catsup during this period as well. Another application was fruit jars, which started to prosper with the invention of the Mason jar in 1858. The Mason jar used a

Three boys and their father, all of whom worked at a West Virginia glass factory, 1908. (Library of Congress)

screw zinc lid to close the screw-type jar. The popularity of the Mason jar in the 1880s helped to standardize molds in the glass industry. Bottles and jars would require Owens' automatic machine to open up the full potential of the market.

While the demand for and usage of glass had increased throughout the 1800s, the "industry" in which Michael Owens began his career in 1869 was small and fractionalized. It represented a cottage industry. Capital requirements were rather small, and few major corporations in the industry existed. New England Glass was an exception, but no fortunes had been made in glassmaking. The glass industry of 1870 was concentrated in the areas of New England, New Jersey, Pittsburgh, and the West Virginia panhandle. Pittsburgh was considered the glass capital, with thirty-three glasshouses in 1870. Most companies were small proprietorships or partnerships and many were short-lived, ending in bankruptcies or partnership breakups. Glasshouse fires were common and led to very high insurance rates. Still, 1870 saw the rise of glass corporations among older companies. Two of these great corporations, New England Glass (Libbey Glass) and Hobbs, Brockunier & Company, would mold a young Michael J. Owens.

CHAPTER 2

American Glass: Libbey

It is hard for any biographer to separate the lives of Michael J. Owens and Edward D. Libbey. They represent a unique symbiotic partnership. E. William Fairfield, Libbey Glass historian, described it best:

> Once in a great while, there occurs a partnership between two men, so talented and equipped to supplement one another in an enterprise that, in retrospect, their success seems almost preordained. Like the warp and woof of cloth, the individual bents of their minds, their personalities, and characters weave a pattern of success. This was the rare alchemy in the partnership.

By their deaths, that partnership would be embodied in a mythical, pseudo-corporation that controlled most of the American glass industry. Yet they were never close friends, nor did they travel in the same social circles. Libbey the Englishman and Owens the Irishman formed an alliance in an age when the English and Irish did not mix. They were both generous but approached that virtue from different points of view. For Libbey, charity came with his social standing; for Owens, it was derived from his religious roots. Libbey loved paintings and art; Owens preferred utilitarian decorations. Libbey saw money as social infrastructure, while Owens viewed it in terms of what it could do. The two men's relationship was founded in Libbey Glass of Toledo.

Edward D. Libbey, 1880. (Owens-Illinois Glass Company Records, MSS-200, the Ward M. Canaday Center for Special Collections, University of Toledo)

History is a defining discipline in studying and understanding the revolutionary advances of Michael Owens. History was also a love of Michael Owens, and from his boyhood throughout his life he often read about the progress of civilization. He particularly enjoyed biographies of great generals, such as Napoleon, Grant, and Lee.

Michael Owens' life was really shaped by two great rivers of influence—Libbey Glass and his own glassmaking experiences. What makes the story so powerful is that both rivers have the same source—Libbey Glass. Libbey Glass itself has deep roots, representing the whole history of American glass. It was the cradle of American glassmakers, and its history changed the nature of glassmaking forever.

American glassmaking dates back to the very first colony at Jamestown. A group of Dutch and Polish glassmakers was sent to the small colony in 1608, and Capt. John Smith said this would be essential for civilizing the New World. While the Spanish sought to establish gold mines there, England searched for glassmaking sites. British restrictions on the use of wood as fuel spurred an interest in the fuel-rich colonies as a base for glassmaking. In 1621, a second Jamestown glassworks was established by smuggling six Italian glassmakers and their secrets out of Venice.

The first significant American retail manufacturer of glass was established near Boston in the 1750s. On July 14, 1752, the *Boston Globe* reported the arrival of 300 glassmakers from Germany, "skilled in the making of Glass, of various sorts," and that "a House proper for carrying on that useful manufacture, will be erected in Germantown [Braintree] as soon as possible." The factory actually became a popular tourist attraction, with the owners charging a shilling admission fee. The major products were flat glass and bottles. The German glassblowers could produce about 720 various bottles a day (a standard that would remain until Michael Owens), but bottle making remained unprofitable. A small profit was made on flat glass, but the company failed in 1762. A number of flat-glass producers did thrive, such as Casper Wistar's factory in New Jersey. Window glass represented a steady growth market in the house-hungry colonies, but bottle making was very cyclic.

The torch of bottle making passed to "Baron" Stiegel in Pennsylvania, who targeted the higher end of the glass business, that of flint (leaded) glass for beauty. Stiegel had come from Cologne, Germany to start work at Elizabeth Iron Furnace in Lancaster County outside of Philadelphia. Within six years, through marriages and deaths, he ended up owning the furnace. A few years later he added a glassworks. The Baron's extravagant lifestyle caused his bankruptcy and imprisonment—and an end to American flint glass. Stiegel glass had become prized as flint glass, but later chemical tests show most of his so-called flint glass was actually soda-lime glass.[1] One area that Stiegel seems to have pioneered is mold-blown glass. Stiegel started using wooden molds to blow the rough shape, thus speeding the manufacturing. Another area of Stiegel innovation was the use of color. His recipes included cobalt oxides to produce rich blue, manganese oxides to produce a violet, and copper additions for a deep green. Probably predating the Baron in flint-glass making was Wistar at his New Jersey factory. Wistar was using lead to clarify window glass. Wistar's plant would represent the American beginning of domestic glassblowers on a par with Europe.

Besides flint glass, both Wistar and Stiegel were supplying the growing bottle market. This market evolved out of an infant beer and whiskey industry in America. Western Pennsylvania was at the heart of the emerging whiskey industry. The production spurred the rise of bottle-making enterprises in the 1790s around Pittsburgh. Another promoter of bottle making was Thomas Jefferson, who started a beer-brewing operation at Monticello in 1810. Jefferson bottled his beer in quart bottles, which were always in short supply. In a letter to a New York glassmaker, Jefferson noted: "I am now engaged in brewing a year's supply of malt strong beer, which however I have no chance of saving but by a supply of quart jugs from you."[2] Eventually, Jefferson even experimented with glassmaking at Monticello. Brewing, construction, and art pieces were creating a boom for glassmakers in the early 1800s.

After the failure at Braintree, 300 German glassmakers were incorporated into a number of glassmaking operations. These glassmakers spread throughout the New England colonies, bringing their expertise to the fledgling American glass industry. One of those early companies was the Boston Crown Glass Company. They made window glass for the growing American market in the early 1800s. This kind of glass was low quality but represented the largest part of the market. This company, however, boasted one of the first glass masters in America, Englishman Thomas Cains. He would become the dean of future American glassmakers. Even as New England developed its industry, America remained dependent on imported glassmakers. As late as the 1860s, agents were sent to Europe to recruit glassmakers.

Cains had been born in Bristol and trained in glassmaking there. He convinced the Boston Crown Glass owners to expand into cut glass and art glass. At the start, however, the company gave Cains only an idle building and an experimental six-pot furnace. He taught these Germans how to make lead-crystal art pieces. The actual production of flint or lead crystal goes back to 1676 in England. The English had rediscovered the sixteenth-century Venetian flint glass known as cristallo. The British held the process as secret as the Venetians, yet glass masters had cracked most of the Venetian code. The secret of lead (flint) glass was the processing of an intermediate material known as red lead.

The key to Cains' entry into the American market was the production of "red lead," a concentrated lead oxide. Red lead is produced by roasting lead oxide (yellow lead or litharge), which increases the lead concentration. Unfortunately, red lead was only available from Europe, which increased the cost of American cut glass. Cains was the first in America to produce fine-cut lead glass equivalent to the prized Venetian cristallo. He achieved this by applying an old metallurgical practice of a bell founder to further improve the density and lead content of flint glass. Because of its weight, lead oxide tended to segregate at the bottom of the glass pots. Bell founders had seen the same problem in brass bell casting. In 1789, P. J. Guinand, a Swiss bell founder, used a fire-clay stirrer to stir molten glass in the pot. The stirring created a homogenous mix of the lead, which ultimately created the optical glass market because of its increased reflectivity.

Cains would be the start of a long line of innovators associated with the beginnings of Libbey Glass leading to Michael Owens. After eight years, Cains opened up the Phoenix Glass Works, which became the leading cut-lead-glass manufacturer. Advertisements in 1816 suggest that he was producing a wide variety of products. These included apothecary's bottles, goblets, inkstands, chemical ware, sugar bowls, salt bowls, and a long list of tableware. Cains perfected his cutting skills and introduced engraving to his products. Wheel engraving, like cutting, required a great deal of skill. Engraving allowed the addition of not only inscriptions but coats-of-arms and scrollwork. Cains also started to experiment with quick-release section molds. Decades later, a young Michael Owens would study these early experiments to develop a new way to produce electric light bulbs.

Several other Boston Crown Glass employees tried to open their own cut-glass factory in South Boston. It failed within three years, but the physical plant became the foundation of New England Glass in 1818.

A group of Boston businessmen came together to form New England Glass and purchase at auction the failed plant and assets. The men were Deming Jarves, Edmond Monroe, Amos Binney, and Daniel Hastings. New England Glass would grow to dominate the industry. It would maintain its competitive advantage via innovation and product development. Its managers would spread out across the industry and develop more premier companies, such as Libbey Glass, Hobbs & Barnes, and Hobbs, Brockunier. Many of these companies and managers would play a critical role in the development of the glass genius, Michael Owens. Hundreds of companies can be traced to New England Glass. Its technology brought new colors, designs, and processes to the glass industry. Its roots run deep, and it deserves the title of the father of the glass industry.

Until Michael Owens automated the glass industry, it was an entrepreneurial industry, where a group of glassmakers could start a company with minimal capital. Competition fostered the entrepreneurial spirit. Again, ironically, an Owens invention would take away part of the industry romance that he loved.

Before Owens, Deming Jarves was prominent in the glass industry. More importantly, Jarves's monopoly on red lead would assure the newly incorporated New England Glass a competitive advantage in the cut-glass market. Deming Jarves became the first general manager of the operation. Jarves's career is every bit a forerunner of the career of Michael Owens. Both men invented new processing advances and formed several glass companies. Both men reduced labor and labor costs in glassmaking. Both men developed American machinery that became the standard for the world. Both men changed the nature of the Venetian system that they loved. Jarves was, in fact, an accomplished glass historian. He was also an experimenter in new methods and glass color chemistry. One of his experiments helped advance the ancient practice of making bottles as well as flatware. This was the three-section mold for glass blowing, which allowed for easy removal of blown glass. Jarves had started the road to automation.

Originally, bottles and containers were blown with the help of an apprentice using hardwood forms to shape the product. By 1800 some half-clay and wood molds were being used. These were two hinged halves that left a seam on the product. The two-part molds were made out of brass, copper, or cast iron. They often caused damage or breakage as the product was removed for further hand working, since the glass tended to stick to the mold. The three-section mold of Cains and Jarves simply allowed easier opening of the mold. It was also used in the production of irregular shapes. The experiments went even further, producing ribs and diamond-point surfaces to compete with cut glass. Jarves pioneered these early experiments in preformed pattern glass in the 1820s. These experiments were the basis of pressed glass, which other ex-New England glassmakers would make a commercial success.

Pressed glass may have been "rediscovered" by Jarves, who was a first-class historian of glass processing. Pressed glass had been used by the Egyptians as early as 1500 B.C. and has been found in the tomb of Tutankhamon. The basic process of pressing is simple. A gather (gob) of metal (molten glass) was put into a cast-iron mold. A plunger was then brought down using a lever, which forced the glass to fill the mold. The process could eliminate several skilled workers. In fact, it could be performed by unskilled labor. Well-maintained molds could produce patterns approaching cut glass at a fraction of the cost. The piece did lose some of its brilliance from contact with the cast iron, but this could be regained by adjusting the annealing. Later discoveries at Hobbs, Brockunier would improve the brilliance with the application of a lime glass (further reducing costs as well).

Jarves developed an economic principle that Owens and even Henry Ford believed in fully. Jarves saw the benefits of automation in substituting unskilled pressers for the blowers. The results were a major decline in production costs from 1840 on. Jarves's analysis of the advances showed that quality, sales, and jobs were increased through automation. First, pressing standardized beautiful tableware patterns. Second, "the tendency has been so to reduce the cost that it multiplied the consumption at least tenfold." Third, with increased sales came huge increases in employment. Pressing even became a highly paid level of glass labor. This study of Jarves would foreshadow the increase of employment that Owens achieved through automation. Amazingly, the union never bought in to the reality of the statistics, choosing to resist automation.

Jarves's pressed-glass trials at New England Glass created fear among the glass workers of the time. Like the British Luddites in the early 1800s textile industry, glass workers formed a secret "protective brotherhood." Jarves's own life was threatened. In a letter, he noted: "The glass blowers on discovery that I had succeeded [pressing glass], were so enraged for fear their business would be ruined by the new discovery, that my life was threatened, and I was compelled to hide from them for six weeks before I dared venture in the street or in the glass house, and for more than six months there was a danger of personal violence should I venture in the street after nightfall." Until its move to Toledo in the 1880s, New England Glass paid pressers a third less than it did blowers, since pressers were considered unskilled. A few decades later, American glass pioneers such as Hobbs, Brockunier, where Michael Owens would get his start, would show that pressed glass would actually increase jobs by taking over the European glass market. John Hobbs had been an associate of Jarves at New England Glass. Hobbs, however, took pressed glass to a level of art, and pressers were paid the same or at times more than blowers.

In 1835, English glass dominated the flint cut-glass market. Deming Jarves set a goal of producing world-class flint cut glass at New England Glass. To that end, he published the earliest history of glass technology, *Reminiscences of Glass*.

Jarves faced several difficulties in achieving his goal. First, English quality was unequaled in the States due to its brilliance and the craftsmanship of the cut pattern. Jarves's challenge to produce quality required both a raw-material change and improved skills.

The key difference in quality was attributed to the use of red lead. As we have seen, red lead is manufactured by roasting yellow lead. In England, the red-lead process was a secret guarded by a handful of glassmakers. Jarves purchased several metallurgy and chemistry books explaining the process. He worked with his glass furnace men to produce a roasting oven for lead ores. Jarves then set up a separate company to produce red lead for New England Glass, but it made him quite wealthy as well. For decades Jarves held a monopoly on red lead, which was not only vital to the American glass industry but also the paint industry. His control of the lead-oxide market gave New England Glass a cost advantage. Jarves was believed to use a "richer" or higher lead content in his flint glass. This made his products noticeably heavier and gave the impression of higher quality. Edward Libbey continued the tradition of higher lead content years later. Jarves's ingenuity would remain unchallenged in the American glass industry until the arrival of Michael Owens.

Craftsmanship presented just as difficult a problem. Jarves needed to import European glass craftsmen, who were jealously guarded by their countrymen. He started a secret project to recruit and smuggle in the glassmakers. One of these would be the famous glass inventor Thomas Leighton, who actually was smuggled in the cargo hold of a clipper ship. By 1855, Jarves had created for New England Glass the international market and fame he had envisioned.

With Thomas Leighton, Jarves had recruited the best glassmaker of the time. In addition, Jarves brought to New England Glass the greatest engraver of the nineteenth century, Louis F. Vaupel. Vaupel's engraving is considered by collectors as the best of the American Middle Period. His famous ruby chalice is thought to be the finest of the time. Vaupel had come from a family of German glasscutters. His work won many awards at the 1876 Philadelphia Centennial Exhibition. He worked with New England and Libbey Glass until 1885. Vaupel's pieces can be found at the Smithsonian Institution and other leading museums. It was around such great artists that Jarves built New England Glass. New England Glass was world class in its art and technology.

It is fascinating that Jarves's great technologic company still held to some of the ancient superstitious practices of the industry. Jarves described the strange pot-setting ritual:

> Dressing in skins of wild animals from head to foot; to this 'outre' garb were added glass goggle eyes, and thus the most hideous-looking monsters were readily presented to the eye. Show was then made of themselves in the neighborhood, to the infinite charm of children, old women, and others. This always occurred, with other mysterious doings, on the occasion of setting the pot . . . the ground was thus furnished for very much of the horrible diablerie connected with the whole history of the manufacture.[3]

While this strange ritual seems out of place for the time, such rites were common to guilds and crafts organization over the centuries. Rituals enforced the fraternal nature of the craft. They built solidarity, loyalty, and romance in the trade. The romance of the craft played an important role in the high quality produced at New England Glass.

The Birth of Libbey Glass

In building his international market, Jarves formed a trading and importing company known as Jarves & Commerias. Through this company, Jarves built two other world-class glass manufacturers—Boston & Sandwich Glass and Mount Washington Glass. But Jarves & Commerias's greatest development was a young clerk who joined the firm in 1855. That clerk was William Landon Libbey. William Libbey was quickly transferred to Mount Washington Glass, where he learned the art-glass business. In 1866, Libbey purchased Mount Washington Glass. His success at the small plant drew the praise of all and led to an offer by New England Glass's board of directors to become general manager there in 1870. Libbey accepted the top position at the troubled firm. The New England glass industry was starting to feel the impact of high-cost, diminishing wood fuel. In the Pittsburgh and Wheeling area, the industry was moving to cheaper coal fuels and immigrant labor. Libbey had held to the use of wood as a fuel as long as possible, believing it affected quality. He started to experiment with coal but it too came at a cost premium in New England.

In addition, these middle Atlantic glassworks were taking skilled artisans out of New England by paying $80 to $100 a month more. The survivors in New England relied on innovation, product development, and marketing. These were the strengths of William Libbey. While many blamed him for the decline of New England Glass, it was market driven, and survival alone was an accomplishment. Throughout the 1870s, Libbey struggled to meet payroll and poured more of his own money into ownership of the firm. By the end of the 1870s, New England Glass was near collapse. There were two major reasons—the cost of bringing coal to New England and a lower-cost "lime" glass being used by its chief rival Hobbs, Brockunier of West Virginia. Another minor factor was imports. Foreign glassmakers had a unique dumping practice, in which packed bottles were used as ballast in clipper ships returning to the United States from Europe. Window glass was even shipped with grain as a protection against breakage.

In 1874, William's son Edward entered the firm. Edward was nineteen at the time. He became involved in marketing and

William Landon Libbey. (Owens-Illinois Glass Company Records, MSS-200, the Ward M. Canaday Center for Special Collections, University of Toledo)

product development. William and Edward's efforts were helped by serendipity. In 1882, Andrew Long, a master glassblower, stumbled on a glass formula that had been lost for hundreds of years. It produced a beautiful deep ruby-colored glass. The formula had originally been discovered (or probably also rediscovered) in the 1600s by a Prussian alchemist, Johann Kunckel Von Lowenstern of Brandenburg, who through much experimentation found that gold added to glass produced a rich ruby color. The ruby glass won much popularity, but Kunckel, with his belief in alchemy, took the secret of gold to his grave. Andrew Long, in the summer of 1882, worked a strange batch of glass that produced a ruby color. He was able to link it to the gold ring that slipped from his finger earlier. William Libbey had seen beautiful ruby-red art pieces throughout Europe. He realized the potential in the beautiful red glass and put John Locke, his best designer, on the project to fully develop the product. Ultimately, Locke patented the formula, but with the death of William Libbey a few months later, the project stalled. Locke's patent called for special reheat practices in the glory hole that could produce a range of colors in the product.

It was Edward Libbey, William's son, who took samples of the new amber glass to retailers and successfully marketed it. In 1884, Edward sold the company's entire stock to Tiffany's of New York. The glass became known as "amberina." Its success turned the company around, and New England Glass reported a profit in 1884 for the first time since 1873. Libbey, sensing a new competitive weapon, introduced several colors and heat-sensitive glasses, such as "agate," "peach," "peachblow," "Burmese," and "Pomona." Metal oxides and special heating achieved the mix of color in these glasses. Libbey combined these new colors with unusual art designs, causing sales to boom. From 1883 to 1886, Libbey used the cash from patent and product sales to reduce debt. The first piece of amberina, a fluted bowl, can still be seen at the Toledo Museum of Art, as well as the first Pomona cream pitcher. Libbey sold the rights of heat-sensitive glasses, such as amberina, to other big producers like Hobbs, Brockunier in Wheeling. Peachblow was an extremely beautiful glass made by the use of cobalt and copper oxides. The Hobbs, Brockunier product was sold as "Wheeling peachblow" and "coral." Libbey also won lawsuits when others tried to "copy" his patents, as Mount Washington Glass did with "peach skin."

This simple, accidental finding had saved the company and allowed it to prosper, as neighboring New England glass firms disappeared. Libbey tried to keep the formula a secret even from his employees. Ernie Pyle reported the following company legend: "Oddly enough, the gold has to be added to the sand-lime-ash mixture before it's put into the furnace, and not after the mixture has become molten. As a result, in the old days Edmund Drummond Libbey used to take a $20 gold piece out of his pocket each morning and throw it into the bin of sand that was going to the furnace that day." As the men caught on, gold had to be added as a powder mixed in.

Still, problems arose again by late 1886. Libbey made his highest profits on the art glass, but part of his successful business formula was the manufacture of high-volume, cheaper products to cover overhead. The fuel and labor-cost disadvantages at New England Glass required Libbey to have high product output to be competitive with "Western" glass plants.

William Libbey had led the company through extremely difficult times, leaving a legacy of innovation when he died in 1883. The struggles of New England Glass through the 1870s and 1880s were no different from those of companies today due to globalization. Like today, Libbey faced a fuel shortage and rising energy costs. His New England location also put him at a serious labor-cost disadvantage compared to the Western plants of Pennsylvania and West Virginia. William Libbey passed on the real key to competitive advantage in such a difficult market. Innovation in products and processes had over and over allowed New England Glass to survive as others failed.

Edward Libbey not only continued his father's passion for innovation but also embraced globalization. From May to September of 1887, Edward made a grand tour of Europe, bringing new colors and design perfection. He sold patent rights for amberina there and toured some of Europe's greatest glasshouses, such as those at Murano. Europe was the World Series for art manufacture, and Libbey was determined to compete in a world market. This philosophy would be part of his product strategy throughout his life. Libbey built strong European ties that would pay dividends in the future.

While innovation would be the future of the company, its New England location and industry practices would require a new response from Edward Libbey. He could be painfully slow in his business analysis, and the decision to leave New England took years. His personal ties to Boston were part of the problem, but there were business issues as well.

One source of financial difficulty was an old glassmaking custom that allowed the gang to use the glass residue at the bottom of the pot to produce and take gift articles home. Master glassblowers produced some great collector's items in this way. Glassblowers called these "whimsies," and they can be seen in museums throughout the world. Libbey's East Cambridge plant had gone too far. Men were not only producing extra product but were selling them on the open market. Even worse, the workers were taking finished cut glass to sell at discount prices. This tended to reduce pricing and profit margin. The problem actually resulted in a stockholder's lawsuit in 1875. Uriah Atherton Boyden had filed a mismanagement suit, claiming the inability of the company to stop employee theft. Theft represented a small portion of the real cost issue. As a result of the suit, a stockholders committee was assigned to look at the company's management and operating problems. They found that fierce competition, lack of fuel, cheap foreign imports, and the westward shift of the end market put the company in serious financial shape. The committee actually suggested to the board of directors that the plant be shut down.

Libbey did not give in to the suggestion. Instead he played to his and the company's strengths—innovation and marketing. In 1876, New England Glass took top honors for its cut glass at the Philadelphia Centennial Exhibition. Collectors generally refer to this period up to the 1915 Centennial Exhibition as the Brilliant Period of cut glass. New England Glass had established itself as the market leader in cut glass. Libbey believed that he could compete in the high-end art market. Still, the directors moved to sell the plant and equipment. Libbey and his father worked out a financial arrangement with the directors to kept the company alive. It was a lease arrangement with a requirement for the Libbeys to eventually buy the equipment and plant. With product innovations, Libbey kept the company in New England, but the dwindling wood supplies doomed its long-term future.

The other problem with New England Glass was unionization. Much is made of the fuel problems, but 75 percent of the cost of glass was in labor. New England Glass had a tough labor history going back to Deming Jarves's battles with the "protective brotherhood." Irish immigrants in many industries, such as mining and steel, had used these secret worker organizations successfully. Still, Libbey had been successful with fair bargaining, even with these secret organizations. The American Flint Glass Workers union was founded in 1878, but it was more successful in the West (Pennsylvania and West Virginia). The Flints had cooperated with the Eastern glass manufacturers, realizing that cost pressures were making their region unprofitable. By 1881, the American Flint Glass Workers were putting pressure on New England Glass to pay what Western workers were paid. The Western workers in Pennsylvania and West Virginia received 25 to 30 percent more than the Eastern workers.[4] A young union representative in West Virginia would indirectly cause that pressure.

Some accounts have Michael Owens playing a direct role in the demise of New England Glass, but these seem to be laced with legend. However, he did play a very important indirect role. Owens had risen to a powerful committee chairman role in the Western branch of the American Flint Glass Workers. At the 1887 Pittsburgh Convention, Owens achieved a major step towards solidarity within the union and, as a result, threatened the existence of New England Glass.

The Flints through the 1880s had been divided by the differences in the Eastern and Western factories. The more successful Western factories and workers had made more progress in wages. The Eastern union leaders were sympathetic to the problems of the New England industry and the dwindling fuel supplies. The New England glass industry had a reputation as a gentlemen's industry. The Eastern representatives were led by a gentleman union leader, James ("Gaffer") Smith of Brooklyn.

The "Gaffer" had held the Eastern representatives in line for a decade. A bit of a dandy, the "Gaffer" dressed in silk hats and carried canes, but he was a tough, fearsome orator whom few challenged. One challenge came from Michael Owens at the Pittsburgh Convention, over the issue of solidarity between the branches on wages. Owens was trained from childhood in debate and combined this with his Irish charm to attack the "Gaffer." Smith used polysyllabic words and long phraseology. Owens used straightforward point-to-point debating, coupled with Irish eloquence. Thomas Rowe, a later president of the Flints, characterized Owens' style thus: "He debated as he had been forced to fight as a boy in the glass factory." Owens throughout his life was known to be highly persuasive. The debate at the Pittsburgh Convention has also become legend. What we know for certain is that wage solidarity carried, and this would break the cost-restricted Eastern factories. New England Glass was one of those marginal factories that could no longer bear the costs of doing business in New England.

CHAPTER 3

Michael Owens:
The Irish-American Glassmaker

Michael Owens was born to John and Mary (Chapman) Owens on January 1, 1859. Both had emigrated from Wexford County, Ireland in the early 1840s to Mason County, West Virginia (then Virginia). They were the first wave of refugees from the great potato famine and British oppression. Michael and his family were fiercely Irish, deeply resenting the English treatment that had forced them from their homeland. One story of Michael in his sixties showed that the resentment lasted throughout his life. Michael was to meet an old friend at Inverness Country Club golf course in Toledo. Upon seeing Michael in knickers and cap, his friend commented that he looked like a "damn Englishman." This fired Michael's temper. On another occasion, during a sales trip for Michael's bottle machine, an English lord baited Michael with a discussion on the problems of Ireland, unleashing Mike's fury. Michael promoted Irish independence behind the scenes throughout his career and was president of the local Friends of Irish Freedom (the American political arm of the Irish freedom movement).

As well as being Irish, Michael was a devout Catholic. There was little money in the Owens home, but any money left over by Sunday was given to the church. Mike honored this Irish tradition of giving generously to the church throughout his life, as well as the tradition that giving was personal, between the giver and God, so it should always be done anonymously.

Michael would often attribute his success to his strong prayer life. He had a deep love for the rosary as well as the tradition of

65

nine days of special prayer known as a novena. Often he would use both techniques to overcome a roadblock at work. He was a rough Irishman, known to swear frequently, but deep down he was a very religious and humble man. He befriended many priests, often consulting them even on business matters. Priests and immediate family were where Michael put his trust. But, true to Irish Catholics of the time, he considered his religion a personal matter to be shared only with a close few.

Mary Owens had passed on a deep faith, but she had also taught Michael about the hatred of Catholics that existed in society. Mary knew oppression firsthand from Ireland, and she taught both prayer and action to Michael. It was well known that Catholics rarely were promoted to management positions in the major industries. Michael's performance would overcome that common bias.

John Owens was a coal miner, and Mike's first boyhood job in the mines was carrying water and lunch pails to the mine for his father. At the age of nine, like most boys in the area, Mike started in the mines beside his father. The wages of the mines left most families needing to employ their children. The family employment was self-perpetuating, as it prevented the children's school attendance.

These were the cavernous mines of West Virginia, where miners swung picks to dig out the tunnels. Mike's earliest experience in the mine was an accident that almost cost him his right eye. A piece of hard coal hit him in the eye, knocking him unconscious at his father's feet. He probably suffered a concussion, but no medical records are available. We do know that he was laid up for some time, requiring his mother to nurse him back to health. Such mining accidents were far from uncommon, but it was one too many for Mary Owens. She forbade Mike from returning to the mines, and this started his career in the glass industry.

The decision to keep Michael out of the mines brought the family to the city of Wheeling in the 1860s. At that time, the family consisted of seven children—Mary, age twelve; John, age ten; Mike, age ten; Thomas, age six; Maggie, age four; Ida, age three; and Anne, age one. John Owens took a reduction in pay because of the move, which then required young Michael to help with expenses. His older brother, John, went into the Wheeling steel mills and became a puddler (the highest-ranking craftsman in the steel-making process). Thomas, his younger brother, followed Mike into the glasshouse. In large Irish families, all the boys and men contributed to the household. Generally, boys stayed in the household until their late twenties or until marriage, and that is what John, Mike, and Thomas did.

Throughout Michael's life, his mother was dominant. Upon Michael's death, Edward Libbey said, "He was the son of a West Virginia miner and a most devoted and unusual mother, who endowed him with many of the finer qualities of his character, and whose influence and guidance played a prominent part in the development of his life." Michael's father had a lesser role in his life. John Owens was a bit of a drifter, moving around to various jobs, never really content. His main career of coal miner was one he hated. He was a skilled handyman, capable of building ingenious devices. Michael always felt inferior to his father because he lacked that mechanical aptitude. Michael credited him as the source of his own inventive genius but little else. In fact, in a 1922 interview, Michael was quite hard on him:

> He would make a wonderful kite and be out flying it, a group of delighted children around him, when he ought to have been at work. That's why we were poor. If he had happened to get into the kind of work he loved, things probably would have been different. But he didn't; and he lacked the initiative, or the understanding, to find the right place for himself. He worked at the thing he hated and played at the thing he loved; and that's a bad program for anyone.[1]

Mike told another reporter:

> My father disliked mine work, but he had no choice. So he found satisfaction in building things. He built everything from wheelbarrows to boats for children—everybody's children. I remember him best surrounded by youngsters.[2]

Wheeling was down the Ohio River from Pittsburgh and in the

postbellum years was making a mark as an industrial town. Wheeling had always been a transportation center on the Ohio frontier. The Indians of Pennsylvania traveling west crossed the Ohio River at Wheeling Island for centuries. In the 1820s, Wheeling beat out Pittsburgh to become a stop on the National Road. In addition to becoming a transportation hub, Wheeling boasted rich natural resources of coal, iron ore, limestone, clay, and natural gas. This positioned the West Virginia panhandle to be a participant in the great American expansion during the Gilded Age. Wheeling contributed to the early roots of coal mining, iron and steel manufacture, and glass manufacture.

All three were dominated by immigrant Irish labor, and young Irish were favored for these labor jobs. The demand for child labor in Wheeling was enormous. While the Irish dominated the labor force and often rose to foreman positions, they were systematically restricted from higher management, which was mainly populated by men of German and English descent.

Mary Owens pushed her son towards the best of the three industries—glass. She remembered how Ireland had made its mark via Waterford glass, and what little wealth there was in Ireland was related to glass. With the Irish control of the lower labor jobs, Michael could find work in this growth industry. The Irish had "lodges," which allowed new immigrants to enter the factory and apprentice system. The lodges were a natural extension of the Irish benevolent societies. The societies in Wheeling helped newcomers find jobs and housing. They supported informal youth groups and schooling at the church parishes. They held dances for the youth, which also raised money for needy families. The idea was to keep Irish youth out of the Wheeling city gangs.

The Wheeling area and Pittsburgh were unusual in that the glass industry preceded the iron and steel industry. In Wheeling, the glass industry started with the firm of Plunkett & Miller. The plant appears to have produced window glass, but it failed in the 1840s. James Barnes and John L. Hobbs, from the cradle of glassmakers—East Cambridge, Massachusetts—then purchased the firm. The New England fuel shortages had started the emigration of glassmakers to the energy-rich areas of Pennsylvania and West

Virginia. These New England glassmakers brought new formulas and technologies that opened new product lines, such as solar chimneys, oil-lamp chimneys, jars, tumblers, cologne bottles, and vials. These Western plants also offered access to farther Western markets. However, the Allegheny Mountains created a barrier to East Coast imports. Also, shipping glass over the Alleghenies resulted in unacceptable breakage. This breakage was even higher with thinner products such as chimneys. Chimneys, representing the highest-tonnage product by 1890, continued to push glasshouses west. Fuel, however, remained the dominant drive in the move west.

Glass firms were mushrooming throughout western Pennsylvania and the panhandle of West Virginia because of fuel availability. Western Pennsylvania was blessed with both coal and natural gas. The New England glass industry had been based on the abundance of local hardwood for fuel, but that supply was dwindling. By the early 1850s, good hardwood had been lumbered out and a new fuel—coal—offered better efficiency. Some New England firms successfully switched to softer woods such as pine, but the consumption of wood by these glass factories was enormous. A factory could easily consume 10,000 cords of wood in a year. In good times, a glass factory would consume a football field of forest in a week! A century earlier, England had banned the use of hardwood in glasshouses because of the navy's needs for it in shipbuilding. Coal was abundant in Pennsylvania and West Virginia, and this fired the emerging glass industry of the area. Glass historian E. William Fairfield summarized the situation:

> The proximity of big coal supplies in the West immediately gave New England's Western competitors a powerful economic advantage. By 1860, the once plentiful wood supply in New England had dwindled . . . hundreds of acres of timberland that had been leased by the New England Glass and Boston & Sandwich had been stripped for fuel. Even had there been hundreds of additional acres available, wood as fuel was no match for the efficiency of coal. . . . It took great quantities of wood, oil additives and powerful drafts to make the wood fires intense enough to melt and work glass.[3]

Coal changed the nature of the glass industry. Two types of

coal were available, a hard coal known as anthracite and a soft coal known as bituminous. Anthracite could be used as a fuel directly, while bituminous needed to be converted to coke. Coking was labor intensive and, like coal mining, depended on cheap immigrant labor. Even though coke in the glass furnaces produced a hotter and more consistent heat than did wood, there was a price. Coke produced a residue known as clinkers, which had to be removed. The bigger drawback was that coke was "dirty." The finished glass product required washing. A glass manager in 1886 described it: "When the ware is pressed and placed in the lears, which are heated with coke, it comes out very dirty, keeping a number of hands busy placing the glass in carrying boxes; then to the wash room, where it is washed one piece at a time, then repacked in the boxes and sent to the packing room. In double handling of ware a great amount is broken."[4] Coal in general was a cheap but dirty fuel. In art- and clear-glass factories, pots of molten glass needed covers to prevent ash from entering the glass.

Coal was driving a glass-industry exodus from New England. Pittsburgh was the first to benefit, as its glass industry was dominant from 1850 to 1880. Coal heating could substantially increase productivity by producing more "metal" per hour with larger pots. Pittsburgh was naturally rich in coal reserves. Coal was often shoveled directly from open seams in the surrounding hills. The Pittsburgh industry was proud but arrogant, driving some of New England's glass masters to the West Virginia panhandle. The transplanted glassmakers at Wheeling's Hobbs, Brockunier brought a new technological edge to the area. West Virginia, of course, was also rich in coal deposits. West Virginia, however, became rich in innovation as well. In 1864, a former New England Glass employee, William Leighton, experimenting at Hobbs, Brockunier developed a new lime glass formula. The formula used lime rather than lead oxide to produce hardness. This cut the cost of the glass by a third. This new formula was an alternative to lead glass, but it lacked the full brilliance and "ring" of lead glass. Still, it was of such quality that it could be widely used for tableware. Lime glass could readily be pressed as well. The combination of lime glass and pressing greatly reduced the price of glass tableware. The art glass manufacturers of New England had to surrender the lower end of their market to the pressed lime glass manufacturers. West Virginia became the center of this new segment of glassmaking.

The glass company where Mike Owens started in Wheeling, West Virginia was not only one of Wheeling's first but had direct ties to New England Glass. The company was the South Wheeling Glass Works of Hobbs, Brockunier & Company. Wheeling was a natural early glass center. First, it was rich in natural resources and fuel such as coal and natural gas. Wheeling had also attracted some of New England's best glassmakers. Even more important was its transportation network. Wheeling is located on the Ohio River downstream from Pittsburgh. The Ohio River flows directly into the Mississippi River and ultimately the seaport of New Orleans. In the 1830s, it was cheaper to use the river route from New Orleans to New York than the Wheeling-to-New York overland route. River transportation was smoother as well and prevented extensive breakage during the trip. The river also allowed for a direct connection to the great coal fields of Pennsylvania and Kentucky.

Glassmaking had come to the Wheeling area in 1821, with a window-glass plant in Wellsburg. When Mike started in 1869, the Wheeling valley included Steubenville, Martin's Ferry, and Wellsburg and employed over two thousand in glassmaking. By 1886, Wheeling glass factories used a flexible mix of fuel, including wood, coal, and distilled petroleum products.

In 1863, two more glassmakers joined the firm from New England Glass. Scottish glass master Thomas Leighton, Sr., and his son William came to Wheeling. The senior Leighton was given charge of all manufacturing. One of the major costs of producing cut crystal glass was the addition of 10 to 22 percent lead oxide in the product (Libbey liked to add as much as 33 percent). Lead oxide gives the crystal its brilliance and durability. Lead adds that heavy feel to cut crystal. It was a costly addition, however. Upon arriving at Wheeling, Leighton started a number of experiments to eliminate lead. He had started these experiments at New England Glass but had not found the key to a commercial product. After many experiments, the main ingredients were found to be Berkshire sand (from New England), Spanish chalk, and bicarbonate of soda. This so called "lime glass" further took market away from the crystal market and New England Glass. This new lime-soda glass could be pressed as well. Prior to the discovery of this lime glass, pressed glass required lead glass to allow mechanical pressing. The new lime glass could be made at half the cost of lead glass. The savings from this formula and from pressing versus full cutting gave Hobbs, Brockunier a major advantage over its rival, New England Glass.

The younger Leighton went on to experiment with new colors such as coral and peach in pressed glass. William Leighton was an inspiration for a young Michael Owens, who joined the firm a few years later. Leighton was a renaissance man, the Thomas Jefferson of glass. He had a science degree from Harvard. He was an author of several books on English history and a lover of poetry. He offered a model for the young Owens of the gentleman glassmaker.

Hobbs, Brockunier & Company became the major competitor to New England Glass in cut crystal as well as new products such as pressed glass and lime glass. By 1886 (the year that Libbey prepared to move his New England plant to Toledo), Hobbs, Brockunier & Company had achieved international fame. The works was producing 150 tons per week, employing 650 men. Cost cutting by the development of cheaper processes and products had created one of the most profitable American glass companies. The *Wheeling Daily Intelligencer* in 1886 reported: "About four hundred car loads of goods are shipped annually to every part of the United States, Cuba, South America, Australia and Europe." The firm was the American leader of ruby cut glass, using large amounts of gold bullion. It had sales offices in Boston, Philadelphia, New York, and Baltimore. Besides quality flatware, Hobbs, Brockunier was making jars, tumblers, oil-lamp chimneys, cologne bottles, and inkbottles. Sales and profits were rising while New England Glass faltered.

Hobbs, Brockunier & Company was an industry innovator. The

company pioneered commercial pressed glass, winning note at the 1876 Centennial Exhibition at Philadelphia.There Hobbs, Brockunier faced the elite of the industry, such as New England Glass, Boston & Sandwich Glass, Bakewell, Pears, & Company of Pittsburgh, Mount Washington Glass of Boston, and J. B. Dobleman of Brooklyn. While the Centennial Exhibition is credited with starting a renaissance in cut glass, the introduction of commercial pressed glass was more visionary. Boston & Sandwich won a gold medal for its art pressed glass, but the real commercial breakthrough was Hobbs, Brockunier's pressed glass. Hobbs, Brockunier introduced a "Centennial" pattern for the exhibition (known as "Viking" or "Bearded Head" by collectors). The motif became an American bestseller in the 1870s. The success of this design and Hobbs, Brockunier's later pressed-glass pattern— "Tree of Life"—made it the largest glass company in 1879. The use of a world's fair as a marketing tool was not lost on a young Michael Owens, who would do the same for Libbey Glass in 1892. The Centennial Exhibition had established Hobbs, Brockunier as the premier pressed-glass manufacturer in the world, creating a huge export market for the West Virginia company.

Pressed glass is substantially cheaper to produce than cut glass, which requires time and great skill to cut in the pattern. It substitutes cheaper labor for glassblowers and eliminates much of the cutting steps as well. Also, it is cheaper to machine the pattern into cast iron only once than to press out thousands of pieces in individual cast-iron molds. Hobbs, Brockunier & Company's pressed glass started to take away the lower end of the crystal flatware market by 1886. The reduction in costs and price resulted in a tenfold increase in consumption during the 1880s. Pressed glass was one of Hobbs, Brockunier's many great industry innovations.

The coal resources of West Virginia had been the foundation of Hobbs, Brockunier & Company, but an even more efficient fuel was arising in the 1880s. From its start in 1845, Hobbs, Brockunier & Company used coal as a fuel in the kilns, but it still used wood in the annealing furnaces. On the day that Owens entered the plant in 1869, coal cost 50 cents a ton and wood $3.50 a cord. As in the past, Hobbs, Brockunier & Company would be the industry innovator. By 1886, it had become one of the first glassworks to successfully use natural gas as a fuel. Actually, Rochester Tumbler Works, near Pittsburgh, lays claim to being first to use gas, in 1875. Gas offered some amazing advantages over coal. It could supply higher heat at about a third less cost. This new fuel further strengthened the company's cost advantage over such competitors such as New England Glass and Pittsburgh glassmakers. The use of gas allowed for more "metal" per hour by increasing the size and number of pots. An average coal- or wood-fired glasshouse might have six pots of 700 pounds each. With gas, the average glasshouse had ten pots of 2,500 pounds each. The potential use of the Siemens gas furnace offered even more savings to area steel makers as well.

Hobbs, Brockunier was also experimenting in 1886 with oil as a possible future fuel. Michael Owens gained extremely valuable experience in the conversion to and use of these new fuels, which would save struggling Libbey Glass a few years later. Hobbs, Brockunier & Company remains an example of effectively competing in a difficult marketplace.

There are many striking analogies between the histories of Hobbs, Brockunier and New England Glass and business today. The 1880s were a time of dwindling fuel reserves and rising fuel costs. Imports controlled the glass market with high-quality and cheaper product. Labor costs were rising due to unionization and strikes. New England Glass chose the traditional head-on competition approach, while Hobbs, Brockunier chose to innovate by finding alternative fuels and developing new processes and products. Hobbs, Brockunier prospered in this difficult time and increased its national and international markets. The difference was in the management. While New England Glass had become the technical college for the industry, Hobbs, Brockunier became the management school that would train industry leaders. More importantly, Hobbs, Brockunier would be the school for Michael Owens.

It was at age ten that Michael Owens came to the creative firm of Hobbs, Brockunier & Company. That day in 1869, Michael J. Owens entered a child-slavery system that he would personally overcome and ultimately eliminate through his inventions, although he felt that child labor was actually a positive, assuming that conditions were controlled and maintained to advance the child. He would start his progression through the crafts system that he loved but would make obsolete through his future inventions. Mike was a self-motivated youth with a desire to learn. As with many mining families, there was a drive in the Owens household to improve their lot in life. Mike's mother would also supply support and motivation. Being an Irish Catholic motivated Mike to find acceptance. That background gave him both hope and endurance in the most depressing environments. Mike did not expect an easy life—in fact, he believed that suffering was the norm—but he hoped for a better future. He was willing to sacrifice since he believed in the future. This attitude of sacrificing for future generations was inherent in Irish immigrants, and it made him a perfect fit for the organization he was about to enter. Hobbs, Brockunier & Company was a company of innovative managers. It rewarded creativity and hard work; age or lack of education was not a handicap.

A reporter in 1930 summarized how Mike's mother's had shaped him:

> Mrs. Owens had high and noble ambitions for her boy. In her fine old Irish heart she dreamed a mother's dream. She saw her son blazing a trail from the humble home in Mason City, W. Va., to the industrial heights of a mighty and pulsating metropolis. He would be loved and respected. And from the heights he would reach down to assist his fellowman. These were dreams and the immediate demands for the necessities of life pointed out a rugged road to young Mike.[5]

Mike started as a furnace boy, firing the "glory hole." The glory hole at Hobbs, Brockunier was coal fired. A number of "corporate legends" still appear in the archives. One of these is that Mike showed up to work the first day with only one shoe and had to dig another out of the rubbish heap to work in the glasshouse. The work was long and hard for even a young man. In addition, it was extremely dirty, coating the body and lungs with coke dust and furnace ash. The extreme difficulty of the job favored the use of young, strong workers. The shift work for a child furnace tender consumed his life, eliminating any opportunity for relaxation. Michael's day at the furnaces started at five in the morning. He worked five hours and returned home for a few hours, only to return in later afternoon for another five hours. The split shift was geared to the two-shift operations of the glass furnaces. Michael kept up this schedule six days a week. He usually brought a meal of fatback sandwiches and sliced cold mush prepared by his mother.

This was the type of child labor that Mike's future bottle-making inventions would eliminate; yet in 1869 children represented a necessary labor source to drive the industrial revolution. Mike loved work because he dreamed of being a glass baron. Still, the factory heat could reach 100-plus degrees in the summer. Heat exhaustion was a common problem, even for the strongest of the boys. Years later, Mike described those early days: "I worked five hours in the morning and when I came out of the pit, I was black as ink there. I went home, washed clean, ate my dinner, and went back for another five hours."

New boys faced a type of initiation that sent many home for good. The new boy always got the label "greenie." Ambitious boys like Owens were anxious to please the boss, and this often attracted the attention of the older bullies. Hazing by these bullies was a common practice that arose from their frustrated childhoods. Owens, however, was no mama's boy but a hardened son of a coal worker. In fact, his mother supported her son in taking a strong stand against any bullies. Mary Owens knew that these bullies had to be addressed as soon as possible or they would torture him for a lifetime. Owens had gone fearlessly into the mines earlier. The bullying did not last long before Mike was charging fists first, encouraged by his wise mother. Owens was a fighter and would resort to fisticuffs throughout his career. He gained valuable street smarts in those earlier years that would serve him as a manager later in life. Owens would refer often to the day when he took on the bullies; his stand against them would become a defining event for him.

Child Labor in the Glass Industry

These glasshouse boys were paid thirty cents a day. This represented a major savings for the factory owners, who paid a skilled worker two to three dollars a day. When Michael started in the glass industry, children made up over a quarter of the industrial workforce. In states like West Virginia, there were no laws regarding their employment. Ohio was an exception, requiring a minimum of twelve years of age and limiting labor to ten hours a day.[6] In 1883, the Pittsburgh Humane Society unsuccessfully sponsored a Pennsylvania bill to restrict employment to boys thirteen or older and the work year to six months for boys under fifteen.The demand for children (eight to fifteen years old) increased yearly, spurring a slavelike trade in children between states. Children were often packed in the infamous "orphan cars," to be transported to factories throughout America. During a strike at the Dalzell Company of Findlay, Ohio in 1888, the company brought in 20 boys from an orphanage in Brooklyn, New York. The 1870 census recorded 700,000 child laborers in the United States. In 1879, of the 24,000 workers in the glass industry, nearly 5,600 (23 percent) were boys, and due to the shortage of boys another 15 percent were women. By the 1880s, boys were in such short supply in the factories that managers offered to relocate and hire entire families who had young boys. The *Bowling Green Sentinel* in Ohio reported the following on September 13, 1888:

> The glass factories [here] could find employment today for 50 more boys from 12 to 17, to whom good wages would be paid. There are plenty of families throughout this section who would do well by moving here; for instance, a laboring man who has one or two boys. He and his boys could readily find employment at any one of the [glass] factories here at good wages. Any one of the factories would be glad to hire them.

The following is from a book on nineteenth-century glassmaking by William Walbridge, the brother-in-law of Edward Libbey:

I shall never forget my first visit to a glass factory at night. It was a big wooden structure so lonely built that it afforded little protection from draughts, surrounded by a high fence, with several rows of barbed wire stretched across the top. I went with the foreman of the factory and he explained the reasons for the stockade-like fence.

"It keeps the young imps inside once we've got them in for the night shift," he said. The young imps were boys employed, about forty in number, at least ten of who were less than twelve years of age. It was a cheap bottle factory—cheapness and child labor go together.

The hours of labor for the night shift were from 5:30 p.m. to 3:30 a.m. The effect of the employment of young boys in the glass factories, especially at night, is injurious from every point of view. The constant facing of the glare of the furnaces, and the red-hot bottle causes injury to the sight. Minor accidents from burning are numerous. From working in draughty sheds, where they are often, or as one boy stated "burning on the side next the furnace and freezing on the other," they are frequently subject to rheumatism and fall readily to pneumonia.[7]

Child labor was a grievous evil, but it was also a paradox. Many of America's greatest industrialists rose from the ranks of child labor. As with any part of business, there is a propensity to abuse it. The opportunity for a job was not a bad thing in itself. And many self-made men, such as Andrew Carnegie, George Westinghouse, Thomas Edison, as well as Michael Owens, had used it to start successful careers. It was not just industrial giants who benefited. My own grandmother, an orphan in Pittsburgh, worked at the glasshouse in the day and went to nursing school at night on the wages she earned. Orphanages did receive financial aid from the factories, and housing was built for the working boys. But the Horatio Alger myths ended in the arduous toil, dangerous conditions, and long hours of the workplace.

Opinions were mixed on the issue of child labor. The glass unions never took on the subject. Glass historian and researcher Jack Paquette did an extensive review of the American Flint Glass Workers archives from 1880 to 1900 and found no references to child labor. The fledgling union seemed to support the use of children in the glass factories, since older workers wanted no part of such physical labor or the second-shift hours. Even Michael Owens' view at times seemed paradoxical for a man who is often hailed for freeing child laborers. He was not opposed to the use of children if the treatment was fair and living conditions good. Owens felt that children should have the opportunity of a job.

Generally, living conditions were reported as good. An Ohio inspector's report on the imported Dalzell Company orphans stated that their house was "scrupulously clean" and they were well fed. The inspector still found the work to be too dangerous for such young boys.

By 1889, the boys of Dalzell organized a strike for better sleeping conditions. They were sleeping three to a bed in the hot summers. Glasshouse boys organized local strikes often and were more aggressive in calling a strike than were their adult counterparts. These young men faced twelve-hour days, excessive heat, lung disease, lead poisoning, and injury. It took a special breed of child to rise above the environment. Other advantages were a strong faith and loving parents, which Michael was blessed with.

In reality, for a child, the glass industry was not a whole lot better than coal mining. The work was slightly less dangerous but just as tiring, if not more so. Still, child labor was an economic necessity for most families as well as companies. It was estimated that 25 to 35 percent of the nation's children were working by 1880. Hobbs, Brockunier & Company employed over one hundred boys in its four hundred-plus workers when Michael Owens started. The glass industry was actually suffering from a shortage of children throughout the latter part of the nineteenth century. Many were using boys from orphanages. In this respect, Michael Owens was blessed to have an Irish mother to prepare his meals, wash his clothes, and make his bed; orphans lived a prisonlike existence on and off the job.

History shows that Michael Owens' bottle machine would eliminate child labor in the glass industry, but Michael remained ambivalent about the hiring of boys throughout his life. The fact that the Owens Bottle Machine reduced child labor was a side benefit, not his motivation, as many revisionist histories suggest.

Owens was not driven by this goal; in fact, eliminating the opportunity for a child to work bothered him. Owens, like Charles Schwab, Andrew Carnegie, Thomas Edison, and George Westinghouse, strongly believed that "children" should work. Of course, they assumed and demanded fair treatment. Owens and these men came out of the school of Horatio Alger, who wrote boyhood success stories. This school of thought saw work as almost a spiritual necessity. Owens was from this mold; he had passion for work. The wealthier he became, the less he was able to disengage from work. Even Carnegie and Schwab found ways to move away from work in their later years. Michael was a true workaholic; work was a drug for him. He dealt with all problems by working more.

Owens put it quite strongly in a 1922 interview:

> One of the greatest evils of modern life is the growing habit of regarding work as an affliction. When I was a youngster I wanted to work. If they [children] went to school, they did odd jobs out of school hours. In vacations they tried to get steady employment. It was good for them, mentally and physically. By the time they left school they had formed habits of industry and knew something of the value of earned money.
>
> A great deal of the trouble today is with the mothers. Too many boys are being brought up by sentimental women. The first fifteen or twenty years of their lives are spent in playing. That's all they do; at least, a great many of them. When they finally start to work, they are so useless and so helpless that it is positively pathetic. The young man who has begun to work when he was a boy has them handicapped.
>
> Work never hurt anyone! The conditions under which you work may hurt you. You will suffer if you don't get enough food and sleep for rebuilding and the rest you need. Worrying over work will wear you out. But the hard work I did as a boy never injured me.[8]

Flint-glass factories such as Hobbs, Brockunier & Company presented another very unique health threat that was not understood at the time. That threat came from the use of lead in the process. Many workers suffered unknowingly from the effects of lead poisoning. One symptom they recognized was the "lead shakes," which occurred in workers over the weekend. It was actually a form of withdrawal from lead in the body. Brass-foundry workers in the area knew it also because of the use of lead and zinc in brass making. One glass historian even attributed the tempers of glass workers to lead poisoning. Lead poisoning in general was not understood until the 1950s. Finished flint glass, which was often 25 percent lead oxide, was a problem itself. The flint-glass decanters that were so popular in Victorian times could leach lead. Research in Canada showed that lead in Scotch whiskey stored in a crystal decanter for a year could reach 1,500 parts per million and in port wine could rise to 2,000 parts per million. This may account for the high level of lead found in hair samples from Andrew Jackson. Still, the popularity of crystal decanters rose from 1840 to 1910.

The 1870s were a decade of growth for both Michael and Hobbs, Brockunier. Hobbs, Brockunier, with its new cheaper lime formula, was looking for other ways to take the lower end of the lead-crystal market. By 1880 it was a major exporter to South American and European markets. In particular, Hobbs, Brockunier had a major share of the German glass tableware market. Again, Hobbs, Brockunier had shown how innovation could trump cheaper European labor. Furthermore, Hobbs, Brockunier added savvy marketing, opening sales outlets in Cuba and most major American cities.

But the real advantage and education that Michael found at Hobbs, Brockunier was its love for innovation. One of its advances was known as "opalescent" glass. This was created by adding bone ash to a heated clear-glass formula. The glass is then reheated, causing a color change.

Hobbs, Brockunier & Company, New England Glass, and Libbey Glass became part of a rare breed of manufacturers that used innovation for competitive advantage. Their art pieces rarely paid the bills, but they stimulated advances in all product lines. Innovations allowed them to prosper over competitors with cheaper labor, natural resources, and capital. They not only withstood imports but also developed exporting divisions as part of the business. This environment of innovation honed Michael Owens for a future of inventions.

Michael's ambition can be seen in his early efforts in self-education as well. His education was dependent on his mother, parish priest, and local Irish organizations. His mother gave Michael his dominant characteristic—ambition. However, he also joined a literary and debate club for young men, which was like Benjamin Franklin's Juno club of an earlier time. His mother attributed to this experience the improvement of Michael's speaking and debating skills, which would serve him well in the future. Later in Wheeling, Owens teamed up with his parish priest to form a youth debating club. Mike was now skilled in both fighting and debating, making him a tough competitor in any arena. He was able to apply logic as well as "Irish eloquence" to any situation. As his confidence in his debating skills rose, and with the encouragement of his parish priest and mother, he backed off the use of his fists.

For working Catholic boys, the local diocese was their only available schooling. Parish priests had the responsibility to teach reading. It was Mike's parish priest who got him interested in the life of Napoleon. Mike read every book he could borrow on him. After his mother, Michael's parish priest was a key influence on him. Michael learned early on to face his struggles with prayer. Throughout his life, this rough Irishman would credit God for his success.

The parish literary and debating clubs also planted in Michael an interest in writing, history, and science. His love of history and reading remained for him a lifelong passion. At his death, Owens would have one of the largest personal libraries in northwest Ohio.

Still, for a young Irish-American, work was the center of one's life. Michael progressed rapidly through the unskilled positions, but each one taught him a piece of the larger system. He befriended the master blowers and found time to experiment after his ten-hour shift. This experience was invaluable and augmented his inventive designs of his later life.

Michael Moves Up

Michael's first semiskilled job was "mold boy." A mold boy cleaned, coated, and readied the cast-iron mold for the glassblower. This was the top of the child positions and offered an introduction to the making of glass product. This earliest experience would prove the most valuable and lead to his first patent. He never forgot working with molten glass and its interaction with the mold. The cleaning of the molds helped Mike understand that reaction. This would be key to his automatic mold inventions of later years. As it turned out, Owens was a true "right-brain" genius, needing to physically handle product and machinery in order to understand it. He was unable to read or draw engineering

Glassblower and mold boy, 1908. (Library of Congress)

Children working the day shift in a glass factory, 1909. (Library of Congress)

drawings throughout his career, preferring verbal descriptions based on physical observation. It was said of him after his death: "He could neither build his machine nor draw the blueprints, but he could describe it so accurately that an engineer could build it for him."[9] He was a unique inventor, more in the vein of Leonardo da Vinci and Thomas Edison than Henry Ford. Unlike many of great inventors of his time, he was neither a mechanic, engineer, scientist, nor designer. Like the glass industry itself, he was able to blend creativity and practicality. Working all the jobs of the gang was the ideal training for this future inventor. The abstract learning of engineering school would have been of little value to Owens. Owens combined work experience and creativity into genius.

Michael always remembered but greatly disliked glasshouse "humor." Mike had a good sense of humor, but throughout his life he maintained a serious demeanor about work. Always anxious to learn the craft of a blower, Owens stayed later to get a chance to learn. The blowers always enjoyed giving him a hot blowpipe or one plugged with chewing tobacco. This type of humor at his expense he particularly disliked. But he endured these rites of passage to advance in the trade. Later in life, he would ban such practices in his plants.

Michael rose very quickly through the hierarchy of the gang. In 1874, at age fifteen, he was a journeyman glassblower. He had advanced at a rate rarely seen. In less than a year, he had moved from fire boy to carry-in boy for the annealing furnace. These two jobs were considered the toughest in the glasshouse. At twelve, he made carry-out boy in the annealing area. He worked also as a mold boy prior to making the step to gatherer at age fourteen. The simple fact is that Owens outworked his fellow employees. Michael's rise went beyond hard work; it was driven ambition. He avoided dances and passed on a childhood in order to achieve his dream of someday owning a glasshouse.

Owens had a practical desire for high wages in the glass industry. The American Flints had been active in the Wheeling area from his earliest days in the industry. Wages were always an issue, as well as a formal apprentice system. The glass workers tended to function as a quasi-guild. The problem was that management would move cheaper workers around the apprentice system. The apprentice system functioned at the favor of management. The apprentice system provided security for the worker and was a major factor in the unionization movement. The more aristocratic part of the industry in New England and Pittsburgh had unionized by the hierarchy of the old Venetian system, but the Wheeling area embraced the more integrated approach of the American Flints. For example, in Pittsburgh, glass unions represented the blowers and the gatherers separately, while in West Virginia, the union organized by plant, bringing the blowers, gatherers, etc., into the same union. The gang therefore belonged to one union. In Pittsburgh's flat-glass industry, Local Assembly 300 of the Knights of Labor had fought hard on output and pay. The container glass workers of the Wheeling area, where art glass was emphasized, wanted work and apprenticeship rules.

This focus was more suited to Michael Owens' romantic view of the industry, and he became involved early with the union. With the formation of the American Flint Glass Workers in 1878, the Wheeling district, known as Local 9, became the lead local. Local 9 had a vision of a unionized craft, which a young Owens supported. However, in the long run, even Michael's romantic view would yield to his drive to achieve.

As the union movement increased in Wheeling, owners started to standardize and reduce the labor requirements in bottle making. The new arrangement was known as the seven-man shop, consisting of three skilled workers and four unskilled boys. Two of the skilled workers were needed for blowing and one for finishing. In the unskilled workers, the mold boy still held the bottle mold for the two blowers. The other boys carried out the bottles and cleaned tools. In many cases, a management foreman, who headed the shop, replaced the gaffer. The seven-man shop did not have the romance of the Venetian crafts system, but it was rooted in the new philosophy of Frederick Taylor's factory system. This adoption of the factory system brought wages down and reduced skill levels. Production of bottles moved from an average of 40 dozen bottles per day to 300 dozen per day under the factory system. The fall of the Venetian crafts system, as much as anything, pushed Michael and his associates towards the union. The union offered a means to salvage some of the crafts and apprentice system while maintaining good wages for the skilled workforce. The union showed almost no interest in the conditions or wages for the unskilled child laborers.[10]

Mike had a lot to say throughout his career, and that made him a natural for union leadership. He had a temper and was not afraid to use his fists, which gave him credibility with the workingmen. While Michael did indeed rise to union leadership, his commitment seemed more pragmatic than philosophical. As an assistant blower at Hobbs, Brockunier, he had faced management control (actually interference), which prevented him from becoming a gaffer. Initially, Owens viewed the union as a way to protect the crafts system and his own career. In addition, the union movement was being led by immigrant Irish who made social security a priority. That is, a worker wanted the ability to rise to a higher level and pay. Helping immigrant Irish was always consistent with Michael's beliefs. Politically, the Irish supported the unionization of the Wheeling steel and glass industries, which was also reflected by the Irish on a national level. The control of the glass industry by English-Americans played into Michael's deep resentment of English control of anything. Also, the union offered another organization for Michael to rise in.

Michael was still struggling to make the jump to blower when the Flints gained control of the Wheeling glasshouses. Michael was quick to understand the potential power of the union, and he wanted to be part of it. However, while he used the union in his youth, he grew leery of its influence in some matters. Later in life, as an entrepreneur, Michael used non-union labor in his first bottle plant. As an owner, Michael did not want to relinquish any control to another group.

Owens started his union career as a contributor to the union newspaper, the *Ohio Valley Boycotter*. While he was a notoriously poor speller, he was an extremely creative writer. He excelled in composition and was able to build a convincing argument.

Owens was always ready to debate. His debating skills made other men look to him to voice their grievances. Mike certainly enjoyed the reputation and became active in union positions. The union wanted him for his natural leadership. In the early 1880s, Michael was working on a number of union committees. In 1883, he was elected as Local 9's national convention delegate. The American Flint Glass Workers convention that year was in the hometown of New England Glass—East Cambridge.

The national convention introduced Owens to a major division in the fledgling American Flints: pay differences between the Eastern and Western factories. The Eastern factories, suffering from high costs, had worked with the union to keep wages down. The Eastern plants had also suppressed new technology and any new skilled laborers such as pressers, but cost control was at the heart of the Eastern strategy. The more prosperous districts, such as Owens' Local 9, had been able to make substantial wage gains. The American Flints wanted a more uniform industry and geographic wage strategy, but the Eastern branches believed survival was more important. The 1883 convention was a rite of passage for Michael into the political nature of a national union.

Michael was an ideal union delegate, armed with debating skills and a likable personality. He was also blessed with a beautiful set of teeth and a disarming smile. In 1884, Owens again represented Local 9 at the national convention. He served on the union's wage committee. Michael became well known and liked among the other representatives. He joined more committees and, as in his career in glassmaking, learned the organization by working all the jobs. In 1887, he was elected to the executive board of the American Flints.

In his career, however, Mike wanted to move into management. By fifteen, Mike had been at the top of his career—a glassblower,

The famous Owens smile. (Owens-Illinois Glass Company Records, MSS-200, the Ward M. Canaday Center for Special Collections, University of Toledo)

which he remained for another thirteen years. Michael's own analysis of his career situation was not hopeful. Looking back, he noted:

> I had been a glassblower when I was fifteen. Now, thirteen years later, I was still a glassblower. I didn't think of that as much progress.

For most, becoming glassblower was a career-defining event, but not for Mike. Neither the crafts system nor the union could satisfy his ambition. Furthermore, he was frustrated by work stoppages and economic cycles. Mike recognized that these had less impact on salaried positions. He made it clear: "I wanted a management position."

Mike was restless and maybe more like his father than he wanted to believe. Both he and his father became restless at any one position, but Michael looked up the ladder, not laterally, to move on. He helped build Union Flint Glass Works at Martin's Ferry across from Wheeling in the early 1880s. It did not fare well, and Michael missed a chance to move into management. He was also bumping against a "glass ceiling" he didn't fully understand. The Wheeling-area industrialists were in a type of fraternity themselves—the Masons. The Masons opposed the rise of any Irish Catholic into industrial management. It was an unwritten rule, and Michael did not want to believe it, but ultimately he accepted the reality. Old friends told him of the strength of the Masons in the Wheeling valley. In fact, the Masons successfully kept Catholics out of industrial management well into the 1960s. Michael would never, however, accept that there was no hope. The Irish of Wheeling had found a legendary glassmaking hero in in the family of the Sweeneys. The Sweeneys had built a world-class flint-glass factory in Wheeling's earliest industrial days (1830s). Thomas Sweeney had handcrafted a mold for a huge punch bowl as a gift for Henry Clay. He actually produced three bowls; one was sent to the London Exhibition. The bowl won the Grand Prize and is in the British Museum. The last bowl became part of Michael Sweeney's granite grave marker. Sweeney Glass disappeared before the Civil War but it was remembered by the Irish of Wheeling as one of the great early glasshouses. Sweeney remained the embodiment of the America dream for the glass-making Irish. Times were different in the 1880s for the young glass genius Owens.

Owens' union affiliation certainly did not help his ambition to move into management. Still, Mike moved to various companies in search of that goal. He had several other blowing jobs in the valley as he improved his skills. One of these was paste-mold blower at Dithridge Glass, where he gained valuable experience. Dithridge Glass was an offshoot of Dithridge and Company of Pittsburgh built at Martin's Ferry. Dithridge had pioneered the use of uranium oxide salts to produce yellow custard glass. Perhaps more important for Owens was the learning the technique of paste-mold blowing. Paste molding used thin cast-iron molds with a carboneous paste baked on the surface. The paste could be a simple mix of wax resin and sawdust. The mold was then saturated with water prior to blowing the glass. The blower then gathered molten glass to be blown. Once the gather was put in the mold, it was closed by the mold boy. The blower blew into the mold as he twirled the blowpipe. The wet surface contacting the hot glass formed a vapor layer (steam cushion), allowing the piece to be twirled and eliminating the mold line at the part. This early experience with paste molding would help Owens obtain his first patent for electric light-bulbs.

In 1884, he was working as a glassblower in another glasshouse across the river from Bellaire, Ohio. He resided in a high-class rooming house for glassblowers. It was here that he met "Molly" McKelvey, his future wife. Mike at the time was working a six-day week, ten hours a day, but he did go to mass at Bellaire's St. John's Catholic Church with Molly on Sundays and found time for a picnic or walk in the park. For many, being a glassblower and twenty-five years old would mean it was time to settle down, but Mike's ambition drove him to achieve. He believed he would run a company someday. Mike's career was the result of well-defined, ambitious goals, not luck. He believed that hard work could overcome any roadblock. Marriage at this time would have moved him into mediocrity. He had not ruled out marriage, but he did have measured goals to achieve first. Breaking into management became a quest, and work was his sword. He also feared becoming a mediocre, though somewhat happy, glassblower, which would be too close to his father's path.

Michael seemed at peace with blowing for a while as he worked at Martin's Ferry and courted Molly. Still, he wanted an opportunity to manage. That opportunity would arise from the new Toledo glass company of Edward Libbey.

CHAPTER 4

Libbey Brings His Company
to Toledo

In researching the life of Michael J. Owens, the striking theme is how the destinies of Owens, Libbey, and Toledo seemed linked. Biographers, of course, tend to make connections, but with Owens the confluence of destinies seems natural, what in former times would have been called Providence. In 1888, Owens' destiny was to be united with the city of Toledo as the glass industry moved west in search of fuel and cheap labor. Owens and Libbey would change the city of Toledo forever. Even today the Owens and Libbey names dominate the Toledo landscape. Toledo was more a product of the Industrial Revolution than a source of products for it. Toledo was the center of the Great Black Swamp, which was a tract of muck and mud across northwest Ohio between Lake Erie and the south side of the Maumee River to Fort Wayne, Indiana. In 1812, a soldier called it the "home of Satan." An observer in 1837 said that there was "perhaps no other more unhealthy place upon the whole continent than at this point of Wood and Lucas counties."[1] The only early civilization was a branch of the mound builders around A.D. 900. These "rampart" builders built two mounds in the Toledo area. By the seventeenth century, traders noted no traces of any permanent settlers. The Eastern Indians seemed to have avoided the area as well, other than the annual hunting parties of the Eries. The later extensions of the Erie Canal in the 1840s brought the first real settlers there. The canal actually started a trading and transportation boom in the area. Even with the difficulties of the swamp, the location of Toledo made it a natural intersection of Indian trade routes.

Toledo had deep roots as a transportation center and western shipping hub. In the 1830s, Toledo became part of an extensive Ohio and Indiana canal system. As a lake port as well, Toledo allowed product to flow from the East via the Erie Canal and Great Lakes. The Ohio canals could then move it west faster, avoiding the Lake Michigan route. Even New England Glass used this Toledo route early on to move glass products to the West. The canal system offered a gentle transportation means compared to overland routes, where breakage was high. Canals, however, opened the West to cheaper glass imports, which the mountains had restricted. Canal building of the 1830s and 1840s also brought the immigrant Irish to the Toledo area, and this would become important in Libbey's decision to move to Toledo.

The transportation network of Toledo allowed it to develop as a manufacturing city early on. Its first reputation was for wagon building, due to the abundance of lumber and the Western transportation system. After the Civil War, Toledo had become an important grain center because of the rails and shipping. Still, growth in the 1870s was extremely slow compared to the town's rivals. Grain and beer were its major products. In particular, Finlay Brewing had been brewing German lager since 1855. Finlay Brewing was shipping throughout Ohio, Indiana, and Michigan when Libbey first visited Toledo. Later, Finlay Brewing would become the first customer of Owens' automatic bottle machine.

The growth of the railroads in the late 1870s opened up new opportunities for Toledo. When Libbey visited Toledo, it had 140 passenger trains arriving and departing daily and handled as much grain cargo as did Chicago. It had a total of twenty-three railroad lines, more than any other city. The Toledo Chamber of Commerce claimed it to be the "greatest railroad center in the world."[2] Toledo's lake port also offered a quick changeover to rail, whereas a long trip through the lakes around Michigan was required from the East to reach Chicago's port and rails. This hub of transportation was essential to the glass companies, whose market was rapidly moving west. Rival locations in Wheeling and

Pittsburgh lacked such integrated transportation for both customers and suppliers. Toledo offered canals, lake ports, rivers, railroads, and good roads to ship product in all directions. Toledo had lacked industrial development, but real progress arrived with the great gas boom of the 1880s. That economic movement was to start south of Toledo in the town of Findlay.

Findlay, Ohio, perplexed early settlers with many strange happenings. Marsh-gas "lights" produced eerie glows at night. There were oily and even burning ponds. Then, in 1859, the nation's first successful oil well came in at Titusville, Pennsylvania, and created a rush in oil and gas exploration. This discovery changed the nation, and Ohioans started to look for the black gold of industry. Findlay, with its gas seepage, seemed a natural place to look. Nearby Bowling Green also found gas, but Toledo never did. What Toledo businessmen did do was organize private gas-line companies to bring gas in from Lima and Findlay. A great pipeline race was on to assure Toledo's gas supplies. The pipeline was turned on July 27, 1887, a few months prior to the initial Libbey inquiries. The "Grand Gas Celebration" was formally held on September 7, 1887, with ex-president Rutherford B. Hayes speaking. Hayes had personally been involved in the northwest Ohio gas rush, drilling wells on his Fremont estate.

With gas supplies assured, the "Toledo Business Men's Committee" (also called the "Businessmen Association") solicited industries to come into Toledo. The committee seems to have grown out of local real-estate men's invitation to "take active steps to derive some benefit from gas development." But just as important was a belief in the industrial future of the area.

The area also had a strong advocate in the *Toledo Blade*. The invitation was mailed on a postcard to every businessman in the city. The group came together on April 8, 1887, at Toledo Memorial Hall to elect officers. A well-known and dynamic hardware-store owner, William H. Maher, was elected as the promotional secretary. Maher's significance seems lost on Toledo and the glass industry today, but the man deserves a bronze statue. In the fall of 1887, Maher launched a major advertising campaign in other cities' newspapers to bring glass companies to Toledo. The campaign emphasized low gas prices and detailed the area's environmental and transportation strengths. This was to bring Edward D. Libbey's agents to the city.

Maher's campaign had targeted the glass centers of Wheeling, Pittsburgh, and New England. Within a few weeks, he had over twenty-five prospective companies lined up to visit. Within ten days, the first company, Toledo Window Glass, signed to start operations in 1888.

Toledo was not alone in such advertising; cities such as Tiffin, Findlay, and Fostoria were out there too. Libbey was actually reviewing a large number of geographic locations; he had taken this on as a personal project. He was clearly frustrated with the union efforts at his New England plant, and this was his main motivation to look for cheaper fuel prices. Libbey wanted to pay the higher wages to the workers, but with New England fuel prices, this would make it impossible to remain profitable. Libbey never viewed the union issue as local but as an industrywide, global struggle. He was always a "gentleman glassmaker," wanting to work with the men. Libbey hated direct confrontation, but the cost pressure had forced him to hold firm with the union. In fact, Libbey, unlike Owens, remained open to unions in all of his plants.

Small strikes and union slowdowns in New England had drained Libbey's corporate and personal assets. Glass historian E. William Fairfield noted: "Sales had fallen to a low point equal to that of 1882 and 1883. Libbey personally had very little money left. For months it had been touch-and-go just meeting the payroll, and now he was faced with a demand for a wage increase that was impossible to meet." Without this cost pressure, Libbey would not have made any geographic move. He loved Boston too much to move west. Still, to the Midwesterners, Libbey and New England Glass had an international reputation. This allowed him to get extremely lucrative offers from many cities.

Libbey spent the fall and winter of 1887 surveying towns in Pennsylvania, Ohio, and Indiana. He was an adroit businessman, realizing that cheap gas was not the overriding factor in deciding where to locate a plant. Libbey had seen coal replace wood as a fuel, requiring dislocation of plants. Still, fuel and labor were over 85 percent of the total production costs and needed to be addressed. Labor was the major cost, but fuel cost was more controllable. Libbey believed that the secret to long-term success was flexibility and innovation, a theory that history would bear out. His corporate and product strategy had to determine the location as much as any cost factor. Libbey also paid attention to the lesser-cost factors such as living conditions, because happy craftsmen were key to high-quality artwork. Libbey's real genius was this type of project management. He personally surveyed all potential sites. In addition, Libbey exhibited patience and discernment in making the selection. His one weakness revolved around his extreme concern for his workers. Libbey believed in the Venetian tradition that quality glass was made by highly skilled craftsmen. The worker represented the heart of glassmaking. Libbey, the "gentleman glassmaker," preferred worker-friendly communities, even over less desirable places that offered him free fuel. He cared about the men to a fault. Libbey's overconcern for his workers often weakened his ability to manage, which would augur the need for a tough manager like Michael Owens.

In the fall of 1887, Libbey made his first visit to Toledo. George Pomeroy, a local realtor and member of the Businessmen Association who would act as his guide, met Libbey at the railroad station. Libbey was taken to an old city lot, which the neighborhhood boys were using as a baseball field. Libbey had seen a number of lots over his weeklong trip, but he favored this baseball field, where Ash Street met the Wheeling & Lake Erie Railroad, because of rail access and a suitable neighborhood nearby for his men. Again, conditions for his men were constantly on his mind, but in hindsight it is clear that Libbey also understood the new role of transportation in the glass industry. He was quick to realize that a good transportation system would overcome any future fuel issue. Toledo, in particular, could deliver coal at Pittsburgh prices and oil at Cleveland prices because of its transportation network. Libbey had learned that fuel flexibility was more important than the availability of one type of low-cost fuel. Any fuel had finite resources, so long-term survival required access to a variety of fuels.

Libbey saw something that the gas boom had masked. Toledo, with its extensive railroads, roads, and lake port, had quietly become the nation's largest soft-coal port. In the early 1870s, Toledo railroads had tied into the great southern Ohio and Hocking Valley coal fields. In 1877, the *Toledo Blade* hailed: "Coal is king of the world and to him that can form the most intimate and firmest relations with his carbonaceous majesty is given power and dominion. Our manifest destiny is clearly outlined; there is no doubt that the future Queen of the West is she who sits at the head of Lake Erie." In 1881, the Wheeling & Lake Erie Railroad opened the West Virginia fields to Toledo. Again the *Blade* hailed the progress: "A magnificent new highway to the finest coal fields in the world. It places us within easier reach of the best and cheapest fuel than any other city in the country." Many believed that Toledo would now become the steel city. The deeper ports of Cleveland, however, allowed steel to move to the Cleveland, Youngstown, Pittsburgh, and Wheeling corridor. Still, coal shipments continued to increase every year. Libbey saw coal as a real plus for Toledo. Coal could offer an alternative to gas, which Libbey was always skeptical of.

A chance meeting that week would also change Libbey's life. One day during the visit Libbey noticed a beautiful young girl in Pomeroy's office and inquired as to her name. The woman was Miss Florence Scott, the daughter of Maurice Scott and a member of one of the oldest families in Toledo. George Pomeroy was the family's real-estate agent and personal friend. Pomeroy was a smart salesman and, noticing Libbey's interest, set up dinner at his house and invited Florence. At that dinner, Libbey met the woman who would be his wife. Florence shared a love of art with Libbey. This meeting probably played a major, but underestimated, role in his decision to come to Toledo. Libbey feared the loneliness that might result from moving to a new city. Florence Scott would offer the romance that was missing in his life.

The only real competition to Toledo in Libbey's mind was not gas-boom cities such as Findlay but the city of Pittsburgh. Pittsburgh offered everything Toledo had but on a bigger scale. Pittsburgh even had a national baseball team that played in the

Boston league. Pittsburgh was also a strong transportation center, but Toledo offered better access to the markets in the West. Fuel, at least coal, was cheaper in Pittsburgh, but Pittsburgh at the time lacked the fuel flexibility of Toledo. The dirt of industrial Pittsburgh was its main disadvantage. Pittsburgh was a coal-burning town. In 1835, Charles Dickens noted that the smoke of Pittsburgh closed off sunlight. To Libbey, the problem was that dust and dirt would require extensive cleaning operations for art-glass manufacture. Art manufacture drove Libbey's vision for his new company. He finally decided that Toledo was the best location.

Still, Libbey continued to hesitate. He loved Boston. His own family went back to Plymouth Rock, so the decision to leave New England was difficult and painful. Unbelievable package offers came in almost daily from Fostoria, Findlay, and Tiffin, which seemed to cloud his thinking. Tiffin had offered free land, free gas, and $25,000 cash! For a brief period he wavered on his Toledo decision. Discussions with his men, however, revealed that few would relocate to such a small town as Tiffin. Glassmakers had a high standard of living and were used to outlets for spending. Toledo offered his men good schools, churches, running water (Tiffin lacked this), professional baseball, lots of baseball fields, and many cultural assets. Even more important to his men was the lack of Irish in Tiffin. . Toledo had a sizable, established Irish population (about a third of the population in 1888). The Irish roots in the area went back to the canal building in the 1830s. The influx of Irish, known as "Lonfords" and "Corkonians," had been the key to the building of an extensive canal system and now offered labor for industry. As the canal traffic declined, the Irish laborers turned to area railroad building. Irish society was well established in Toledo, and the political bosses were ready to welcome the new influx of Boston Irish.

Libbey was reluctant to break his ties to Boston, but he knew that ultimately he had to. His managers were not decisive either. Libbey lacked a manager who could evaluate the risks and make a decision, someone he needed badly in his organization and would soon have in Mike Owens.

Libbey continued to seek miraculous ways to remain in New England right up until the minute that he stepped on the train to move to Toledo. Concurrently, he was facing a new strike at the East Cambridge plant. The fight centered on a pay discrepancy between the old Eastern glassmaking districts and the more profitable Mid-Atlantic and Western ones. The cheaper fuels in Pittsburgh, West Virginia, and the Midwest had allowed for higher wages to be paid there—$80-100 a month for skilled workers, which was 25 percent more than in the New England shops. The American Flint Glass Workers, who had been brought about those wage increases in the Midwest, were urging East Cambridge workers to stand fast. Libbey personally negotiated with the workers, which shows the serious financial position of the company. In the end, the workers struck under pressure from the union national headquarters, giving the final blow to the company. This was the final push Libbey so badly needed to make the decision. Libbey actually understood their position, and in the end he would meet the American Flints' demands at his new Toledo plant.

Libbey explained the situation in an 1888 newspaper article:

> The business has gradually been changing. Glass manufactories began to be opened in the West [western Pennsylvania, West Virginia, and Ohio], and with cheaper fuel the goods could be made for less money and the West has gradually absorbed the business on the cheaper grades of goods—pressed glass, etc. Our works make nothing now but the finest grade of blown glass goods, not being able to compete with the West in the cheaper grades and pressed goods. We keep alive by means of specialties in fine ware, which cannot be made to advantage in the West . . . the present trouble has indirectly come from the effects of the Western manufacturers to force us into paying the same rates for work as themselves. Since the majority of glass workers are in the West, and since they do not wish to lower the wages of the workmen there, they had rather bring about an equalization of wages by raising those of the Eastern workmen and making an increase here. The workmen here are not responsible for the present movement, but have habit forced upon them by the National Union whose control is in the hands of Western workers. . . . There are about 40 men still out, but we don't believe they will be out many days. We will give them but one week in which to return, to

come back at the old rates, after which all who do not come in will be refused work again at our works. We have always treated our men as well as we knew how, and those that are now out do not seem to stay out because they believe in the wisdom of the strike, but rather from a sense of loyalty to the Union. They cannot see that the interests of the workmen in the East and West are not identical, and that they are working against themselves. . . . Our action is not to be understood as a blow at the local unions of glass workers, but is a blow at dictation from the West.[3]

Some histories have suggested that Mike Owens, a West Virginia union representative, was behind the strike at East Cambridge. Some depression-era stories even have Michael Owens going into Libbey's New England office and demanding wage increases for union members.[4] This legend has found its way into many histories of Toledo, but it seems unlikely. A more recent 1960 company history of Libbey-Owens-Ford Glass notes the following:

Legend has it that Michael J. Owens who was active in union work at the time was one of the agitators who finally shut down the East Cambridge factory. William Walbridge who knew Edward D. Libbey from childhood, in later years expressed his doubt as to the truth of the legend, however. He said that Libbey would never have hired Owens, if such had been the case. John D. Biggers, former president and now a director [1960] and chairman of the finance committee of Libbey-Owens-Ford Glass Company, who was well acquainted with both Libbey and Owens through years of daily contacts, confirmed that there was no truth to the popular legend.

However, we have seen that there was some truth behind it, in that Owens was part of an East-West solidarity movement in the American Flint Workers that ultimately doomed companies such as New England Glass.

Libbey's hesitation after his November Toledo visit bothered the Businessmen Association. He had actually decided that if he moved to northwest Ohio, it would be Toledo, but his wavering kept the contest going. The strike now forced a decision, but he pondered his choices again. West Virginia made a last-minute argument that Ohio gas supplies were limited, and rumors of low pressure were common. Libbey was well aware of pressure variations throughout the area in November of 1887. In addition, Toledo was at the edge of the Ohio gas deposit.

In December, William Maher went to Boston to further plead Toledo's case. Maher was aware that strike pressure was building, and Libbey would have to make a decision. Maher never assumed that the deal was closed, and he pushed until Libbey's company agreed to sign.

Toledo had no glass companies in the fall of 1887 but had contracted for a pipeline to run from the Findlay gas fields for potential glass companies. This pipeline would be key in opening up Toledo to glass manufacturing. Maher and the Businessmen Association moved quickly to add further incentives to the pipeline package. Raising the necessary funds was a true community effort. The association enlisted 231 local businesses to finance a fund to purchase a factory site for Libbey. The money was collected in mostly $20 contributions, the largest being $500 from Northwestern Natural Gas Company. This assured the deal with Libbey, and New England Glass's secretary, Solon O. Richardson, Jr., was sent to Toledo to sign the papers. The contract was signed on February 6, 1888, and the *Toledo Blade*'s headline of February 8 proclaimed, "Glass is king." Before leaving town, Richardson set up a display of cut glass at Bell & Powell's Monroe Street store. Lines formed at the storefront for days as the public marveled at the brilliant cut glass, comparing it to "cut diamond."

Cut glass was Libbey's strength, and he had positioned his company to benefit from its rising popularity. He had tough American competition, but even tougher European competitors in the Bohemians. The Bohemians controlled most of the world market with their cut and color glass. They produced enormous amounts of cut glass in various quality levels. Libbey, however, could compete with anyone on the high end of the market. His cost structure in New England had lost most of the middle and all of the lower end of the glass art market. Libbey stood committed to the highest quality, but he hoped the better cost structure of the Toledo location would help him regain the lower and middle part of the tableware market.

Libbey Comes to Toledo

Libbey Glass produced the highest quality leaded (flint) glass for cut-glass products and art pieces. It was already an established company prior to moving to Toledo. It had built up a good reputation for its artistic design and patterns. Among these were the Victoria, Florence, Kimberly, Wedgemere, and Stratford. The Kimberly pattern was named in honor of the Kimberly Diamond Mine and was famed for its diamondlike luster and brilliance. These patterns were used in a full line of products, including nut dishes, jelly trays, celery dishes, ice-cream sets, punch bowls, flower vases, goblets, and champagne glasses. Libbey even pioneered the use of gold or silver gilding on art products. The higher-end art pieces sold for around $30 ($700 in today's dollars). The Toledo public was impressed with the beauty of the displayed pieces, which would also help Libbey sell stock in his new company.

Libbey Glass was a truly world class company. All future works would have an engraved trademark—an eagle in a circle, surrounded by another circle with the words *Libbey Cut Glass, Toledo, O.,* and that would be part of the reward for the Businessmen Association. The company also produced many mundane items, which would require cost control and lower-cost raw materials. Toledo offered some of the badly needed cost reductions.

Still, the key to New England Glass was its reputation for quality. Libbey maintained a very high level of lead in his products to assure the feel of quality. That quality depended on the skill of his glassmakers, his technology, and the quality of his raw materials. Libbey planned to move his men and technology, and Toledo seemed to have the raw materials with two exceptions. One was the special recipe of sand from France, and the other was very special fine clay from Germany to make the crucible pots. This unusual clay would have to continue to be imported well into the twentieth century. Libbey had hoped to find another source, since demand and price for this Bavarian clay was increasing. One reason for the demand was some innovative work of Henry Thoreau, American writer and pencil maker. Thoreau had experimented with the clay from New England Glass in the making of graphite pencils. Thoreau discovered that this fine clay was the secret also to high-quality pencils. Ultimately, Thoreau entered into the business of glass crucible production.

In December of 1887, Libbey's last efforts to reach a compromise with the American Flint Workers failed, and the move had to be made. He had studied the various locations of Pennsylvania, Ohio, and West Virginia as a project manager would today. Libbey turned down other attractive incentives and chose Toledo for the long run. His decision has stood the test of time. Amazingly, Libbey had no hard feelings towards the workers or union, whom he offered to move with their families to Toledo. The American Flint Glass Workers would also organize his new plant. Libbey would even improve their wages in the next few years. He was truly a gentleman and a very ethical owner, but he also knew that in the art-glass market, which he loved, skilled workers were the main assets. The blowers, gatherers, cutters, and engravers were particularly critical to art-glass production.

Once Libbey made the decision to move, he still had one last hurdle to overcome. He was short of cash for the move. The company had lost over $40,000 in 1887, leaving nothing for the move. Libbey borrowed heavily from his friends and relatives. Both his sisters, Sarah and Alice (wife of future director William Walbridge), lent large sums, even borrowing against insurance policies. He issued a stock offering in a newly formed company— W. L. Libbey & Son—at a capitalization of $100,000. Libbey would use stock issues over the years to great advantage. Toledo bankers helped with additional loans. Libbey once again had proven his ability to raise money in times of need. At the age of thirty-four, he was now ready to launch America's glass empire.

The original Toledo plant was designed for a capacity of thirty-five tons of glass a day. The plant was three stories high, located on fifty lots that became known as "Lower Town" or later as Glassboro.

Ultimately, the plant would take up four acres on Ash Street. The factory complex included a thirteen-pot furnace. The furnaces were gas fired but designed to be adapted to coal, oil, or even wood if necessary. In addition to the furnaces, steam power drove the mechanical equipment and heated the plant.

Many historians have been critical of Libbey's business style, but his multifueled furnaces showed genius. Libbey was quoted in 1888 on the furnace design: "When the gas rates reach a point where we cannot afford it, we have other sources for fuel which, when we located in Toledo, we were not mindful of. Our furnaces are so constructed as to use gas, oil, or coal, and we shall always avail ourselves of the cheapest."[5] No other glassmaker had learned so well from the fuel shortages as Libbey or shown as much insight as to how to survive.

The plant's estimated employment was 300. The majority of the workers would be transferred from Boston, with the balance being local women and child labor for unskilled positions. The *Toledo Blade* reported that hundreds of girls and women applied for less than a hundred unskilled openings. Women were needed because northwest Ohio had a shortage of young orphans, who had been hired by the earlier glass enterprises in Bowling Green.

The groundbreaking had been planned for mid-March but had to be postponed because of the Great Blizzard of 1888 (March 11-14). The actual groundbreaking occurred on St. Patrick's Day, much to the joy of the Irish employees.

Libbey planned to move not only his workers but also all essential plant equipment. The logistics of such a move would challenge the best of companies. Fifty railcars of equipment were dismantled and packed. The value of the transported equipment was over $25,000 (over $1,000,000 today).

The key manager of the new company was Ed Libbey, who was only thirty-four years old and, by his own admission, was a businessman, not a manager. Second in command was Libbey's boyhood friend and company secretary, Solon Richardson. Sol Richardson's expertise was, like Libbey's, in the financial realm. The plant manager, John Hopkins (the "Gaffer"), was the most experienced operator, with nearly four decades in glassmaking. The Gaffer was an easygoing manager—really more of a craftsman. He was just one of the boys and more interested in the artistic product produced. Joseph Locke was the plant superintendent, who functioned as the technical guru for the operation. He had designed many great glass product lines, such as agata, peachblow, amberina, and Pomona.

Bostonians from New England Glass filled all the skilled worker positions, such as skilled cutters. The most skilled positions joined management in the move. While Libbey had convinced most of the skilled laborers to come to Toledo, there was an almost endless hope that Libbey might move back to Boston. This was a tough move for the immigrant Boston Irish, many of whom were making their second big move within a generation.

Their arrival in Toledo was theatrical. The Libbey workers and managers boarded the train in Boston on August 16, 1888, for the thirty-six-hour ride. Ed Libbey joined his men on board, but wives and families were left at the station to follow later. Most of the workers were unhappy about the move, but they realized it was the economics of the time. Like today, the men understood the effect of globalization on their jobs, even though they resented it. During the ride, they planned a company baseball team, baseball being their favorite pastime in Boston.

A large, enthusiastic crowd gathered at the Toledo Station for the August 17 arrival of Libbey. The *Toledo Blade* had primed the city with the morning headline: "All Toledo welcomes you to the future glass center of the world." Mayor Hamilton had set up a popular band (Tony Leon's Grand Army of the Republic Band) to welcome the train and form a parade to the site of the new factory. The crowd remained enthusiastic, waiting through a constant drizzling rain on a hot, humid afternoon. Upon arrival at Toledo, Libbey stepped first off the train to make a short presentation. The Libbey employees had prepared placards: "Give Us Boston Beans and We Will Stand," "We Are the Advance Guard of Glassworkers . . . With Free Gas More Will Follow," and "From Boston to Boss-Town We Have Come to Stay." Some signs suggested their unhappiness—for example, "Natural Gas Has Forced Us from Our Native Heath." Toledo housewives had prepared picnic food for the workers. After the talks, the band led a parade three miles to Ash Street. Cheering Toledoeans lined the route. The description by the *Toledo Blade* was loaded with superlatives and unbounded optimism. There was plenty of drinking for the Irish to ease their arrival. Still, for most of the new arrivals, Toledo could never replace their beloved Boston.

Many biographers of Libbey have characterized him as a poor businessman, but just the opposite is true. What he lacked in operations management, he more than compensated for in finance and marketing. Libbey had over and over saved the company through these avenues. He was ahead of his time in understanding the globalization of business, developing European markets to enhance and complement his domestic operations. Libbey created an interlocking network of corporations that allowed him to stealthily build a monopoly in the glass industry. While other industrialists of the time faced almost constant government scrutiny, Libbey ran his empire quietly from his Toledo base. His project-management approach to the selection of Toledo was brilliant. It is true that he lacked operational and direct management skills, which a Michael Owens would augment perfectly in later years. It was the early operational failures at Toledo that held Libbey back and tarnished his record. Once his young genius, Michael Owens, got the operations under control, Libbey's own genius would surface. Owens' automation changed the nature of work in the glass industry, but Libbey changed the very nature of the glass industry. Libbey would form huge partnerships and interlinking directorships, which ended the entrepreneurial nature of the industry. This new era of Libbey glassmaking started in Toledo and would later be called the "Toledo Glass Faction" or "Toledo Faction." The Toledo Faction would represent one of the most unusual and extensive monopolies in American history. It would also control world glass production on a level with the Egyptian priests and Venetian craftsmen of the past. The "Napoleon" of this great world monopoly would be Michael Owens.

It all started with the first "blow" at the Ash Street plant on August 22, 1888. The startup went smoothly, thanks again to the business savvy of Libbey, who excelled in planning. The beginning production focused on lower-end products, such as soda-fountain glasses and battery jars. Libbey was considering a new line of products that fit his new Toledo location shipping advantages. For example, oil-lamp chimneys were in great demand at the western end of the Toledo rail system. Libbey, the marketer, had also gotten his manager, Solon Richardson, involved with Thomas Edison on the development of electric light-bulb prototypes. And Libbey was focused on the high end of the market, with his success at Tiffany's. His love would always be the art-glass market. Libbey envisioned a full line of art-glass and utilitarian products. He used volume to cover some high-end art-glass costs and high-end profits to cover some break-even utilitarian tableware products. It was a unique operations/marketing strategy that integrated plant resources.

Yet Libbey's personal as well as corporate weakness remained plant operations, which would dog him throughout his career. After a few weeks, the optimism waned as serious operating problems surfaced.

CHAPTER 5

Toledo: The Glass City

Jack Paquette, glass historian, started his book, *Blowpipes*, with a quote that best describes the nature of competition in the glass industry. The Darwin quote was: "It is not the strongest of the species who survive, nor the most intelligent, but the ones most responsive to change." Libbey's decision to come to Toledo would change both the city and glass industry, but more importantly, it was a strategic response to change. The *Toledo Blade*'s famous headline of "Glass is king" heralded the birth of the glass city in 1888. This would set the stage for the arrival of Michael J. Owens and his complex of glass companies. The Libbey-Owens partnership, known as the "Toledo Faction," would dominate the glass industry for the next fifty years. It would control the glass industry both vertically and horizontally in all phases and types of glass manufacturing. The Faction ruled monopolistically over prices and wages through a complex web of interlocking corporate directorships. Libbey arrived in Toledo with less than $100,000 and Owens with less than $1,000. By 1920, the companies they owned or created had $60 million in assets. Toledo as a city was not much better off at the time than Libbey and Owens were, but, like them, it had a vision. Its strength was in the dreams envisioned by its businessmen, who foresaw the city as a manufacturing center.

The early days of Toledo as a city were far from stellar. In the 1840s, it amounted to a frog- and mosquito-infested swamp with few redeeming virtues. The swamp was the root of Toledo's earliest nickname—Frogtown. Roads were mud paths requiring wood planks to make them marginally passable. Road and railroad building struggled in this mud. One visitor in 1846 said of Toledo, "Of all the new towns I ever saw, I think it is the most miserable." Another visitor called it the "rendezvous of bedbugs for all the western country." The canal system allowed Toledo to hang on even with all its drawbacks, and that system would form the foundation of a future transportation network. The visions and dreams of the citizens, however, would be the city's major asset.

In 1870, prior to the rise of the glass industry, Toledo and the metropolitan area of Lucas County was home to 31,584 people. Toledo ranked third in Ohio population, behind Cincinnati and Cleveland. Nationally, it ranked thirty-ninth in population. It ranked behind Cincinnati, Cleveland, Dayton, Akron, Youngstown, and Columbus in industrial production. The leading industry was flour milling, followed by lumbering and carpentry. On a smaller scale, Toledo manufactured bicycles, foundry products, plumbing, wagons, and railroad supplies. Wagon making strengthened the transportation network because of the need to bring large supplies of lumber from northern Michigan.

The swamp environment of Toledo produced some of the best building oak wood in the nation. This oak had been favored for federal shipbuilding from the 1850s. Oak had become a major lake-shipping commodity, hence the name of nearby Oak Harbor.

Along with lumber, the transportation network brought in grain. Toledo had become known as the "Corn City" because of its grain processing. Later, one of Libbey Glass's most popular patented designs was "Maize Art Glass," which had a pattern based on corn kernels and husks. Corn and grain helped build the initial transportation network of Toledo. The canal development, along with railroads in the 1840s, had driven its role as a grain center. As a major port and railroad center, Toledo established itself as the granary of America. Almost all grain for the Toledo mills arrived by rail, and 20 percent left by boat.[1] In 1870, Toledo was even ahead of Chicago in grain processing, but the end was on the horizon by 1870.

Still, the grain boom of the 1860s and 1870s spurred a number of different enterprises. Toledo was known in Germany as the "clover-seed capital of the world," being at the center of the northern Ohio, southern Michigan, and northern Indiana red clover growing area. The second largest railroad in Toledo, the Toledo, St. Louis & Kansas City, became known as the "Clover Leaf." The Germans used the clover as a soil improver and cattle forage. Also, Toledo's ports and railroads allowed it to be a major export center. The Clover Leaf Railroad was narrow gauge, however, which limited its future growth. Ultimately, the standard-gauge railroads, such as the Pennsylvania, won out, moving the clover business to Chicago in the 1880s. Most Toledo grain moved on the standard-gauge Wabash Railroad, which allowed Toledo to remain an important, but declining, grain center into the twentieth century. Grain, however, would lay the rails for the future glass industry.

Another industry closely allied with grain was beer making. Toledo was not far behind St. Louis and Milwaukee in brewing in the 1870s. Beer making came to Toledo in 1851 with Peter Lenk of Wurzburg, Germany. Beer requires boiling a corn and barley malt. The type of German lager beer popular in Toledo used a lot of hops as well. The Germans liked a bitter beer of barley and hops. In 1855, W. J. Finlay started the Finlay Brewing Company. It produced several types of lager beer. The bitter lagers were similar to those still being produced by Pittsburgh Brewing (Iron City Beer). The year that Libbey Glass opened in Toledo, Finlay Brewing was supplying beer throughout the Midwest and had achieved an output of 80,000 barrels.[2] Beer was sold in barrels in 1870, but hand-blown expensive quart bottles might be used inside a bar, filled from the tap. Finlay Brewing would be the first company to use bottles made by Owens' machine, a practice it would continue into the 1970s.

By 1896, Ohio cities such as Fostoria, Findlay, Tiffin, and Bowling Green that had contended for the title were minor glass producers at best. Findlay, for example, attracted twenty-five glasshouses during the boom; by 1908 all were gone. At its prime in 1890, Findlay was second to Pittsburgh in glassmaking. By 1893, almost all of Findlay's glasshouses were gone. Toledo's distribution network allowed it to overcome the loss of gas and offer other fuels. Libbey was one of a few to see the strength in the Toledo location early on. While the other cities' roles faded in the industry, Toledo's boom in glass would occur in the twentieth century, driven not by natural resources but human creativity.

Toledo railroads represented a far-reaching and high-tonnage network to all points. In 1888, Toledo had twenty-three railway lines. Between 500 and 1,000 trains came through the network each day. Toledo citizens had to get used to sleeping amid the rumble of the rails and the whistles of the trains throughout the night. Toledo had fifteen roads to the seaboard towns of New York, Boston, Philadelphia, and Baltimore and two West Coast connections to Portland. Internal routes included five to Chicago, four to Detroit, four to St. Louis, three to Cincinnati, three to Columbus, and three to Buffalo. Toledo was in an excellent position to reduce market transportation costs in the glass industry.

In the early 1870s, Toledo was rivaling Chicago not only in grain shipments but also coal. It would have surpassed Chicago except for the control of the railroads by the "trunk lines" such as Baltimore & Ohio and the Pennsylvania Railroads. These made it cheaper to ship from Chicago to the East Coast than from Toledo. Still, these railroad connections made coal very cheap in Toledo, to the point of rivaling costs in West Virginia and Pennsylvania.

A lesser-known advantage of Toledo was a seam of sand running from Sylvania through Monclova to Otsego Falls on the Maumee River. The vein was a pure type of granular sandstone known as quartzite, very prized in the manufacture of flint glass. Potash treatments were required to remove the few impurities, but Toledo offered potash as a natural resource as well. The firm of Card & Hubbard had worked the quartz site since the 1860s. Libbey was aware of the high quality of this Toledo sand and considered it a major plus to locating in Toledo. Several short railroad spurs such as the Toledo Glass Sand Railroad were built in the 1880s to supply direct shipments to Wheeling, Pittsburgh, and New England. By the late 1880s, the purity levels were reduced as the higher-quality quartz had been skimmed off.

Libbey showed real business savvy in his selection of Toledo for his factory, and Edward Ford, future Toledo glassmaker, confirmed his analysis in 1901.

Toledo has almost everything necessary to manufacture of plate glass. . . . Right at her doors is found the raw material from which plate glass is manufactured. There is white sand in abundance at Monclova and Holland, within fifteen miles of Toledo, at Port Clinton is found the gypsum rock so necessary to us, as we manufacture our own plaster of paris [used as bedding for glass on

Edward Ford. (Owens-Illinois Glass Company Records, MSS-200, the Ward M. Canaday Center for Special Collections, University of Toledo)

grinding tables], and there is nothing to excel Toledo white lime for limestone. When a coal famine exists Toledo can nearly always be relied upon to furnish the needed fuel. Coal is almost as cheap in Toledo now as in Pittsburgh, Toledo offers special lumber market in which one can buy very cheaply.[3]

Oil was a similar story, with Toledo's rail connections to the Cleveland refineries. Libbey had preceded Edward Ford in looking at all these advantages, not just at the gas boom in the 1880s.

An amateur Findlay geologist, Dr. Charles Osterlen, had observed oil slicks and "marsh lights" in the area for years. These were similar to the sightings around early Pennsylvania wells; the first successful oil well came in at Titusville, Pennsylvania in 1859. In 1884, Dr. Osterlen's drillings hit gas under Findlay in the Trenton limestone formation. This formation ran under most of northwest Ohio and parts of Indiana.

The real gas boom started, however, when a Findlay butcher, Louis Karg, struck gas on the south side of the Blanchard River. The Karg well was of enormous commercial value, with a flow of 20 million cubic feet daily. Optimism broke out all over northwest Ohio. The size of the Trenton limestone formation suggested the presence of a huge oil reservoir. Radical geological theories were put forth. On August 11, 1885, the *Toledo Blade* quoted Prof. J. P. Lesley of the Pennsylvania Geological Survey as saying that the gas formations were self-generating. Furthermore, he suggested "it would be impossible to sink a well any place within this basin without finding gas, if the well were drilled to the proper depth." Test drilling accelerated throughout the area, with oil being found in Lima. Eastern capitalists rushed in with cash and plans. Fremont, Fostoria, North Baltimore, and Bowling Green, among others, became boomtowns. Glass companies in particular were attracted to the cheap source of fuel. These companies tended to be the most mobile. Unlike steel, oil, and other industries, glass required little in the way of permanent machinery; its equipment could be moved by rail. The framing of the plants was wood, which could be found locally. Between 1870 and 1910, it was common for whole glass plants to be moved to areas of cheap fuel.

Libbey went counter to the herd, analyzing many economic, transportation, and geographical factors as well as gas availability. Findlay's short gas boom proved him right. The region's first glasshouse was the Findlay Window Glass Company, formed by investors from Bellaire, Ohio. Findlay Window used the cylinder method and first blew glass in 1886. Over the next two years, 3 more window-glass companies settled in Findlay. These factories were plagued with fires as glass men learned to tame the new fuel. Most companies failed as a result of the great gas shortage of the winter of 1891-92. Findlay built 25 glasshouses the very first year of the boom (1888), and by 1892 most were gone. It was estimated that over 130 glasshouses settled in Ohio and Indiana during the boom, and by its end in 1893, only a tenth of these factories were operating.[4] Bowling Green, twenty-three miles north of Findlay, had a similar boom history. Toledo's location north of the Trenton limestone formation turned out to be key in its success.

Much has been made of the gas boom of the 1880s as a stimulus to glass companies coming to Toledo. At that time, a major structural shift was taking place in America. The Eastern and even the Midwestern states were running out of cheap, clean fuels such as wood. This was forcing the iron and glass industries to switch to coal, which was more efficient, abundant, and cheaper.

Maher's Toledo Businessmen Association did what most old industrial centers are trying to do today—morph into a new economic base. Maher today would be an excellent consultant to those cities trying to counter the effects of globalization. His immediate concern in 1888, however, was to ride the nearby gas boom to bring in industry. Toledo would require gas pipelines to compete, at least in the short run. Maher pushed for gas development while looking to the future of coal and oil. His brilliant strategy would be at the core of Toledo's industrial success for over a century. Maher's name has undeservedly been lost to history, but his short-term tactics made headlines. Maher had fostered a great gas pipeline competition to supply gas from the Lima fields.

The Toledo newspapers followed the pipeline race daily. It was the talk of saloons and business luncheons. The race was between Northwestern Gas and Toledo Natural Gas. The latter was actually owned and organized by the Businessmen Association. Maher was the company's vice-president. More importantly, the company employed a number of experienced Standard Oil men. The race began in February 1887 with Northwestern workers digging ten miles of trench before Toledo Gas had received the permits. Both lines followed a parallel path close to today's I-75 corridor. The major obstacles were the Maumee River and many miles of downtown streets needing to be thrown up, trenched, and repaired. Toledo Gas was to cross the Maumee via the Perrysburg Bridge and then come up the west side of the river into downtown. Northwestern crossed the Maumee south of the Cherry Street Bridge by going under the river.

On July 27, 1887, at 10:00 A.M., the Northwestern pipeline reached the Cherry Street Bridge on the east side of downtown, and a flame was ignited (Northwestern claimed victory, and the press obliged). There was a cheering crowd there. Eleven hours later, at 9:00 P.M., Toledo ignited a flame downtown at St. Clair and Madison streets. They used a perforated pipe to spell out "THE TOLEDO NATURAL GAS CO." The "victorious" Northwestern still had to traverse the river! In the end, Toledo Gas was first to supply fuel to a residence (August 28) and factory (Toledo Nuts and Bolts, August 29). Ultimately, it would also supply the Libbey plant.

The immediate effect of the Toledo pipeline was an influx of glass companies. The first glassblowing operation in Toledo was an enterprise headed by Charles J. Hurrle, a former superintendent of Quaker City Glass. Hurrle was given an acre of land and $6,000 to "re-locate." The enterprise and others seems to have been lured to Toledo by a combination of political and promotional efforts. Hurrle argued that is reason for selecting Toledo was "lower rates on fuel, glass sand, lime, lumber and freight."[5] He started his factory on September 1, 1888, a few months ahead of Libbey. The company was incorporated as the Toledo Window Glass Company.

Hurrle's Toledo Window Glass was a twelve-pot factory capable of producing 10,000 square feet of glass a day.[6] The plant employed sixty employees using the cylinder method, which was a major advancement over the earlier crown method. The plant was producing the largest cylinder glass plate in the world. A master glassblower at the plant could produce as many as 120 cylinders in a day. In the 1880s the union limited production to 72 per day. Charles Hurrle was said to be able to produce a cylinder 100 inches long, giving him superman status.

Toledo Window Glass ran for only a few years, failing because it was unable to adapt to the gas shortages. In December 6, 1890, the *Toledo Blade* reported that the plant shut down for lack of gas. Toledo felt the gas shortage first, as pressure dropped in the pipelines and southern cities such as Findlay restricted flow. Toledo Window Glass tried to convert to oil in March 1891, but final shutdown came a few months later. The all-gas design had left the plant incapable of making the necessary conversions to oil. Libbey, on the other hand, had from the start designed in conversion flexibility for Libbey Glass. The shortsightedness of Toledo Window was based on the fact that its plant was to be a promotional center for gas. Some window-glass plants survived the gas shortage by moving to a coal gas or producer gas fuel. The Siemens regenerative process popular in the American steel industry and European glasshouses produced coal gas. The apparatus was expensive and most companies could not obtain the needed cash for conversion. In the end, it would be Toledo's oil pipelines that would establish it as the "Glass City."

Another of the "gas boom" plants that Maher brought to Toledo was the Glassboro Novelty Glass Company. It lasted only four months, but it was a colorful experience, mostly due to its self-styled inventor, "Colonel" Christopher W. McLean. McLean was one of those great Victorian tinkerers and dreamers. While well published in the glass industry, he had lost some credibility with his proposals for all-glass homes and glass coffins. The latter idea resurfaced in 1918, and it is rumored that Michael Owens had a financial interest in it. However, glass coffins were too heavy to gain market share. McLean's actual first proposal for the Toledo operation was for a glass bathtub factory.

Maher's alternative strategy included bringing oil to Toledo as well. In fact, by 1892, there was a small pipeline bringing in oil. More importantly, four oil refineries located in Toledo during the 1890s. The railroads again were the key asset, with most of the early oil coming in via tank car. By 1900, Toledo was an important regional oil center in the Midwest. The *Toledo Blade* summarized the role of oil in 1898.

> Toledo has grown and flourished as no other young city in the country. The oil production is, in a greater degree, responsible for our thrift and advancement than any other industry that has ever had a foothold here. When the country was on the verge of financial collapse in 1893 did any one for a moment ever have the remotest suspicion that any of the monetary institutions of Toledo were the least shaky? Not for a moment! . . . Twelve times a year, every month, money flowed in from the oil fields all over the northwestern portion of Ohio. . . . The farmer received his run checks right along every month and he could go to the office of the Standard Oil Company or some kindred institutions and get his cash. . . . Oil was his salvation. . . . Our wholesale houses depend largely upon the revenue of the oil producing sections. . . . Oil is the real cause of Toledo's growth and prosperity during the past ten years.[7]

As we have seen, Libbey had the foresight to build his plant with the capability to use different fuels. In fact, the Toledo Libbey plant was working on conversion from gas to oil in early 1891. Maher and Libbey's visionary fuel plans made Toledo the glass capital.

Libbey also factored in another advantage of the Toledo area: raw materials. Toledo had an excellent band of limestone and "Oriskany" quartzite, as has been noted. This quartzite was ideal for Libbey's art-glass production. Geologists refer to the strata formally as the Helderburg Limestone. Like the Venetians' ancient river quartzite, the Oriskany quartzite was high silica with little impurities. Flint glass, such as window glass, requires the very highest silica content of sand. This is why the Venetians handpicked river sand for their flint-sand artworks. The Oriskany deposit was on a par with those in the East. This was key to Libbey, whose East Cambridge glasshouse was located near some of the best sand for flint glass known at the time. The Oriskany sand had been shipped to West Virginia and Pittsburgh art and window glasshouses since 1862. Libbey had the Toledo sand tested at his Cambridge plant, and his workers reported it to be the finest sand in the U.S.. The Toledo area quarries of Monclova and Sylvania at their peak could supply 160 tons per day. High-quality sand for window making was mined out by 1895, but lower-grade silica deposits served Libbey into the 1920s. There were also soda (sodium carbonate) deposits in nearby Michigan. The deposit at the little hamlet of Wyandotte, Michigan, a few miles north of Toledo, did more than anything to make Toledo the glass capital. This deposit caught the interest of another famous glassmaker, Captain John B. Ford.

After the gas boom, in 1897, Ford Plate Glass split off from Pittsburgh Plate Glass and came to Toledo. Ford Plate Glass would ultimately cross the path of Michael J. Owens and become Libbey-Owens-Ford in the 1930s. The main reason that Captain Ford and his son Edward Ford came to Toledo was not cheap fuel or sand but the Wyandotte soda deposit. Soda was a critical raw material for clear plate glass. Captain Ford had learned glassmaking from English plate makers, but his first venture into glass was in pipe. He developed a method to produce glass sewer pipe. Being a great salesman, he sold famous engineer Peter Cooper on investing in a glass plant, which he built in 1882 at Creighton, Pennsylvania, twenty miles north of Pittsburgh. Glass pipe, like glass coffins, never found a market. The plant never made glass sewer pipe, but it did become the major producer of plate glass—Pittsburgh Plate Glass.

Captain Ford had learned from the master of Pittsburgh, Andrew Carnegie, that profits came from controlling all resources needed, known as horizontal control. It was that desire that attracted Captain Ford to the soda deposits of Wyandotte. He eventually purchased the deposit, forming Michigan Chemical. In his many trips to Wyandotte, he took the train from Pittsburgh to Toledo, then boarded for Detroit. This was how he learned about Toledo. In 1897, the Fords broke with Pittsburgh Plate Glass to form a new company in Toledo. Besides the

Wyandotte soda deposit, Toledo offered nearly all the materials they needed: white sand, white lime, cheap coal, and lumber. Ford's glass company would ultimately come under the Owens empire and the "Toledo Faction."

Problems Arise at Libbey Glass

The core of the glass capital would be the art-glass manufacture of Libbey Glass, which had been passed the torch of industry leadership from New England Glass and Hobbs, Brockunier in the 1890s. But Libbey would have to struggle much to take the torch. While the mechanical and engineering problems of starting up the plant emerged, so did an unexpected problem—homesickness among the workforce! Libbey-Owens Glass historian E. William Fairfield described it:

> They were growing increasingly irritable. . . . Beneath the dissatisfaction there was a general, gnawing, almost overwhelming homesickness that grew with each successive failure. By the end of the first three months, 35 men gave up and returned to Boston. The loss of these skilled artisans and the difficulty he would have replacing them was another blow added to the many that were undermining Libbey's own confidence.

The problems of Libbey Glass were bigger than the company alone. The year 1888 had been the beginning of a national economic depression. By 1893, more than 2.5 million would have lost their jobs. Businesses fared no better; 15,000 failed, including 600 banks and 50 railroads. Crime was increasing throughout America, and the urban poor frequently experienced tuberculosis epidemics. Northwest Ohio was bucking the national trends, but Libbey's markets were outside the area. The great urban markets for art glass had slowed significantly. One piece of good news was that Libbey had a signed contract for natural gas at 3 cents per 1,000 feet, which many businessmen called a crime, since fair market value was at least 7 cents. The total gas bill for the first year of operation was $4,246, versus $12,000 a year for coal. Still, operating problems at the plant had offset the gas advantage. Libbey Glass was losing large sums of money.

Even more problematic was that Edward Libbey appeared to be slipping into a personal depression. The mechanical problems of the equipment coupled with the loss of skilled operators soon weighed on him. Libbey was unable to manufacture the higher-quality products that his firms had been famous for. Operating and quality problems by September of 1888 were creating a financial crisis that Libbey had not planned for. Great planners like Libbey tend to be great worriers too, and Libbey had good reason to worry. He was having problems meeting the payroll each week. He had risked all of his sister Sarah's money as well as his own to cover early operating costs. Every day Libbey would walk anxiously from the Madison Hotel to the post office to check his postal box for orders. When a week's orders could not cover the payroll, he borrowed from local banks. Libbey Glass existed virtually one day at a time.

By October, Libbey was near despair. Sarah Libbey had moved to Toledo with him. E. William Fairfield, glass historian, described Libbey's low point:

> Discouraged, constantly worried about meeting operating expenses, and faced with the loss of more of his best men, Libbey himself began to long for Boston. One evening, after a particularly trying week, Libbey was having dinner with Sarah. . . . . He was all but entirely discouraged, he told her, and feared that the entire move to Toledo had been ill-advised, a ridiculously foolish gamble. Worse, he went on he had probably lost his sister's money as well as his own and that of his friends and other businessmen who had trusted him.[8]

Sarah would become his best advisor in this depression. She became his source of much-needed strength. Sarah pointed to how their father decades before had risen above the tribulations of the changing glass market to save the company.

Sarah believed that his main problem was a simple case of homesickness.[9] She continued to push Edward into utilizing his strength as a planner in order to save the company. What Libbey lacked in management skills, he made up for in business sense. Finance, investment, marketing, and recruiting were his strengths.

Libbey did come up with a plan, and part of it involved a number of trips to Pittsburgh and Wheeling to recruit skilled replacements for the men he had lost. One of those trips would result in finding the seed of Libbey's future success—Michael J. Owens. Libbey and Owens would change the glass industry forever. Libbey Glass and a network of glass companies formed by Libbey and Michael J. Owens crowned Toledo as the glass capital.

CHAPTER 6

Owens: The Last of the Victorian Managers

Near the end of Edward Drummond Libbey's career, one could not miss the picture of Michael Owens hanging in his office. Few managers are given the unusual tribute of having their pictures hanging in the boss's office! Yet Michael Owens deserved such an honor. His management style had saved Libbey Glass, while his inventions had revolutionized the glass industry. Owens was part of a rare breed of American Victorians, such as Charles Schwab in the steel industry, who changed managerial attitudes and practices. He also represented a group of Victorian industrial geniuses who formed the structure for modern research and development centers. This league of "new" managers of the Industrial Revolution worked their way up in the factory while learning technology and science in their leisure time. They believed in and had demonstrated a work ethic since childhood. Their expertise arose from their work experience, leadership skills, and knowledge of the process. They were highly respected, having worked their way through the ranks, but generally lacked formal education. They were natural leaders in any environment. These Victorian managers stood on the principles of leadership, which at times allowed them to apply unconventional practices. The common model of leadership admired by Owens and many other Victorian managers was Napoleon.

To these Victorians, management was merely a matter of working with other workers. They were straightforward in their approach and at times raw. Their objective was to integrate the corporate vision with the workers' vision. The insight of having been a worker gave them the perspective needed to achieve this difficult integration. Managers such as Owens had the ability to compromise, but they could stand determined as well. His Irish roots influenced Owens; often he used his fists to get his point across. This was typical of the leadership required in a hard-drinking, immigrant industry. Theirs was a type of peer leadership, common on playgrounds. Besides a temper, Owens had a large Irish heart as well. He was known to help a worker who needed money for a family crisis. Victorian managers approached their positions as paternal, but they demanded much. Owens' work ethic tolerated nothing less than commitment to hard work. Owens believed that management needed to lead and set the tone for the workplace.

The Libbey Toledo plant that Owens would come to as glassblower/foreman was in disarray. Some of the start-up problems at the plant were mechanical and equipment based. In addition, no one had any experience in process change. New England Glass had been a stable process environment for years. Formulas, times, and temperatures were routine. Finally, the skilled New England glassblowers became homesick, and their move back home aggravated the disarray. This homesickness seemed to flow down from Libbey himself.

Quality dropped dramatically, which in turn bottlenecked shipping and the ability to meet orders. In 1889, Libbey paid for newspaper ads in Pittsburgh, Wheeling, and the glass towns of southern Ohio to help replace skilled laborers and supervisors. Mike Owens answered an advertisement in a West Virginia newspaper for glassblowers and foremen for the new Libbey plant. He was interested in being a foreman, thus breaking into management.

Though the story of the Libbey and Owens meeting varies, the original source appears to have been a 1967 interview of a mutual friend—John Biggers. Libbey had gone to Wheeling and signed up a surprising number of glass men. As he prepared to leave his hotel room, Mike Owens strode in, introduced himself, and announced that he was coming to Toledo to work for Libbey. Libbey apologized, explaining that he had all the men he needed. Owens replied:

"Oh, no, you don't! You need me!" and Libbey said the man's appearance and self-confidence just stopped him. "So I offered him a job and he came . . . to Toledo with me."[1]

The aggressive young man no doubt took Libbey by surprise. The attitude that Libbey saw that day remained throughout his association with Owens. Libbey saw a positive, hard-driving man, not common in the glass industry. A bond seemed to have formed from the first meeting. Certainly, Libbey realized that Mike's aggressiveness and confidence might be needed. The glass industry was a "gentlemen's profession" in that management lay back and yielded to the craftsmen. Owens' drive and focus would stand out in such a gentlemen's club. Libbey saw Owens as the missing link in his glass company. The attraction was mutual; Libbey remained one of the few Englishmen that Owens held in high esteem. Owens to the day he died respectfully referred to him as "Mr. Libbey."

Throughout Owens' career, Libbey praised his confidence and willingness to take on tough assignments. Reporters hailed Owens' later motto, "It can be done," which Owens proudly displayed on a plaque in his office. And time after time, Libbey would turn to Owens to do the impossible. In his eulogy of Owens in 1923, Libbey remembered that first meeting. "I first met Mr. Owens, then a young man full of energy and ambition, when he came to Toledo and entered the employ of the Libbey Glass Company. Without any school training, without much technical knowledge of the manufacture of glass, without recommendations other than his personal character (which impressed me greatly), he was engaged by me to fill the position of a glass blower."

Actually, Owens came to Toledo as a second-rate glassblower known as a "servicer," but his dream was clearly management. He felt that he could make the move to management quickly at the Libbey plant. Even Libbey believed that the fiery Irishman from Wheeling could somehow make a difference in morale.

The Toledo plant was a far different environment than the one Owens grew up in. Libbey Glass represented the aristocratic Eastern arm of the union, not the hard-driving Western arm of

Owens' experience. The Libbey plant lacked a strong work ethic.

As a glassblower, Owens was part of a guild of master crafts-men. It had taken hard work to rise to glassblower. While the glassblower was a union man, he was also a craftsman and a "professional." Owens had achieved the crafts position of glassblower at the age of fifteen. His move from Hobbs, Brockunier & Company to Libbey appears to have been due to restlessness, a longing for adventure, and a hope for advancement. The Libbey plant would have been a challenge for even a seasoned manager. Owens, however, had brought with him a diverse background in glassmaking. He also realized that the Midwestern fuel of natural gas would replace the coal of Pittsburgh and West Virginia.

Libbey had brought a number of glassblowers from his New England plant, whose only experience was with wood and coal furnaces. The management and a large contingent of Irish workers had also come from New England. The massive requirements for child labor were met locally. About 100 of the 500 employees were to be unskilled women and children. This initial employment estimate took years to be fulfilled. Workers dissatisfied with their wages came to Toledo also, even though their wages were still under negotiation. The New England workers were not only unhappy about wages but resented the move from Boston.

This dissatisfaction surfaced in major drinking problems and poor productivity. The drinking was occurring on and off the job. In the glasshouse, glass melts were to be ready Monday morning for the start of the glassblowers' shift. Hangovers and on-the-job drinking had disturbed the routine, and often glassblowers were kept waiting. The workers often purchased contracts at the local bars to have ready for them a daily morning shot and beer before they entered the glasshouse. The superintendent of the plant ignored the drinking problem. Drinking in the workplace was not unusual in the Victorian era; the goal was more to manage and control it. Many higher-level managers of the time chose not to address the well-known problem, instead pushing control and discipline to the frontline managers. Through hiring and firing, work rules, use of sober foremen, and some union support, drinking on the job could be limited. As a compromise, most

American factories of the time did not provide holidays to the workforce. Judging from the unusual references to the problem at the Toledo plant, drinking must have been significant there. The supervisors were totally frustrated, homesick, and demoralized over the fact that the labor problems from New England had only gotten worse. They accepted poor performance as the norm. Libbey himself appeared to be depressed, homesick, and expecting failure.

Owens was appalled at the operation. He saw the drinking problems, lackadaisical management, poor worker attitudes, and overall lack of work ethic in the New England crews. These men had enjoyed the original prosperity of the industry and then chosen to take no notice of the economic forces of change in it. They were happy to work limited production schedules at a set pay rate. This had been the root of the split of the Flint Workers into East and West factions. West Virginian workers had worked until the last of the day's melts were completed, and they were paid on output. Fairfield described work practices at the Libbey plant: "But no amount of urging could change an attitude that was tacitly approved by the old superintendent. Each evening at quitting time, the men promptly put aside their tools, unworked glass was left to cool, the plant emptied in a matter of minutes . . . a practice condoned in the old New England glassworks but completely averse to what young Mike had been taught in the glass factories of West Virginia."[2] The "union" problems of the New England Glass Company had followed it to Toledo.

The Libbey plant was running heavily into the red each month. The advantages of cheap resources, low-cost child labor, low transportation costs, better market access, and favorable taxes could not offset the attitude problem. The work rules, drinking, and weak work ethic had sped the demise of New England Glass, but the situation in Toledo was even worse. Certainly, the fact that the moved workers had taken a significant pay cut in Toledo contributed to their poor morale. There was a natural propensity to adjust the amount of work down for the lower wages given.

In three months, Owens decided the operation was doomed. He was not alone, as Libbey was thinking of closing and going back to Boston. Libbey was even facing a lawsuit from one of his stockholders for mismanagement. After thirty-six years of profits and dividends, Libbey had failed in the last two years to produce either.

Libbey and the superintendent were clearly too easygoing, and the middle and frontline management lacked leadership abilities as well. In general, management felt no drive to change and had no knowledge of how to improve productivity. They were still plagued by start-up problems, but technical problems arose too. Libbey's older plant manager, John Hopkins—"The Gaffer"— seemed incapable of dealing with the issues. Hopkins was a fifty-year-old ex-glassblower and artist and a born and bred Bostonian with not much liking for Toledo. Like many of the workers, he longed to move back to Boston. As plant manager, Hopkins had to take most of the blame, but his backups tended to be great artists, not managers.

John Locke, the plant superintendent and a famous designer (he had developed the Pomona, peachblow, amberina, and agata art lines), also seemed to ignore the problems. His position gave him full operational authority. Locke was a great artist but no manager. The August 18, 1888, edition of the *Toledo Blade*, on the arrival of Libbey Glass in Toledo, said of Locke: "He is genial, popular, and obliging, and is liked by the 500 men employed by the company. He is a talented man in other lines, being an artist and musician of considerable reputation in Boston." The blend of artist and manager always presented a problem in the glass industry. Locke, like Libbey, viewed the glass industry as a "trade of gentlemen." Management rose through the ranks based on their talent for working glass, but managing men required a completely different set of skills. Such a system rarely produced capable managers. Locke and Hopkins had managed well enough in the tranquility and prosperity of the New England glass industry, but these new economic challenges overwhelmed them.

The Venetian crafts model was breaking down due to globalization of the glass industry. High wages were no longer assured, nor were skilled positions. Imports increased, forcing lower prices and profits. The economic factors had dislodged craftsmen from their towns. They felt more like factory resources than craftsmen. Drinking and depression were the results of this new personal struggle.

A new model would be required. The situation called for true leadership, which was lacking with Locke and Hopkins. The workers had to understand the economic reality and the need for cooperation. Locke and Hopkins probably did not understand the problem themselves. They longed for the good old days of New England Glass.

The hardworking Michael Owens, as a glassblower, was at the center of the failing operation and had a clear insight into the problem. He represented the solution, and it appears that Libbey realized it. The need for strong leadership was apparent to Owens from his first days at the plant. He could supply sober leadership, tough management, and worker support. Owens realized that he could not work in the conditions he saw, nor could most of the good men at Libbey Glass. The proper English management style was failing; a tough Irish approach was needed. The company was going down, and everyone seemed to be accepting it. In fact, the men and management seemed to want failure so they could return to Boston. Certainly, Libbey wanted to return home as well, but he was in too deep. The men needed to understand that Libbey had saved their jobs by taking them to Toledo. Libbey believed that Owens could make them understand. And sure enough, when Libbey gave Owens the opportunity, he turned the company around.

Stories and legends abound about how Owens got the job as superintendent. William Boshart, a later associate of the two men, reported that Libbey took more notice of Owens due to the latter's constant stuffing of the employee suggestion box. Libbey even provided a suggestion box just for Mike. Finally, Libbey gave in and made Owens manager of part of the plant.

The following is a summary of the story related some years later by their friend John B. Biggers.[3] Owens after three months was said to have walked into Libbey's office to give two weeks' notice. When asked what was the matter, Owens replied: "I don't know anything about your books, but I know something about glassmaking, and I can tell that you're not making a success of this business and I don't want to go down with a sinking ship." Libbey was facing extensive deficits for the year and even the weekly payrolls were not assured. He asked what Owens might do if he were superintendent. Michael's response was: "Well, I'm not!" Finally Libbey offered the job to Owens. Owens is said to have waited until the next morning to accept. The acceptance was provisional on Libbey staying out of the direct management of the plant. The story goes that Owens wanted Libbey's door to the plant nailed shut! Every decade, upon the anniversary of Libbey-related milestones, news services have repeated this story, making it, like Owens' original hiring and his introduction of the bottle machine, a legend.

Personal interviews suggest that Libbey hated to deal with more than one or two men at a time.[4] The part about nailing the door shut seems a stretch, since Libbey preferred to delegate as much as possible. However, he would move into a management void if it existed. Libbey would interfere at times. He liked to wander around the plant and have certain things, such as the chemical formulas, under his personal control. So there is, of course, some truth in these well-nurtured corporate legends.

There is evidence that this "official" story may not be the full truth but a story deliberately promoted to mold corporate history. A few years before Libbey died, he started a project to produce a classic account of his companies, similar to Bridge's famous story of the Carnegie steel empire, *The Inside Story of the Carnegie Steel Company.* Warren Scoville, in researching his book, *Revolution in Glassmaking,* found evidence suggesting a more scaled-down story.[5] The building of corporate legends appears to have begun with Edward Libbey, who loved heroic tales of business.

Libbey was inspired by Carnegie's use of department heads and prominent employees. Also, Libbey used company stock to motivate his managers, the same way that Carnegie did. Carnegie offered a model that Libbey emulated throughout his life. One of the key employees credited with the success of Carnegie Steel was Bill Jones. He was a fiery Irishman and a natural leader. Jones was a franchise employee from the working ranks. Libbey's Bill Jones was to

be another fiery Irishman, Mike Owens. The personalities and stories of Jones and Owens are hard to separate. Libbey would look
back to Owens as "his Jones." The analogies are endless. Owens was,
of course, the exact thing that Libbey read about in the Carnegie
organization and exactly what his failing company needed.

Libbey had taken a liking to Owens, but Libbey's close associates were shocked to see him give Michael the superintendent job
at the Toledo plant. Owens was rough around the edges and did
not fit into the social world of officers such as Libbey, Solon
Richardson, and Jefferson Robinson. Richardson, Libbey's right-
hand man and boyhood friend, resented the move, as did longtime sales agent Robinson and Libbey's chief financial officer, Bill
Donovan. All of these officers were aristocratic, gentlemen operators. They felt that the problem at Libbey was a technical one that
they could resolve. The technical issues, however, were more a
result of a problem than a cause. The real problem was that
Libbey's officers were young and not objective. Owens was an outsider, but it was clearly time to go to an outsider, and Libbey knew
it. Yet Owens was also Irish and therefore a natural leader of the
Irish workers. His West Virginia style was also raw and straightforward. Maybe just as important, Libbey realized that many old
Bostonians would need to go, and his managers were not up to
the task of firing them. It was the type of job that Owens could do.

Libbey realized that the business was failing and Owens' glassmaking background was impressive. Libbey did not know at the
time that Owens' real asset was his management style. Owens was
the antithesis of Libbey and therefore overcame Libbey's weak
points in frontline management. Libbey was the financier and
marketer, and Owens became the operations man. Ultimately,
the Libbey-Owens partnership would rival that of Andrew
Carnegie and Charles Schwab. E. William Fairfield described it
best: "Once in a great while, there occurs a partnership between
two men so talented and equipped to supplement one another in
an enterprise that, in retrospect, their success seems almost pre-
ordained. Like the warp and woof of cloth, the individual bents
of their minds, their personalities, and characters weave a pattern
of success. This was the rare alchemy in the partnership of

Edward Drummond Libbey and Michael Joseph Owens."[6] In a 1920s *Saturday Evening Post* advertisement, Libbey-Owens Glass hailed the following:

Edison in Electricity
Bessemer in Steel
Marconi in Wireless
Libbey-Owens in Glass

Owens and the Turnaround

The Libbey-Owens team functioned at many levels. Owens, however, was the organization maker and Libbey the marketing genius. Owens loved to make decisions, feeling confident at every turn. Libbey hesitated to make decisions in areas outside marketing and finance. He agonized for days over the simplest issues. His deliberation served him well in financial decisions but restricted him in operations. Owens sized up issues and then charged forward. Libbey totally empowered Owens to make the operating decisions. Owens' hands-on experience with the jobs and equipment would prove invaluable to Libbey over the years. Their partnership was a perfect fit of weaknesses and strengths with no overlap, and that's what made it so unique. It worked best when each kept to his expertise. The partnership eliminated personal competition between the men and fostered cooperation. It weakened as Libbey slowly reopened his "door to the plant," but at least initially Owens kept him out of the factory.

Owens' first few weeks as a manager were dramatic and decisive. He was passionate and ambitious in his new position, driven by the joy of achieving it. Owens had wanted to be a manager for long time, and he had studied, dreamed, and observed. He did what only a few managers had the guts to do. It is a credit to Owens that he perceived that attitude could not be changed in most cases. Furthermore, he did not have the time to cajole and argue for change. Lesser managers would have tried—and failed. What Owens did was more revolutionary than his bottle machine. He shut down the operation and fired all the employees! Then he individually hired back the men he knew to be hard workers. Negative and lazy workers were gone. Owens reasoned correctly that it was the only way to attack the cause of the problem. The negativity of some could not be changed, and that required organizational surgery. Furthermore, he replaced the fired workers with hard-driving men from the Ohio River-West Virginia corridor. In three weeks, Owens had transformed the attitude and work ethic of the plant. Productivity moved up quickly.

Owens supplied the type of leadership that the workers could follow. He arrived before sunrise and left twelve hours later. He was not afraid to get dirty or pitch in if necessary. He was involved throughout the process, asking questions and correcting problems. He led by doing, and with his background, no worker could question his expertise. Owens knew the union better than most of its members did. He was never afraid to make a decision. Maybe more importantly, he understood the very nature of the worker. He was a product of the workforce and of the Irish immigrants who made up the workforce. He understood their fears and hopes as well as their weaknesses. He lived and worshiped with them. He was with them in the community, workplace, and church. He might be resisted, but he was always trusted. He had the same passion for their homeland—Ireland. He supported high wages but demanded hard work in return. Workers could not fool him, and this allowed him to boost productivity to new levels.

The miracle at Libbey Glass should be taught in Management 101. Most managers would have tried to change attitudes, and the company's future and ultimately the manager's career would have been doomed. Mike Owens believed that you could not change attitudes directly, but you could regulate behavior in the workplace. So many companies spend their energy in trying to change the attitude of a few negative people. Owens got on the floor and pushed the men where needed. His longtime friend and chief engineer, Richard LaFrance, looked back on those days: "A plant manger had to be tough in those days. Mr. Owens had a temper but he mellowed in later years and I seldom was caught in the path of his storms. One of his good traits was that he tried to be fair and judicial in the Solomon fashion."[7] Mike did manage with his fists in those early days, although actual encounters were probably exaggerated. Owens' approach was typical of a breed of twentieth-century managers known as the Industrial Victorians, which included men like Carnegie and Westinghouse. This style was tough but paternal. A manager punished in order to correct and improve workers. Tough and strict, such a manager, like Owens, often gave money out of his own pocket to help a worker with a personal problem. He would maintain the role of corporate father. It was a management style that fostered a kind of worker's loyalty not often seen today.

Owens believed in quality as the basis for success. His approach to quality was unique in the industrial era, but it was clearly a remnant of his crafts background. Quality and productivity were integrated in Owens' approach. He would often inspect the shipping floor for excellence in workmanship. Imperfections resulted in him throwing the piece to the floor to illustrate the importance of quality. He was also known to kick a worker producing shoddy work. The last year of his life, while recovering from a tonsillectomy in California, he wrote a letter to his chief engineer about poor-quality Libbey saltshakers at the hospital, demanding that corrections be made. No matter how much automation was implemented, Owens demanded that output meet the quality standard of the hand craftsmen. This passion for quality was an extension of his perfectionism. His inventions always focused on quality and reliability. He never rushed to market unless his machines could meet the most demanding requirements. His painfully slow progress on development projects often infuriated higher management. Even the frames of his equipment were built to last; nothing cheap was used. Many viewed this type of perfectionism as a costly corporate virtue. However, Owens' commitment to quality would allow his bottle machines to dominate the industry for decades.

Such a strict and tough approach to work and quality may seem strange to today's manager. The Irish workers at the plant were a tough gang. They understood and respected a tough, physical boss. Many times, a worker's main tool of intimidation was bodily threat. The Libbey gentlemen managers had a hard time with this intimidation and usually backed down, which only increased the problem. Drinking tended to make matters worse. But with Owens, they ran into an Irish bulldog, trained from his earliest days to be aggressive. He had learned from those first days at the glasshouse in Wheeling, where he was taunted as a boy. Owens was not only able to stand his ground in the face of aggression, but he could move through it. This forceful, proactive approach allowed him to make some tough choices and stick with them. The shutdown and firing of the workforce had required that type of determination.

Owens also reasoned that he was doing the fired workers a favor. He is quoted in the corporate archives as saying:

> And the others, I did a great favor. When a man has lost his bearings, nothing less than a shock like being fired will put him back on course. Many a good man will tell you that he traces his success to being fired, for that was when he really took stock of himself, what he was doing and where he was going.

Owens saw negativity as a cancer in an organization that required surgery. Cutting out negative people was necessary to assure good workplace behavior and to improve the individual. It can be viewed as tough love, but the very men he fired would later praise it. Benedictine monasteries had advocated such an approach for centuries. This type of courage and insight is rare in a manager. Today we see reorganizations that merely reshuffle the players, avoiding the deeper issues. Negativity is rarely identified and addressed as the root problem. Owens reemployed workers based on their work ethic and positive outlook. At times he reinforced the new discipline with tough language and his fists.

While Owens became popular with Libbey and the men, the old-line conservative Libbey managers disliked this newcomer. Solon Richardson, in particular, continued to distrust Owens. Clearly, this was due partly to Owens getting so much of Libbey's attention. Owens challenged Richardson's title as Libbey's right-hand man, as the *Toledo Blade* had dubbed him. Also, Owens did not fit the Libbey image of a gentleman glassmaker. He was too liberal and volatile for traditional New England organizations, but the Toledo plant was far from a traditional organization.

Drinking on the job was another issue that Owens took head on. It was a common problem throughout America in the immigrant-laden industries. Bars and saloons were located near factory gates. In some areas, beer was considered a way to get more productivity out of a man, an idea still held today in Japan and Germany. Most managers of Owens' time merely looked the other way and hoped it would not interfere with work. But Owens firmly opposed drinking on the job. He watched the factory entrance each morning to be sure he had a sober workforce. He might show up at a local bar to check on his men as well. In addition, he had little patience with those who came to work hung over. Work came first and Owens felt that drinking prevented peak performance. It was difficult for any hard-drinking man to meet the performance requirements of Michael Owens.

With a new organization, Owens turned to improving customer satisfaction as his next step in making the company profitable. Again we see the amazing depth of business insight in the young Owens. He realized that the customers controlled profits. Delayed delivery had resulted in a loss of customers and the customer confidence needed for increased business. Focusing on delivery brought Owens to the underlying problem of poor quality. Poor quality caused endless "remakes," which put orders behind. Many historians believed that the poor quality and delivery resulted from the switch from wood and coal to gas as a fuel. Gas fuel supplied a rapid heat that needed to be adjusted for. The East Cambridge workers could not apply the precise control of heat they had achieved in New England. Owens had solid experience in the switching of fuels at Hobbs, Brockunier, but he worked best by using the experience of others. He spent days with the furnace men and gaffers to adjust the heating. Chemical formulas had to be adjusted as well.

My own research suggests a more significant problem: sand chemistry. A very small impurity such as iron or manganese can result in major processing and quality problems. Industrial chemistry at the time did not fully understand this.

Early American glassmakers had to bring pure sand from Europe, usually as ballast on cargo ships. In New England, Libbey had access to some of the purest sand in the world in Berkshire County, Massachusetts. This Berkshire sand had become the standard throughout the flint-glass market. Even Libbey tried to maintain shipments of it to Toledo. As early as the 1850s, Berkshire sand was being shipped to West Virginia and Pennsylvania.

Pure silica sand was critical for making Libbey's high-brilliance flint glass. The local sand sources did not meet these high purity needs, yet Toledo sand was excellent in less-demanding applications and used throughout the country. Large amounts of Toledo sand were shipped to Pittsburgh and Wheeling glass factories from the 1860s to 1890s. At the peak, Toledo supplied 100 tons of sand a day to the sand industry in the East. The difference in purity, while critical, was difficult to identify except for trial-and-error batches of glassmaking. Cleaning agents such as potash can be added to remove discoloration caused by impurities such as iron oxide. Very minor impurities and trapped elements such as iron oxide can give a green tint to glass. Impurities of just a few thousandths of a percent can cause discoloration, which can make art glass substandard. The source of these impurities can be extremely difficult to find in a new operation. Libbey was probably initially blending New England sand with some local sand, which had a higher impurity level. Plant management had focused on following the recipes and standard operating practices versus undertaking the needed industrial experimentation. This was good scientific management, but what was needed was an experimenter. Michael Owens was just the type of manager needed. He started an in-depth review of how glass was made at Libbey. Owens became more and more convinced that sand and fuel type worked together to affect quality.

Libbey's wood-fired formulas, based on New England sand, were hundreds of years old. In New England, Libbey used many of the Venetian practices, which were based on wood as the fuel. The formulas needed to be adjusted via experimentation. Libbey's high-end product was particularly sensitive to small quality shifts. For example, green-bottle makers saw no problem in

changing fuels. Green is the natural color of lower-quality or recycled glass. Art glass was the highest-quality product.

Owens' experimentation was to be a painfully slow process. It
also required the knowledge of an experienced furnace operator.
Owens had this hard-won experience. In particular, he had experience in fuel changes with diverse products on his West Virginia
jobs. The problems at the Libbey Toledo plant were not entirely
the fault of the workers, as Owens later found the furnace design
to be incorrect.[8] These gas furnaces were some of the first gas furnaces used in industry, and design problems could be expected.
Libbey tried to buy time by keeping the East Cambridge plant
running, but within a few months the exodus of men and equipment from New England further crippled the operation. At the
time of the full-capacity switch to Toledo, the problems were far
from resolved. This was where Owens' knowledge of the overall
process paid off. He could instinctively locate process problems
that eluded others. Owens again brought in the right people to
get the furnace problems corrected.

The improved and adjusted furnaces went a long way towards
increasing productivity and customer satisfaction. As Owens
improved quality, delivery improved, since costly remakes were
avoided. He saw quality as an integrated part of the process, inter-
related with all measures of performance. This integrated
approach to productivity, quality, and delivery was revolutionary—almost a hundred years ahead of its time. Dr. Edward
Deming in the 1980s would successfully echo Owens' views.

With this new attitude, Owens could quickly address the quality issue through worker training. He also strengthened the
apprentice program to support his integrated view of manufacturing. Owens started reorientation programs for his "new"
employees, clearly defining quality, delivery, and reliability as the
mission. Within a year, quality and delivery had improved and
Libbey Glass was known for reliability. This reputation remained
for over a hundred years. Libbey Glass had regained its lead position in the industry, thanks to the skill and resourcefulness of
Michael Owens.

One area that continued to frustrate Owens was Edward

Libbey's control of the batch-mix formulas. Experimentation slowed because of Owens' inability to make mix changes. Libbey had always maintained that secrecy was required in the art-glass industry. He had the advantage in some unique glass chemistries and products. Even Libbey's basic flint-glass formula was unique, requiring more lead content than his competition. Libbey would personally supervise the mixing of new batches, so Owens had to wait for him. Probably just as important to Owens was that he felt, as a manager, he had a need and a right to know the formulas. He started to call Libbey during dinner at the Secor Hotel, where he lived. Libbey would have to come to the plant to prepare a new mix. He finally caved in and gave Owens the formulas. To Owens, knowing the formulas was the highest form of control and power in the art-glass industry. Unfortunately, one of his shortcomings was overdoing things. For the rest of his career, Owens played with new batch chemistries, often with disastrous results. And he held just as tightly to his knowledge of formulas as Libbey had. He refused to the very end of his career to hire a professional chemist. Still, Owens was a great asset to Libbey, even with his shortcomings.

Michael Owens was not the only management asset on the Libbey team. Libbey had brought from New England a scientific manager—Solon Richardson. As noted, Richardson had grown up with Libbey. At the time that Owens took over, Richardson was corporate secretary. Even though Richardson was a great administrator (a skill lacking in both Owens and Libbey), his envy and resentment led to infighting. While Owens and Richardson seemed to always be squabbling for Libbey's attention, they each had an important role to play in the overall success of the company. Back in East Cambridge, Richardson had done some pioneering work with the Edison people on the manufacture of light bulbs, which would lead Libbey Glass back to profitability. Richardson, at twenty-five, was Libbey's right-hand man, having been on the payroll since boyhood. He remained Libbey's friend to the end and was named in Libbey's will, but Owens was always the son Libbey never had.

The rivalry between Owens and Richardson throughout their

early careers was more personal than professional. Both men saw Libbey as a father figure and jockeyed for the position of favorite son. Owens was known for his fiery temper and sharp tongue as a manager but is said to have rarely argued with "Mr. Libbey" (as Mike always addressed him). When a disagreement with Libbey occurred, Owens' strategy was to just leave the room or walk away.

The real genius of Libbey was that he realized the unique skills of both men, and he harnessed their skills and personalities into a successful business enterprise. This was not done in a controlling manner but in a paternal way. Libbey often created separate companies to deal with personal or operating problems. Ultimately, he tried to separate Owens and Richardson, using Libbey Glass and Toledo Glass, but Owens would not be held by paper boundaries. Owens roamed all of Libbey's operations as if they were one entity.

Owens was an energetic, goal-oriented manager. He was typical of many Industrial Victorian managers, who had worked their way up through the ranks. Owens was an operational lion, focused on the big picture and bigger goals. Details and procedures could be set aside for the sake of the goal. Owens was driven by sheer willpower. He was a glass-processing genius whom no one could question. He searched for efficiency in all methods as well as a reduction in labor hours. Performance was the criterion for employment. Owens lacked patience for low energy in the plant. Achievement was his workplace religion. Everything—procedures, education, science, etc.—was secondary to achievement. Owens worked directly in the operations, with little regard for the company's organizational structure. He symbolized the shop master, overseeing all phases of the operations. He tolerated little interference from above and none from below. Owens needed a laid-back boss like Libbey in order to be successful. Owens seemed born to manage operations, but his direct, driven approach applied to managing research and development as well.

Richardson came from a completely different school of management than Owens. This school evolved out of the Industrial Victorians and in the twentieth century would develop into the "Industrial Edwardians." They were followers of Frederick

Taylor's scientific approach. Richardson was also a line-and-staff man, which ran opposite to the non-organizational approach of Owens. Where Richardson loved defined organizations, Owens loved no formal structure. Richardson believed in procedures and set methods, whereas Owens changed things quickly to address a problem. Deviation from procedures often resulted in production problems, but Owens saw this as a discipline issue, while Richardson saw it as a system problem. Richardson also designed his industrial experiments, whereas Owens just experimented. Richardson's scientific approach was very much in vogue in the 1880s, but it required well-defined operating standards. Richardson's approach was powerful and he was an excellent administrator, but he lacked the turnaround punch of Owens' methods. Richardson could never have transformed the company; still, he would play an important role in the future of Libbey Glass. Once Owens had reformed the organization, then Richardson's procedural approach could be applied. Richardson's scientific approach worked best to stabilize and institutionalize organizations.

Owens and Richardson were excellent managers for their own level and environment. Owens represented the model middle manager. He was flexible, people oriented, and goal driven. Richardson was much more the executive. He was interested in organization and job design for the long run. Richardson saw a need to blend marketing, financial, and operating strategies, while Owens saw a need to maximize operating strategy.

Later in life, Owens would be uncomfortable in his more executive positions. His management style would erode organizations; he obeyed no organizational chart or reporting structure. Owens' success depended on Libbey allowing him to run free. Owens was a difficult employeed to manage. Libbey was one of the few bosses he ever accepted. Libbey always tried to control Owens indirectly through corporate boards. Still, the Libbey-Owens team had magic in it, and Libbey knew it even better than Owens did. The Libbey-Owens combination rivaled the Carnegie-Schwab combination as one of the most productive in the history of industry. It is truly unfortunate that we rarely see these great management alliances today.

Given a stable environment, Richardson's methods contributed to success. However, problems such as sand chemistry could actually be made worse by overdependence on scientific management techniques. Also, scientific management was not a strategy for adjusting serious attitude problems. Richardson's efforts at Libbey had been diluted because of the floor disarray and poor morale. Richardson respected Owens' results but loathed his bulldog approach to achieving goals. He and Owens often clashed, but for the most part, they pulled together for Libbey's sake. In the end they learned from each other, even though they never liked each other. Owens supplied the innovation and Richardson the scientific procedures. Libbey knew which man to go to as well. In new projects, new plants, processes problems, and new technology, it was Owens; to stabilize existing operations, to institutionalize processes, and to develop a lasting organization, it was Richardson.

In the long run, it was the Libbey-Owens team that would change the glass industry. An associate noted:

> The whole advance rested on the shoulders of Mr. Owens and Mr. Libbey. Their association was indispensable to improvement. Mr. Owens was the genius who supplied the constructive imagination. Mr. Libbey had the breadth of view to recognize this genius and risk the capital investment necessary to turn the vision into reality.[9]

Such teams are rare. It is difficult to gauge the impact on the glass industry of Libbey and Owens individually. They worked together, augmenting each other. Neither had shown the ability to stand alone. What one could not do, the other could. Libbey and Owens, collaborating on a 1919 article in *System Magazine,* put it this way:

> Moreover—and this is quite as significant—both recognized their own limitations, had full confidence in each other, and so could coordinate their efforts. Owens would say the company's great success was due to Libbey. Libbey would tell you his part was merely incidental and that Owens did it. The truth is, success came because each did his part well, and understood the importance of the other's part.

Certainly, Michael Owens would be the dream manager for any business owner. With his reorganization in Toledo, he would do what other very skillful managers of Libbey could not have done. Owens' success can be seen in the balance sheets of 1890 through 1892. At the start of 1891, Libbey reported a loss of $3,000. Within eight months, Libbey had turned a $50,000 profit, and by year end it was $75,000. The furnace and fuel problems had been resolved. The workforce had been retooled as well. The company had gained a reputation for reliability. Just as indicative of the success was Owens' confidence in his new career. In the summer of 1890, Mike felt he had the financial security to become engaged to be married.

In addition, the Toledo plant had greatly improved its product lines by moving into a small product line of electric light bulbs. Most of these bulbs were for small manufacturers, since the Corning Glass Works in Corning, New York, owned the General Electric contract. Bulb production was where Owens showed his first mechanical genius and obtained his first patent. Richardson, however, was a visionary like Libbey and would lead the marketing turnaround. In fact, Libbey showed little interest in bulb production, preferring art glass. Bulb production had been one of the few things for which Richardson was willing to take a risk. Electricity represented the new consumer frontier, with the potential for explosive growth. Bulb production would be where Libbey used the talents of both Richardson and Owens.

CHAPTER 7

Edison's Light Bulb Lights the Way

Edison's successful electric-lamp experiment occurred on October 19, 1879. One of the seven men present was Ludwig Boehm, his glassblower. The first few bulbs were hand blown from laboratory glass tubing using flame heating. The next year, Edison produced 30,000 lamps with this method. He started a Harrison, New Jersey, plant, and with a force of forty-five men in 1881, he was able to produce 700 bulbs a day.[1] At that rate, implementation of electric lighting would have been greatly slowed. It would be Michael Owens who would make glass light bulbs commercially successful and help Edison light the world.

The Corning Glass Works, of Corning, New York, in 1890 accounted for 95 percent of the total U.S. production of glass light bulbs. The remaining 5 percent was divided among several companies, the premier one being Libbey Glass. In all cases, the glass bulbs were produced and sent to Edison General Electric for the manufacture of incandescent bulbs (lamps). Libbey's role was directly attributable to Solon Richardson's early work with Thomas Edison while he was in East Cambridge. Even at the new Libbey plant in Toledo, Richardson reserved a small fraction of production for bulbs. Richardson was convinced of the bright future of electric lighting, and he wanted to position Libbey Glass to benefit from it. Libbey was less enthusiastic, seeing the company's future in art glass. In December of 1890, a crippling strike hit the Corning Glass Works, which would change the future of Libbey Glass and bring Michael Owens into the national spotlight.

Thomas Edison in one of his New Jersey labs, circa 1910. (Henry Ford Museum)

The strike at Corning evolved from the union's desire for a "closed shop," requiring union membership. The company held strongly to the "open" shop approach of optional union membership—that is, an employee was free to decide whether to join the union or not. The relatively new glass union—the American Flint Glass Workers—had made a lot of progress and was ready to challenge Corning management. The Corning plant fell under the jurisdiction of the Eastern branch of the American Flints. The Flints had continued to push all Eastern glasshouses to meet or exceed the Western plants in union membership as well as wages. In general, the weak profitability of the Eastern glasshouses had slowed the progress of the American Flint Glass Workers. After a ten-year struggle, Corning was a profitable plant in 1890. It controlled 95 percent of America's newest growth-glass market— electric light bulbs. Corning management was firmly anti-union and willing to fight a long battle. The lines were drawn for a long and difficult struggle. Neither side would compromise on its stand, even knowing that Edison General Electric would be forced to find an alternative manufacturer. Fortunately, there was no other manufacturer with the expertise to take over the business. Edison General Electric held on for a few weeks, but its patience was turning to panic. It would be crippled, just as it was fighting to corner the nation's lighting business. All involved realized a new manufacturer would be needed soon. This fear resulted in a unique arrangement with Libbey Glass.

Libbey Glass had been one of the first companies involved in bulb production for Edison. Solon Richardson had started work with Edison Electric prior to moving to Toledo. Spending many days at Edison's laboratory with his glassblowers, he had become a true expert in this new field. While Libbey Glass had less than 1 percent of the business in 1890, it had the expertise. It had been blowing a limited number of bulbs for various Edison competitors as well. The fragile bulbs were considered specialized and difficult to produce, and most glass companies were not actively pursuing the business.

The union took the lead in working out an arrangement between Edison and Libbey Glass. Despite Libbey's expertise in bulb production, its Toledo plant was struggling to solve overall manufacturing problems. The company hesitated to take on such a large and difficult project. The union members at Corning realized that their jobs would be lost if Edison did strike a deal with another bulb manufacturer. They came to Libbey with a revolutionary idea of temporarily supplying the men and expertise to produce bulbs at Toledo during a Corning strike. This radical suggestion was made to Libbey in early January 1890, well ahead of the formal strike in December. The proposition was summarized by glass historian Jack Paquette: "If Libbey would take over

Libbey employees, 1890. Mike Owens is on the back row, third from right, in a dark jacket with his elbows out. (Owens-Illinois Glass Company Records, MSS-200, the Ward M. Canaday Center for Special Collections, University of Toledo)

the Corning contract for the duration of the strike, the union would supply whatever additional number of glassblowers the company would require. Further, the . . . workers guaranteed that blowers would stay on the job throughout the strike period." This is an amazing agreement even by today's standards. Corning management was blessed by such a forward-thinking union (which in the end lost the strike). The plan was a true win-win for all. The union members would keep working while preventing Libbey blowers from gaining the skills to compete after the strike. Corning could prevent loss of the business in the long run. Libbey would position himself for the future growth of electric lighting.

Richardson and the Libbey board approached the project enthusiastically. Libbey himself reluctantly went forward with the proposition but with the restriction that work would be done at a rented location. His struggling Toledo plant was in no position to take on such a major project.

The product also did not fit Libbey's art-glass strategy. Light bulbs would always be a high-volume item requiring cost control and special skills, yet the potential for profit and growth was enormous. The market for bulbs, however, was not yet established, and production problems such as breakage would easily increase costs. Richardson, however, was confident in the future of the market.

Libbey assigned Michael Owens to locate a plant facility. Again, this demonstrated his belief and trust in Owens. Of course, it was a source of friction with Richardson.

Owens' success at the Toledo plant gave him a future he lacked in the Wheeling Valley. Typical of Victorians of the time, Mike felt he needed to be financially secure before marrying. He had been dating Miss McKelvey for six years. Before Owens took over the Findlay operation, he married Mary ("Molly") McKelvey of Bellaire. Mike was thirty-one and his career had just been launched. The marriage took place in the summer of 1890 at St. John's Catholic Church in Bellaire. Owens was extremely private with his family affairs, protecting them from any reporting. It is a challenge for any biographer of Owens to track down family details. Owens would not discuss his family with the press or business associates. He asked that his charitable donations remain secret and even had church records purged of his name. Mike brought his wife to Toledo and moved into a six-bedroom Buffalo Street cottage across from the boardinghouse where he first lived. Later, the family lived in the very fashionable West End of Toledo but interacted little with the neighbors. While Mike was known to play cards with them occasionally, he preferred solitaire. Molly would stay in the background, but she was an active member of several churches. This went beyond making donations; she always volunteered to do physical work also, such as cleaning. She, like Mike, believed that good deeds should be performed in private and without fanfare. Such a humble philosophy ran counter to the Victorian view of philanthropy. Owens would eventually move Molly's sister to Toledo to provide companionship for his wife. Owens was a loving husband, but for most of his early career he was a workaholic.

Mike Owens and his wife (left) with Thomas Rowe and family. (Owens-Illinois Glass Company Records, MSS-200, the Ward M. Canaday Center for Special Collections, University of Toledo)

Owens favored a Findlay, Ohio, location for the new bulb facility because of gas availability and vacant plants. He moved to Findlay in the late summer of 1890 to search for a site and start up the plant. The plant found was the old Globe and Chimney Works, which had opened in 1889 but failed in 1890. This was mainly due to its management's inability to find enough skilled glass workers. Libbey luckily had the manpower agreement with the Corning union. He signed an eighteen-month lease in January and put Richardson in charge of the operation. Richardson had the management and product expertise. The Corning union made good on its promise, supplying 150 workers by the end of the month.

Bulb production began on February 2, 1891, at what would become known as the "Richardson Glass Factory." The operation would run seventeen months and totally reverse the financial status of Libbey Glass. Richardson created the operation, bringing the facility, men, and raw materials together, but Owens made it work efficiently. The rent for the plant was high at $1,800 a month, but the gas supply was extremely cheap. The town of Findlay hoped to make the factory permanent. A local paper predicted: "It is confidently stated that the entire Libbey factory will eventually remove to Findlay where there is a certainty of an abundant supply of gas at all times."[2] The operation had a well-managed startup, which is attributable to both Owens and Richardson.

While Richardson was general manager, Owens was made plant superintendent. Libbey now had his best managers in place for this critical project. At a personal level, it was a shaky alliance but a necessary one. Richardson despised Owens' management approach and resented his creative genius. Still, they would work together, with Richardson proving to be the superior administrator, and he was in a position to assure he received the credit for success.

The production numbers were amazing. Initially, bulbs could be produced by hand blowing at the rate of 1,200 per eight-hour shift. This rate was a little better than Corning's, which was estimated at 2 bulbs per minute from a gaffer and an assistant.[3] In the first six months, the plant had achieved the unbelievable rate of 250,000 bulbs a week! These exceptional production rates were attributed to the first inventions of Michael Owens, which automated portions of the process. Historically, bulbs were blown using hand-operated molds. The gatherer would gather molten glass and hand it to a blower. The blower would blow it into a two-piece cast-iron mold operated by a mold boy. The boy held the mold in place for the blower, and after the blower finished, the boy opened the mold and removed the bulb. Another boy took it to the annealing furnace. He also washed the mold for the next batch of glass. Mold boys made up a substantial part of the glass-blowing workforce. Owens had originally been a mold boy and had an in-depth understanding of the process. He had started designing in his mind years ago the machinery to replace the mold boys.

Owens the Inventor

This process of mental design was how Owens functioned as an inventor. As he worked and handled jobs, he thought of things to improve. Some creative people call this mental process " percolation." It is characterized by the confluence of ideas and physical work. Ideas come to one's mind and are evaluated mentally over time and with experience. This mental evaluation and physical experience feeds creativity. Eventually, the ideas are transformed into a mental picture of what is needed. It is at this point that the invention is conceived—the rest is mere routine. Percolation was the genius of Owens.

Owens created, but he depended on others to draw blueprints and build initial models. This is more typical of today's academic-based engineers. Creativity, however, would be the hallmark of his inventions. His lack of mechanical ability held back his early creative ideas, such as the mold opener, but with confidence, Mike's creativity could not be restrained. He did not need drawings or mechanical principles, because he created based on hands-on knowledge gained by work experience. It is not surprising that a mold device would be his initial invention, since that is where he started—as a mold boy.

In many respects, Owens was a lot like Thomas Edison. Both prized their raw creativity, often leaving the details to specialists, such as mathematicians, scientists, and mechanics. Both men in their later years built huge research and development operations around their creative ideas. Both Owens and Edison managed research by hand drawings, hiring draftsmen to convert them to engineering prints. Drawings appear to be a key characteristic of Victorian inventors. Ford, Bessemer, Bell, and many others used them to communicate their ideas. Many, like Owens, were actually poor artists. While Edison made his drawings in hundreds of notebooks, most of Owens' were on a blackboard in his office, thus they were lost to history. He had blackboards installed throughout his plants. Edison, Owens, and even Ford could not read or make blueprints. Blueprints give two-dimensional views, while these great inventors clearly thought and created in full three-dimensional mental views. Owens, however, more than Edison or Ford, developed a new model for industrial research.

Owens was actually a very unique inventor who does not readily fit the norm. At some level he resembles a Leonardo da Vinci or the auto designer who drew concept cars in the 1950s. These designs, like Owens', were not engineering drawings but artist conceptions. The problem with the analogy is Owens was poor at drawing pictures. Still, he was a designer like them. In fact, these designers were artists by nature and, in most cases, by training. Auto engineers had much to do to bring the car of the artist into reality. Often, some of the original art had to be sacrificed to allow the engineering to proceed.

Owens was ultimately motivated to design his imagined semiautomatic process for bulb manufacture when the Findlay mold boys threatened a strike. The mold boys had gone outside the agreement with the Flints, but they realized that they were a labor resource in short supply. They formed their own "union" and demonstrated solidarity in their negotiations. With the gas boom of the late 1880s, Findlay had offered economic incentives for large families with young children to move there and supply unskilled labor for the new glass companies. The boys who came, many of them orphans imported from the East, were street smart and soon realized that they had leverage. They were actually paid double the national average because of the labor shortage in the area. The strike could have ended the great success of the Findlay operation.

Owens started to work with the plant blacksmith, James Wade, on mechanization of the process. Owens supplied a rough drawing on a piece of yellow paper and Wade engineered it. The device was operated by a foot pedal and left the blower's hands free, thus eliminating the first mold boy from the process. The second mold boy was still required to remove the bulb and take it to the annealing furnace, but the number of boys needed was greatly reduced with the semiautomatic process. The machine was an immediate success, increasing productivity and reducing labor costs. It was hailed as the first breakthrough change in glassblowing in 2,000 years. More importantly, it resulted in production levels that could keep up with the demand for Edison's light bulb.

This gadget (which became known as the "dummy") made a significant impact on the use of child labor in the glass industry. In 1880 child labor made up one-fourth of the glass-industry labor force, representing about 20 percent of the cost of glassmaking. The human cost was even greater, with ten-year-old boys working fourteen-hour days at thirty cents a day.[4] Often, child labor was obtained from local orphanages. It was estimated that the Owens mold-opening device eliminated 1,200 mold boys industry-wide. It brought the price of a sixteen-candle-power incandescent bulb down to eighteen cents, which helped bring electric lighting to the homes of average Americans. The semiautomatic bulb process positioned the glass industry to support the world boom in electrical power.

The paste-mold process came into being as Owens perfected the automatic mold opener. As a mold boy, Owens had been aware of sticking problems between the mold and piece. The paste-mold process allowed for quick, defect-free release. A wax/oil paste is smeared on the cast-iron mold. The heat of the glass forms a carbon layer, which prevents iron pickup and facilitates release. Again, productivity and quality were improved. The idea of a paste mold was not new to Owens. He had experimented with it as a glassblower at Dithridge Glass at Martin's Ferry (near Wheeling).

A ball team composed mainly of glass workers, 1908. (Library of Congress)

Owens applied for a patent in 1892 and started to produce the simple devices for the Findlay plant. While Libbey Glass technically owned the rights, Owens was permitted to sell the devices to United States Glass for a sum of $5,000. However, Richardson had convinced Libbey that the Owens patent would be of little value. As a result, Libbey Glass never paid Owens anything for his invention. Owens felt cheated by the internal review of his patent but remained confident that he would win Libbey over. Libbey did allow Owens to establish an experimental shop at the Toledo factory to further automate the bulb production.

In 1894, Owens was awarded a patent for both the automatic mold opener and the paste-mold process. He would continue throughout his life to improve the automation of bulb manufacturing. Furthermore, this engineering breakthrough was the basis for the Owens' automatic bottle machine.

After four months of operation, the *Findlay Republican* hailed the Richardson plant as a success, "nationally celebrated for the superiority and beauty of its product of electric light bulbs." This article specifically praised Richardson for his achievement. The Eastern press similarly trumpeted the plant's success. Richardson reaped the glory and personal gains. The board of directors approved a major salary increase for him. Richardson's exemplary work also earned him a number of shares in Libbey Glass. The usually outspoken Owens stayed in the background, allowing him to take the publicity and further gain Libbey's confidence.

The success of the operation was not based on lower wages, which amazed industry followers. In fact, blowers at Corning only earned twelve dollars a week, while at Findlay they made up to twenty-eight dollars a week. The plant worked around the clock, employing 200 workers.

At this time, New England Glass formally changed names to Libbey Glass, with a capitalization of $2 million. The new officers were president, Edward D. Libbey; vice-president, Solon O. Richardson, Jr.; secretary and treasurer, Jefferson D. Robinson; and assistant treasurer, William F. Donovan. While all were friends of Libbey, they were much more conservative than he was. The Findlay operation poured both needed cash and profits into Libbey Glass, but that help lasted a brief eighteen months. It had given the Toledo operation the time needed to smooth out the operation, and Libbey had time to pay back his creditors. Still, the Toledo operation's profitability was marginal. The plant suffered from the declining market for art glass.

The Corning union began to recognize that not only was the Findlay product better than Corning's, but so were the labor relations with Libbey. A visit and report by F. N. Hollingsworth, Corning union president, gave the operation extremely high marks, further increasing the worries back at Corning. The Findlay press supported and fostered the reputation of the operation. General Electric was very satisfied as well. Libbey started to plan for the possibility of bringing the bulb operation to Toledo after the eighteen-month Findlay operation expired, but more space would be needed.

The city of Findlay hoped to retain the plant. The plant had proved to be one of the most profitable in the industry. Certainly,

William F. Donovan, 1889. (Owens-Illinois Glass Company Records, MSS-200, the Ward M. Canaday Center for Special Collections, University of Toledo)

Owens had formed strong friendships in the area and favored remaining in Findlay.

Findlay was ready to offer land and free gas if necessary to keep its jewel. Libbey, however, was starting to believe that the gas supply was fast diminishing. Maybe just as important, he was convinced that his company could produce bulbs successfully and that Toledo could accommodate large plants. Libbey had already decided that expanding the Toledo plant made more sense than staying in Findlay. He had excess land available there, and bulb production could help balance the declining market for art glass.

The Richardson plant would be an example of the future of glass in Findlay. Even before it closed, there was an omen of future doom. The plant had low gas pressure in the colder winter of 1891-92, which indicated a problem on the horizon. Actually, outside the geographic area of the Findlay wells, the pressure started dropping in late 1888. On November 13, 1888, the *Toledo Blade* carried the headline, "Natural gas—is the supply failing?" On December 18, 1888, the gas supply to Libbey's Toledo plant failed and wood burning was required to save the glass pots. Throughout the month of December there were extensive general supply failures across Toledo. By 1890, Libbey had started, along with the scores of other northwest Ohio glasshouses, to look for alternative fuel. Toledo had been aggressive in bringing fuels such as oil and coal to Libbey's plant in the 1880s, and so it gained the advantage over Findlay.

In the autumn of 1892, Libbey completely converted the Toledo plant to oil use. The equipment had been designed for flexibility, allowing for the alternative burning of coal and/or producer gas. Oil prices in Toledo were extremely competitive, due to the Standard Oil Company being located in Cleveland. By 1893, the Rockefeller Standard Oil Company brought down oil prices so that it was cheaper than gas.

Libbey Glass was becoming the low-cost glass producer nationally. Libbey's foresight led the way for the glass industry in the area. The time he had invested in reviewing the move from New England was paying dividends, and his marketing of new products was moving the company to profitability. Furthermore, Owens' automatic bulb-mold success and creation of an experimental shop within a factory formed the basis of the Victorian model for industrial research. These simple ideas encouraged the development of automated bottle and bulb machines that revolutionized the industry.

Bulb production in Findlay ended formally on July 1, 1892. The Corning plant had successfully defeated the Flints' effort to unionize. As early as 1878, the Flints had called the Corning plant "the life-long enemy of organized labor." In fact, the American Flints would not unionize the Corning operation until 1943.

Another setback for the union was the loss of nineteen glass workers. On July 3, 1891, a train from Ravenna, Ohio, hit a train that was carrying the young glass workers. In April 1893, the American Flints erected a large stone monument at St. Mary's Cemetery in Corning, New York.

The Findlay operation had rejuvenated Libbey Glass, and Libbey's foresight had prepared him for the future loss of gas supplies. As the Findlay operation closed, Libbey completed his new ten-pot factory extension in Toledo to produce electric light bulbs. Owens' automation had given Libbey a significant advantage in this booming new market. The higher wages and loss of the union fight with Corning brought most of the skilled labor of the Findlay plant to Toledo. The success of the bulb operation and Owens' patents made Libbey the second biggest bulb producer in the country. This also ensured Libbey Glass's overall success.

The Financial Turnaround

The influx of cash came at a time when Libbey Glass was being challenged by a new merger of flint-glass companies. The United States Glass Company, known as the "glass trust," was formed on July 1, 1891. United States Glass was headquartered in Pittsburgh but immediately brought in Columbia Glass Company and Bellaire Goblet Company of Findlay; Nickel Plate Glass, Fostoria; Beatty and Sons, Tiffin; and Ripley and Sons, Pittsburgh. This new company was clearly a trust; the only major flint-glass maker outside the trust was Libbey. United States Glass challenged Libbey in all markets, including bulbs and art glass. Famous glass designer John Locke went to United States Glass in 1891 and helped them launch a series of patterns and colors to represent each state. The states series even today is extremely popular with collectors. United States Glass had major cost advantages from its sheer size and economies of scale. Labor problems, however, were inherent in this merger because of its aggressive approach to reducing wages. Since the glass trust controlled the art and flint market, they were confident that they could isolate the union and force it into lower wages. The union, however, hung just as tough in its resistance. This Goliath might have crushed Libbey had the situation not ended in the longest and costliest strike in glass industry history, from 1894 to 1897. Libbey Glass actually gained market share as the only company producing outside the trust. Libbey worked with the powerful American Flint Glass Workers to maintain production. The excellent relations with the Flints can be partly attributed to Mike Owens. Good management, good union relations, and the Findlay success allowed Libbey Glass to defeat this new challenge.

Demand for incandescent light bulbs by 1897 had outstripped General Electric's ability to supply them. The Cleveland firm of Crouse and Tremaine, realizing Libbey Glass's cost advantage, decided to build a plant in nearby Fostoria and use Libbey's glass bulbs. The Fostoria Incandescent Lamp Company began business in 1897. Libbey supplied it with glass bulbs and barrels of straw. The bulbs were supplied in an un-annealed condition, with a "crack-off end" to be removed and the remaining bulb to be placed in a metal base. Edison supplied a secret solution to produce filaments from cotton thread. The Fostoria plant used mainly cheap female labor to assemble the "lamps" by hand. They were sold under the brand name of Fostoria and sold for eighteen cents.

By 1910, the bulb business required Libbey to build another plant at Sandusky, Ohio. In 1904, bulb production accounted for 60 percent of Libbey sales, and its total market share was equal to Corning's. Between 1904 and 1917, for example, Libbey's bulb sales amounted to $14,406,977, while all its other glassware brought in $10,312,772.[5]

On December 12, 1918, Libbey sold its bulb-making rights to General Electric, ending its role in this market. Richardson's business knowledge and Owens' operating inventions had given Libbey Glass a nearly thirty-year record of success in the glass light bulb market. Owens' work would inspire more experimentation in the industry, which would lead to full automation in glassblowing. He had paved the way to the establishment of the *National Glass Budget* newspaper, which was a significant, historical step forward in glassmaking. The *Budget* itself stated, "Mike Owens struck an original lead far from the beaten, footworn path of experimenters, and demonstrated that what for ages had been deemed impossible, was entirely within the reach of the practical glass blower of an inventive bent of mind."[6]

Owens continued to refine the semiautomatic bulb process by using compressed air in place of lungpower. His patented machine of 1895 could make 400 bulbs an hour by 1899. It would take five blowers to match that production rate. The machine ultimately reduced production costs by 90 percent by eliminating the need for blowers as well as gatherers. Only skilled laborers were needed to operate the process.

The real success story of the Findlay bulb plant success was years away. The invention of the semiautomatic process had awoken the creativity lion in Michael Owens. He began a lifelong process of percolating on ideas for automated production.

A glass factory, circa 1899. (Library of Congress)

Owens also gained confidence in seeing his mental pictures become machines. He started to believe in his ability to invent, even with all his limitations. Success breeds success, and Owens was now sure of his mental designs. Libbey also was more confident in his manager. Owens' star was rising.

At the board meeting of February 3, 1892, Libbey had made a proposal that ended the jubilation over the company's recent successes. He suggested that they build an on-site glass factory at the upcoming World Columbian Exhibition in Chicago. The estimated cost was a quarter of a million dollars. The board was taken aback by the proposal. Libbey Glass had nowhere near the cash reserves to support such a project. Conservatives Richardson and Robinson forcefully opposed the motion. The battle was heated, but Libbey prevailed. Still, the board approved spending only $50,000. Their opposition would continue after the meeting, however, as Libbey tried to secure the necessary loans. Libbey would ultimately succeed in the financing, and he would call on his young lion to build and operate the exhibition. The dream alliance of Libbey and Owens would be an alliance of dreams as well.

CHAPTER 8

The Columbian Exhibition of 1893

The Great Exhibition of 1851 had hailed British industrial might, and the proposed Columbian Exhibition was to do the same for America. This world's fair would be the grandest of them all. The world's greatest companies were lining up to be exhibitors. Since the Great Exhibition of 1851, these world fairs had been a marketer's dream. The Philadelphia Centennial Exhibition of 1876 trumpeted electrical inventions, such as the telegraph and telephone. Philadelphia had also been the launching point for the new wave of art glass and tableware. Libbey wanted to be at the 1893 fair, but he faced aggressive opposition from his oldest friends. Richardson and Robinson were not interested in marketing or risking the company's newly found cash reserve. They were bookkeepers at heart and believed in financial prudence. There was also a product-strategy split, with Libbey still favoring art glass and Richardson more interested in bulbs. Libbey was aggressive in his art strategy and felt that was where his company would leave its mark. Richardson and Robinson held firm against Libbey. They were conservative by nature and wanted to strengthen Libbey Glass before launching another major project.

Libbey's idea was not a simple presence at the fair but a role equal to those of Edison Electric and Westinghouse Electric. He wanted to build a large working factory there. The idea was not without precedent, since Gillinder and Sons of Philadelphia had built a small factory on the grounds of the Philadelphia Centennial Exhibition. Gillinder and Sons had shown that the fair could lead to long-term name recognition as well as short-term profits. They were extremely successful, selling over $96,000 worth of souvenirs at a profit. These souvenirs were beautiful cut-glass pieces. More importantly, Gillinder and Sons caused new interest in cut glass throughout the world. Libbey had studied this operation and felt he could produce a bigger success. The Libbey Glass directors saw it as a waste of resources even if it operated at a profit. The physical plant would be only temporary, and Libbey's proposed ten-pot exhibit would take skilled operators away from the newly turned around Toledo plant. Considering the startup problems at the Toledo plant, starting one in Chicago in less than a year seemed extremely risky. Libbey could end up with an embarrassment instead of a marketing success. Richardson argued hard to convince Libbey to drop the idea. Libbey was, however, confident that he understood the mistakes of the Toledo move and that he could now build a plant anywhere. Secretary Robinson argued that Libbey Glass lacked the cash to launch such a project and the company already had substantial debt. Still, Libbey believed that the project would be a breakthrough.

Libbey held over 50 percent of the company's stock, but he was still dependent on full cooperation from the board. When the board finally approved only $50,000 of the estimated $250,000 needed, John B. Ketcham, a Toledo banker, offered Libbey another $100,000. Libbey went on to raise another $100,000 for the project. He was therefore personally in control of it. He created another company, Libbey Glass Company of Illinois. He commissioned a Toledo architect to design the pavilion. Then he surprised the board by choosing Mike Owens to build and manage the ten-pot glasshouse. It was a vote of confidence in his young manager. Owens, as usual, enthusiastically accepted the project, knowing that it was Libbey's baby and that the board had opposed him. It was an opportunity for Mike to show what he could do. Libbey knew he needed the positive drive of Owens to make it a success, and while the board had overlooked Owens, Owens was the man behind Libbey Glass's turnaround. Owens' assignment was particularly disturbing to Libbey's boyhood friend, Richardson. Yet, considering Richardson's own negativity, Libbey had no choice but to go with Mike Owens. Libbey recognized that Owens was the only manager he had for such a risky business venture. The building of a functioning glasshouse in such a short time would represent a major challenge for the most seasoned manager.

The pavilion was to be located on the midway, which required a concession fee of $5,000. In return for Libbey's investment, the fair officials gave Libbey Glass exclusive selling rights for glass souvenirs. Libbey's readiness and capital put him in this excellent position with the fair board. The midway, or Midway Plaisance, was an isthmus separating the two major sections of the fair— Washington and Jackson parks. It functioned as the main thoroughfare for the visitors. It would by design see the most visitors, and this is where Libbey wanted to be. Reporters described the midway that year as "exuberant" and offering "Barnumesque eclecticism." It was the ideal place to sell souvenirs and articles. Unlike glassmakers at previous fairs, Libbey planned an interactive exhibit. This was something new at a world's fair, where companies generally displayed goods rather than manufactured them. The pavilion was to be a fully functional glasshouse producing Bohemian and Venetian art glass. The palace was designed to hold 2,000 visitors. Its entrance would be flanked by twin towers and topped with a 100-foot dome (which was actually a chimney). The pavilion had beautiful living quarters for Libbey and his wife. The full process of glassmaking, including cutting operations, could be observed by visitors. Libbey supplied more than 200 employees, including his best craftsmen. Each visitor would be given a spun-glass bow on the end of a stickpin. Libbey would sell paperweights, cut-glass tableware, doorstops, candy-striped canes, and fair souvenirs. His colossal exhibit would match the fair itself.

The Columbian Exhibition was huge in every respect. It covered 1,037 acres versus 236 for the Philadelphia fair. Attendance would reach 7 million visitors, of which the Libbey exhibit saw 2 million. The big attraction was the "great wheel," better known today as the Ferris wheel. It could hold an amazing 2,160 passengers.

The fair debuted not only Libbey Glass but also Pabst Beer,

LIBBEY GLASS CO'S FACTORY AT WORLD'S COLUMBIAN EXPOSITION
IN FULL OPERATION DURING THE FAIR

Dimensions: 150 ft. wide, 200 ft. long.   Height of Tower, 100 ft.   One of the most interesting features of the Fair.

MAIN FACTORY, TOLEDO, OHIO, U. S. A.

THE FOSTER PRESS   CHICAGO

Libbey Glass ads for the 1893 Chicago exhibition. (Owens-Illinois Glass Company Records, MSS-200, the Ward M. Canaday Center for Special Collections, University of Toledo)

Aunt Jemima syrup, "ragtime," Cream of Wheat, and Juicy Fruit gum. It was the first major public exhibition of electrical lighting. It was a fair of industrial giants, who were America's celebrities. Some of the greatest inventors of all time, such as Edison, Westinghouse, Bell, Benz, Krupp, and Carnegie, had exhibits. For a young Owens, these were inspiring icons.

The cultural impact of the fair ran deep. The fair introduced postcards, carbonated soda, and hamburgers. One historian called it a "dry run for the mass marketing, packaging, and advertising of the twentieth century." Nothing could have suited Libbey better. Many hailed the exhibition at Chicago as a celebration of the new American consumerism.

The midway took in $4 million of revenue. Libbey took a substantial share. Ultimately, he was able to repay the $250,000 plus return a considerable dividend to the shareholders. Libbey, more importantly, became the perceived leader in art and cut glass. Sales increased for years after the fair and an active foreign market was created. The Libbey trademark was known throughout the world after the Chicago fair.

Another glassmaker, Louis Tiffany, got his break at the 1893 fair. He had a very small art-glass works operating in 1878. Tiffany, like Libbey, was a student of marketing and the use of world fairs. Libbey and Tiffany had worked together early on. Tiffany was one of the first to purchase the patent rights to amberina glass from Libbey. Libbey, on the other hand, was interested in Tiffany's Favrile Glass ("favrile" meaning "belonging to the craftsman or his craft"), an iridescent glass produced by metallic surface treatments. It was an old Roman technique that appealed to Libbey's love of art and color. Tiffany's lamp products found much more success at the fair than did his art glass. But Tiffany and Libbey's fair exhibits started a new movement in art glass that would last for decades.

Still, success for Libbey Glass came only with the tremendous effort and leadership of Michael Owens. Owens had worked hard to have the glasshouse in operating order for opening day, May 1, 1893. It was a dreary and rainy day. What few souls ventured out in the rain bypassed the Libbey exhibit to kiss a nearby replica of the Blarney stone. The lack of interest, even with a free admission, was disheartening to both Owens and Libbey. Owens hatched a plan to hire 250 people off the street to enter the exhibit, hoping to create a buzz and redirect the flow of the crowds on their way to "Castle Donegal." The plan worked as the day wore on. Libbey decided that the free admission was also a mistake and they decided to charge twenty-five cents. By the end of the week, the exhibit had more visitors than it could accommodate. Libbey and Owens found themselves in the opposite position. They moved the price to fifty cents and attendance dropped more than planned. Still, attendance and entrance fees would not be enough to pay for the ten-pot glasshouse. Miss Rachel Fell, one of the women in Owens' crew, suggested that the ticket price could be used toward the purchase of produced glass articles. Within a day of implementation of this plan, all the stock was sold. More needed to be ordered from Toledo, and the on-site glass souvenir production was taken to capacity. Now, with sales and the glasshouse running smoothly, success was assured.

Libbey's exhibition glasshouse was an amazing factory and showroom. Libbey and Owens brought more than 130 craftsmen to the operation. Libbey's best gaffer, Joseph Rosenberger, was highlighted at the fair. Rosenberger developed a number of new cut patterns at the fair, which became national bestsellers. His punch bowl of hunting scenes won the exhibition's gold medal for cut glass. This success would foreshadow Libbey Glass's greatest art piece—its 1904 punch bowl for the St. Louis World's Fair. That bowl made Libbey's glasscutter John Denman world renowned. The bowl weighed more than 130 pounds, held ten gallons of punch, and included cut glasses. Today it is among the Toledo Museum of Art's prize pieces. In 1899, Libbey produced a famous punch bowl for President McKinley. Libbey would saturate the market with advertisements of these successes for years.

Princess Eulalie of Spain's enchantment with the glassmaking process was another marketing success for the company. The princess, accompanied by a relative of Christopher Columbus, attracted much press. She was particularly taken with a spun-glass dress created for Georgia Cayvan, a famous actress of the time.

Punch bowl, stand, and cups made by John Denman for Libbey Glass, 1904.
(Owens-Illinois Glass Company Records, MSS-200, the Ward M. Canaday
Center for Special Collections, University of Toledo)

The dress itself was a publicity stunt, but it attracted crowds. The
production of the dress had cost $5,000. Libbey made a duplicate
for the princess, who in turn named Libbey chief glasscutter to
Spain. The press loved the story and played on it for weeks.
Libbey used the publicity to market Libbey glass throughout
Europe. Actually, it appears that Libbey was secretly developing a
spun-glass business in Toledo. He had brought the inventor of
"spun glass," Herman Hammesjahr, from Germany to Toledo and
had set up or at least helped finance a spun-glass operation.
Hammesjahr started to produce neckties, napkins, and other products for Libbey's exhibition, but nothing ever came from the venture. At one point, Hammesjahr had forty-five girls learning the art
in Toledo. Even the success of Libbey's dress did not produce the
hoped-for market in spun glass. Yet, it is an example of how Libbey,
the entrepreneur, loved new technology and products.

Libbey throughout his career proved to be an unequalled marketer. Owens learned marketing at the fair. He prospered in this

new endeavor of sales and product marketing. He proved himself a solid salesman. This experience would be key to Owens in his future as a technology salesman. To a large degree he was a natural salesman, and the Chicago experience gave him new confidence. Libbey was also pleased with the success of his new marketing apprentice. Libbey, of course, was already impressed with Owens' operational and project-management skills. The two men's strengths augmented each other, and the partnership covered their individual weaknesses. This type of symbiotic relationship could not be found with Libbey's other managers, such as Richardson. The close work over the months cemented the personal bond between the two. With both living at the fair, they became friends as well, although socially Owens and Libbey would never mix. Libbey was the type of man who never forgot a favor, and Owens had stood alone with him in the building of the Libbey Glass exhibition. Owens had also proved that his management skills could stand on their own.

One of the often overlooked advantages of the Libbey glasshouse at Chicago was the experimentation of Owens. He is believed to have continued to experiment with semiautomatic glassmaking techniques during the fair. Mike was also known to visit all of the industrial exhibitions, making his famous bad drawings of devices. There is even a corporate legend that Owens got the idea for his bottle machine from the Chicago slaughterhouses (although I could not corroborate this). The story goes that Owens toured the notorious Chicago slaughterhouses often. These were the same houses detailed in Upton Sinclair's *The Jungle*. There were automatic dipping sheds, which were mechanical novelties at the time. An assembly-line type process clamped steel tongs around squealing pigs. The pigs were then moved to a vat of boiling water and dipped. The line paused momentarily to assure the death of the pig, prior to moving to the slaughterhouse. The story goes that this inspired Owens to use a dipping movement in his bottle machine. There is some similarity to the trip device in his bottle machine, as well as the sequencing of opening and closing. More likely Owens was simply inspired to envision automated operations, the same way that Cincinnati slaughterhouses inspired the assembly line of Henry Ford. There is no doubt that slaughterhouses were marvels of automation, inspiring many industries. They offered models of automation, waste reduction, and efficiency. There always seems to be some truth in these Owens legends. Certainly, he would spend his life trying to fully automate glass plants.

Owens was an extremely curious person, even in the smallest things. He loved to observe the operation of mechanical devices and processes for hours. He was known to ask questions as he observed, making mental notes of dimensions. While many would marvel at the mechanical parts, Owens marveled at the overall systems. Mike would always start with the big picture and then work backward to the parts needed, usually turning over the details of individual part design and implementation to mechanical specialists.

The Chicago fair gave Mike the inspiration he needed to move forward with his dreams and industrial inventions. After a few weeks, the glass factory was running smoothly and Mike could spend most of his time observing and experimenting. He later often stated that the concept of the automatic bottle machine was percolating in his mind for those months at the fair. Richardson also confirmed years later that Owens was working and experimenting at the world fair on the idea. Another member of the exhibition team, James Hill, noted in personal letters too that Owens had been talking of automated glassblowing machines at the fair. This percolating was characteristic of Owens' approach to invention. Many have compared him to Edison, but this type of mental experimentation is more reminiscent of Nikola Tesla. This "imageering" would be the touchstone of Owens' genius.

After the world fair, Owens returned to Toledo to manage the plant and expand bulb production. Mike's family expanded as well in July 1894 with the birth of his only son, John Raymond Owens, named after his father. Owens had to get back to where he left off in Findlay as well. Before the Findlay bulb plant had closed prior to the Chicago fair, Owens was working on an improvement of his mechanical paste-mold bulb device. While the device was not fully operational at the close of the Findlay plant, Owens had applied for a patent. The semiautomatic machine was being used with success at the new bulb production plant in Toledo. The machine substituted compressed air for the lungpower of the glassblower. At the original Findlay operation, Owens had only augmented the lungpower of the glassblower. This greatly increased production by allowing a blower to operate two bulb machines at the same time. The idea of compressed air was first suggested by Ishmael Robinet of France in 1820. Robinet used a type of air pump in these early experiments. New England Glass had experimented with compressed air in the 1870s.

After the fair, Libbey gave Owens a shed on Ash Street and the freedom to work on his own projects. Then Libbey took a long vacation, traveling around the world. Owens never took vacations and continued to improve on bulb production. With the fair's success and Libbey out of town, he had a free hand to pursue his interests. Libbey was pushing art glass throughout Europe, but Owens was building the foundation of Libbey Glass in bulb

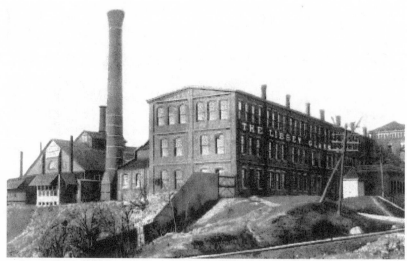

Libbey Glass on Ash Street, 1895. (Owens-Illinois Glass Company Records, MSS-200, the Ward M. Canaday Center for Special Collections, University of Toledo)

production. In addition, Owens' interest in automated glassmaking took him into a new area—tumblers.

With Libbey gone, Mike Owens was uncontrollable in the eyes of the Libbey Glass board. Solon Richardson was particularly upset with Owens doing his own thing. Yet Richardson realized that his old friend Libbey could not say no to the Irishman.

The Birth of the Owens Automatic Machine

Owens continued his development of automated glassmaking until Libbey's return. Some apparently revisionist stories tell that Owens showed Libbey's brother-in-law, William Walbridge, the rough semiautomatic machine before Libbey would see it. Walbridge had been brought in as a manager for Libbey. Walbridge would play an important role in the early development of the tumbler machine, but it is unlikely that Owens went to him before Libbey.

Using his earlier basic patents, Owens had developed a workable semiautomatic tumbler machine by the time Libbey returned from Europe. Owens was the first to bring together the ideas of a semiautomatic mold and compressed air in an automated machine. He showed Libbey his new equipment. The experimental machine used compressed air to produce a number of products. There was the potential to break into two big new markets—tumblers and lamp chimneys. Libbey, as expected, hesitated after seeing the machine. He was concerned that Libbey Glass lacked the resources to develop equipment, and it was not in his product vision.

Libbey's early rejection is contrary to later legends that claim Mike showed the machine to William Walbridge first, and Libbey accepted it with Walbridge's support. This Walbridge story is clearly inconsistent with Libbey's propensity to struggle for weeks to months over any project that was not his own. In addition, Walbridge had just come from the furniture business in Boston and would have been clueless in evaluating a glass machine. Furthermore, Libbey would not make a decision without consulting Richardson and Robinson.

In any case, Owens went to his friend, Father Mullenbeck of St. Ann's Church of Toledo, disappointed. Owens lacked local associates, and his closest friends were local priests. His mother had taught him to trust only a priest in major decisions, and he would follow her advice on this throughout of his life. Father Mullenbeck had encouraged Mike, like the parish priests of his youth. Now, Mullenbeck suggested he strike out on his own if necessary, but Mike was hesitant to do that. Mike liked the security of a salary and had no interest in owning a company or having stock in one. They jointly decided to start a prayer novena (nine days of prayer to the Blessed Mother for help). Mike had a strong devotion to the Blessed Mother from early childhood, and prayer was a natural reaction to setbacks for Owens. On the ninth and last day of the novena, Libbey agreed to finance the machine, which was a great relief for Mike. With Mullenbeck's support, Mike had also started to explore his idea with West Virginia glassmakers, which further pressured Libbey.

Mike, who viewed his Catholic faith as a personal issue, kept the prayer success private. He was extremely dedicated to the rosary but rarely talked of his prayer life. This quiet approach to Catholicism was typical of immigrant Irish who had known repression in Protestant Ireland. It was only after Mike's death that Father Mullenbeck revealed this story of the novena, until then known just to Mike's family.

Libbey had little interest in making tumblers; his own vision was to be the premier producer of art glass. His excursions into practical glass applications were limited to tableware. The bulb production had been a concession to the need to generate a profit. Going into machine development represented a move too far, but again Libbey realized that profitability would require volume product, and he was a bit of a gambler. Libbey's board was more conservative, believing developmental work to be a cash drain. Their opposition was reminiscent of their earlier stand against a fair exhibition. Libbey's real reason for considering Mike's proposal was loyalty. It was Mike who had helped with the realization of Libbey's dream in Chicago, and that meant a lot to a man like Libbey. Furthermore, Libbey had become close to Mike at the fair. Libbey was at least open to helping Mike out.

Libbey was now willing to move on further development, but like the Findlay bulb plant, the Chicago exhibition, and his secret spinning operation, he wanted to keep it a separate entity from his art operations. He also realized that this research and development effort was bigger than Libbey Glass and would require a different set of resources. Plus it was a way to get Owens out of the sight of the Libbey board. Both Libbey and Owens had a love for experimentation and development that the conservative Libbey board had no time for. Libbey and Owens decided to form a new company with a new focus. In 1895, Libbey and Owens formed Toledo Glass Company. On December 17, 1895, Toledo Glass was born, and the Libbey-Owens partnership was defined. The new company took over all the Owens patents owned by Libbey Glass as well as all rights to future patents. Libbey and Owens owned the majority of the capital stock, and the company was completely separate from Libbey Glass.

The story of the formation of this partnership is a very telling one. Libbey, who idealized Andrew Carnegie, believed in giving stock ownership to associates. Libbey's generosity led him to give Owens the controlling share (800 shares) in Toledo Glass.

Owens, just as typically, could not take the lead role over his mentor, according to the story. He returned 400 shares to Libbey. Contrary to the company-promoted story, Owens wanted dollars versus stock. He cared little for stock, preferring a large salary. Owens would later often give stock away with little regard for its value. He gave stock for services as well, a practice opposed by the Toledo Glass board. His lack of trust in stock was common to Irish immigrants. Stock was considered a type of paper used by the ruling class, not on a par with cash. To Owens, stock was the money of the rich but of little value to the common worker. Once, in a childish fit, Mike sold all his stock to show how little it meant to him.

Still, E. William Fairfield noted: "He regarded Libbey almost as a son does his father . . . he respected Libbey's business acumen to aspire to control the company himself."[1] This could be seen in Owens calling Libbey "Mr. Libbey" his whole life. Furthermore, the fiery Owens never raised his voice to Libbey, always leaving the room instead. Owens showed such respect to few. It appears that Libbey, who never had children, substituted Owens for a son. Libbey always referred to him as "Mike."

Owens from the start preferred to stay in a junior partnership position with Libbey than to strike out on his own. It represented a change for Owens, who previously had been ready to move on to advance his career. He was one of those Victorian managers driven not by money but accomplishment. His interest in money was more as a measure of success than for any materialistic reasons. Owens loved also the freedom that he had to pursue his interests, unencumbered by business and financial concerns.

The Libbey-Owens team would be one of the most unique and successful industrial partnerships ever. They were both dreamers and gamblers but traveled in different worlds. Libbey was a natural entrepreneur, while Owens was the ideal intrapreneur. Owens preferred to work in the comfortable environment of the corporation, free of financial and capital concerns. He threatened often to go it alone, but his heart was never in it. He wanted someone to pay him to be creative. While Owens preferred the security of the corporation, he was a manager's nightmare. He demanded freedom. He took direction poorly. Libbey found a way to allow his creativity but harness it also. What Libbey came up with was a new approach to research and development.

Toledo Glass was planned somewhat like a large Menlo Park (Edison's compound). Libbey even envisioned a worker's villa of Venetian architecture to support a new group of skilled glass artisans. Still, it was an experimental operation, and Owens was not interested in villas. But he did envision an invention house modeled after the Venetian crafts system. Owens would be the "housemaster," or master inventor with the ideas. He would have a team of apprentices and journeymen to support the practical development of his ideas, like the gaffer's work gang. Also like the crafts system, the finished product would bear only the signature of the master.

Toledo Glass formed what others would call "research and development centers." In fact, Owens and Libbey pioneered the whole concept of corporate research and development. In addition, Toledo Glass was the first "engineering firm." One of its first actions was to hire a chief mechanic and engineer, to support the creativity of Owens. Henry Colburn became the chief engineer and would be the man to turn Owens' ideas into iron machines.

Owens and Colburn quickly set upon the completion of Owens' automated tumbler machine. Owens and his inventive gang successfully made the automatic tumbler machine commercial. In 1897, Toledo Glass sold the exclusive rights for the tumbler machine to Rochester Tumbler Company of Pennsylvania. Rochester used the machine to produce an array of tumblers, finger bowls, lemonade glasses, and stemware. In addition, Toledo Glass sold the rights to the automated machine to Libbey Glass.

The infusion of cash allowed Toledo Glass to invest in its first factory. Libbey brought in his brother-in-law, William Walbridge to help. The "experimental" factory was built in the Auburndale area (Delaware and Monroe streets) of Toledo. It had a fourteen-pot capacity and Owens immediately put it to use producing lamp chimneys with an experimental semiautomated machine.

Walbridge became the financial manager of the company. Libbey realized that his own Libbey Glass board would have never accepted Walbridge, a "lowly" financial manager, into their glass-making club, so he gave him an administration position at Toledo Glass. He also knew that he would not put another glassmaker in with Owens. Walbridge and Owens, however, made a beautiful team, at least initially, balancing their strengths and weaknesses. Owens and Walbridge would become lifelong friends, but their business relationship did weaken. The initial result, however, was a new semiautomatic glassmaking machine. This machine sent waves throughout the industry. Lamp chimneys were the art of the glass craftsman. Now Owens was automating the heart of the glassmaking art. He had perfected the semiautomated system. Still, since it was not fully automatic, it required four skilled workers and six boys, eliminating only two skilled workers. The bottom line results were, however, significant for any chimney producer. Libbey Glass's cost of chimneys produced went from 23.13 cents per dozen for hand blown versus 10 cents per dozen on Owens' machine.[2] The output was also impressive.

During this time, Libbey stepped down as general manager of Libbey Glass. This was done to appease Solon Richardson, his heir apparent, and allow him to take over. Libbey would, of course, remain at Libbey Glass as chairman of the board. Board member William Donovan, another Boston man, would play a coordinating role between Libbey Glass and Toledo Glass.He was one of the few board members whom Owens trusted, probably because he was an Irish Catholic and both belonged to the local Knights of Columbus. Ultimately, Donovan distanced himself from Owens because of his role on Libbey Glass's board.

Owens still used men and equipment at Libbey Glass with little concern for Richardson's objections. Owens always considered Libbey's assets to be part of a larger, almost mythical company known to outsiders as the "Toledo Faction." Many saw Owens as the true leader of this nonexistent company that represented a real mass of glass-manufacturing assets. This mythical leadership was much resented by Solon Richardson. Libbey, however, clearly viewed Libbey Glass as "his" company, with Mike Owens as "president." In the early years, only Libbey and Owens shared seats on the boards of Libbey Glass and Toledo Glass.

Libbey and Owens felt that Toledo Glass should remain developmental and not get tied down by day-to-day production. In 1898, Toledo Glass proceeded to form a new company—American Lamp Chimney Company. Toledo Glass remained the parent and controlling company. The semiautomated process was further improved by a two-part mold that produced a tumbler and chimney in one mold. As expected, traditional handcrafted-chimney companies became seriously concerned with Libbey controlling such developments. George Macbeth and Thomas Evans of Pennsylvania represented these organizations. Macbeth and Evans worked with Libbey to purchase the new company of American Lamp Chimneys. In 1899, a new company emerged as Macbeth-Evans Company, which took over the Toledo plant. Libbey became vice-president, Walbridge became manager, and Owens became plant superintendent. Toledo Glass would have a substantial share of stock in the new company of Macbeth-Evans. Owens would, of course, continue on with Toledo Glass as well, using the Macbeth-Evans plant as a base of experimental operations. Thus Macbeth-Evans became part of

Macbeth-Evans glass plant in Toledo. (Owens-Illinois Glass Company Records, MSS-200, the Ward M. Canaday Center for Special Collections, University of Toledo)

the invisible "Toledo Faction." Ultimately, through additional licensing arrangements with Rochester Tumbler Company and National Glass, the "Toledo Faction" had effective control of the tumbler and chimney market. The new Macbeth-Evans Company actually merged several companies with additional plants in Pittsburgh and Indiana. Such a merger today would be unlikely because it basically gave control of the chimney market to one company. The Macbeth-Evans chimney plant ran until 1925, when the oil-lamp chimney market fell to electric lighting.

In addition to these semiautomatic glassmaking machines, Owens successfully completed some minor projects. One of these was a method to remove plunger marks from pressed art glass. His process, known as fire polishing, removed the marks by surface melting with a torch flame. This allowed for very deep cut press-pattern molds that could rival cut glass. This "minor" invention of Owens at Toledo Glass is often overlooked, yet it reduced the cost of producing heavy cut glassware (40 percent) by allowing the substitution of pressed glass. Owens was granted the patent on July 4, 1899.

Toledo Glass, with these successes, became independent of Libbey Glass. It would function as an engineering and developmental company for the Libbey empire. Libbey then faced the problem of how to control Michael Owens. Libbey could not say no to him, even when he disagreed. And Owens' new project of a fully automated bottle machine seemed too far-fetched for Libbey. He worried that Owens would use up the corporate assets. Libbey turned to another partner, Clarence Brown. Brown was an investor as well as the corporate lawyer. E. William Fairfield related the following story.

> "Clarence," Libbey is reported to have said, "I want to form some kind of board with you at the head of it, to handle all the new things that keep cropping up in this business. I confess it's getting a little beyond me."
>
> Brown knew Mike Owens well . . . was familiar with his ideas and his "hell-for-leather" approach to turning them into reality. . . .
>
> "Well, it's the first time I have been retained to be a wet blanket," Brown replied, "but I think you need one!"

The story is probably revisionist history, but it accurately reflects the role Brown played.

Clearly, Libbey created a board for Toledo Glass of forceful personalities in the hope of controlling Owens. The board consisted of William Walbridge, Libbey's brother-in-law; Clarence Brown, Toledo lawyer; F. L. Geddes, Brown's law partner; Edward Libbey; and Michael Owens. Clarence Brown made a substantial investment of his own capital in Toledo Glass. Like with any group he belonged to, Owens rose to become the natural leader and, for the most part, a friend to all. But in time, the lawyers, Brown and Geddes, would mount opposition to Owens' control.

This new corporate board created a schism with Libbey's old friends at Libbey Glass—Richardson, Robinson, and Donovan. Richardson, in particular, continued to be resentful of Owens and his partnership with Libbey. Donovan, however, did continue to represent Owens in patent work. Owens continued to function as a consulting manager to Libbey Glass, and he acted freely in the operations and use of equipment. This particularly bothered Richardson and widened the schism with Libbey.

The boards, however, would be the least of Owens' problems over the next four years. Libbey had good reason to be disturbed about Owens' new project. Owens' idea of an automated bottle machine was not a natural evolution of his earlier semiautomatic machines but a quantum leap in technology. That leap would cost millions. For the next four years, Owens launched an Edison-style assault on the new technology, backed by a corps of Toledo Glass engineers and mechanics.

CHAPTER 9

The Owens Breakthrough

In 1959, the centennial of Mike Owens' birth was celebrated in thirty-three cities by the mounting of glass plaques at the plants of Owens-Illinois, Libbey-Owens-Ford, and Owens-Corning. The invention of the Owens Bottle Machine changed not just the glass industry but also the packaging, retailing, distilling, and beer industries forever. The world after the invention of the Owens automatic bottle and container machines was very different from the one before it. The cost of hand-blown bottles restricted any real commercial use of glass bottles. Take, for example, the simple filling of a prescription prior to 1900. The customer had to supply his own bottle or purchase a hand-blown one for his medicine. Standardizing weights and measures was not possible because of the size variations among hand-blown bottles. This variation, combined with the low volume of production, restricted the evolution of automated filling of bottles. Beer and whiskey came only in kegs to be distributed by taverns. Pittsburgh Brewing (Iron City Beer) was the first to use the Owens Bottle Machine, but the rest of the industry rapidly moved to bottles. Pasteurization of beer progressed from bottles and allowed for increased shelf life as well. At the time, milk was distributed by a wagon, and the customer came with a metal can to take it home. Pasteurization was, of course, impossible with this distribution method. Baby bottle-feeding was unheard of. The food industry was totally dependent on canning, Now cheap glass containers allowed for long-term preservation of acidic foods, glass being inert to acids in fruits and vegetables. Automated bottle making would be a major factor in the elimination of child labor in the glass industry and American industry overall. Owens had truly started a cultural revolution through his application of progressive research and development techniques.

Whereas Owens was in his element starting and managing glasshouses, running a research and development center would have seemed a stretch. Glass historian Warren Scoville profiled Owens in 1949.

> It is surprisingly difficult to discover the precise nature of his genius or, perhaps better still, his greatness. . . . He could neither draw nor read blueprints. . . . Whenever he had an idea to communicate to his draftsmen or engineers, he called them together in conference and drew rough sketches of the device he had in mind on a blackboard. In other words, he provided them with the crude idea, and they tried to translate it into manageable engineering terms.[1]

Owens is clearly the antithesis of a modern director of research. Yet he can be fairly compared to James Watt, Thomas Edison, George Westinghouse, Henry Ford, and Steve Jobs (Apple Computers). Owens focused on a goal like a bulldog. He combined his experience with his creativity to find new ways to make glass pieces.

At a technical level, Owens best matches Edison. Consider the following description of Edison by historian William Pretzer: "The Wizard had the curiosity, envisioned the goal, and established the outlines of the puzzle; others provided many of the pieces required to solve it." Owens and Edison have many similarities. Both men used large support staffs, which were kept in the background, out of public view. Both lacked formal training and resented the new breed of university-trained engineers. Both borrowed freely from the work of others. Both wove together the smaller ideas of many into an "impossible dream" to chase. Both appeared to be jealous of their better-educated subordinates. Both were overdemanding and difficult to work for. They were both prone to overwork their employees. Still, these Victorian industrialists demonstrated excellence in leadership, patience, and perseverance. They wanted to dominate their industry. They were often driven by "internal devils."

Marshall Dimock in 1949 studied the "pecuniary" motives of the turn-of-the-century American executives:

> Up to a certain point, rising executives seek increased income first of all; it gives them the comforts and luxuries they want, plus a sense of security. But eventually, varying somewhat with the individual, this financial urge is superseded by a desire for power and position—the chance to make and change policy, and to do things one's own way. This in turn gives way to a desire for recognition, for prestige as a result of work well done. Finally, this egotistical yearning is appeased and top business executives seek an opportunity to work at something where public spirit and altruism are primarily involved.[2]

When researching the corporate records of Owens' earlier years, one cannot escape the parallels with Steve Jobs of Apple Computers. Certainly the tempers and rough personalities are striking, but more so you can see dreamers of little education driving technical experts. The images in national magazines of Steve Jobs drawing on a whiteboard for his subordinates are familiar. Their corporate and industry visions are clearly parallel. Both men represent a corporate dreamer who is necessary to launch a revolution. They were project and product champions. Both had little time for organizational structure. They deserve the credit because without them there was no invention. They are a rare breed. Owens and Jobs could advance technology in quantum leaps, whereas today's well-managed research and development center makes steady but slow progress. The analogy often used today is putting individual bricks in the wall. Owens and Jobs built a wall all at once. They integrated research and development throughout their organizations, giving them competitive and innovative advantage. They invented new technology and directed technical expertise to meet their visions. They functioned outside the box and were not inhibited by previous technical paradigms or functional departments.

Owens was more like Henry Ford and Edison with his fear of publicity for subordinates. Owens hired the expertise he needed but was careful not to bring any more than that. He favored hiring expert batch mixers versus chemists, often ignoring requests of the board. Like Ford, Owens allowed no subordinate to draw any public attention. It seems certain that Owens used an "espionage" network to keep tabs on his management subordinates. He had good reason for concern. Board members Brown and Geddes wanted to gain some leverage over Owens. Historian Scoville accused Owens of firing rising stars: "Several capable men resigned or were discharged because they had been a little too successful in their accomplishments or because they had been outspoken upon occasion."

The selection of Owens' chief engineer is instructive. Emil Bock, his first engineer, deserves a great deal of credit for the invention of the famous bottle machine, which many noted. The board hired him to "help" Owens, but in reality, the board was looking for an inside man capable of replacing Owens, or at least one who could understand what he was up to. Owens, realizing this, never fully trusted Bock. Owens referred to him as the "damn Dutchman." The board caused much of the problem with their constant reference to the "Owens and Bock" machine. Owens clearly did not like this one bit. Bock had a major role in the machine's development, but it was always Owens' idea and concept.

In 1901 Owens added to his team a brilliant engineer, Richard LaFrance, who at the time was in high school and posed no threat. LaFrance remained loyal throughout Owens' life. Owens developed LaFrance as a father would a son. The paternal approach was the hallmark of Owens' management style, but it would be a liability with an experienced and self-motivated employee. Of course, the strength of a paternal organization was the reduction of internal conflict, freeing managers like Owens to focus on creativity. In fairness to Owens, he also took on the role of the obedient son with his boss, Edward Libbey.

Managers realize that personal competition within the organization is the root of poor morale, office politics, and destructive internal fights. It erodes the organization's effectiveness in achieving corporate goals. Andrew Carnegie and his early managers were some of the first to recognize this fact. A team has to be loyal and focused on the corporate goals. The teams of Carnegie, Libbey, and Owens were tied to overall objectives by blocks of company stock. Owens was never stingy with recognition, but he tolerated little publicity for his managers. Many believe that the problem with glass and most other industrial research today is the lack of Owens' type of bulldog control to produce results. Instead, you have credential-based dukedoms competing within the research kingdom for "publicity." For years now, industrial research centers have behaved like universities. Credentials, not ability and results, rule the infrastructure. Egos rule over any team effort. Toledo Glass was a far different organization. It was a kingdom but a highly productive one.

Owens demanded this type of loyalty and also gave it. He gave his whole life to Libbey, never going out on his own. Certainly, Owens felt a little inferior to the new wave of university-educated managers who were taking over the business world. The greats like Owens and Edison feared that credentials would rule over ability. My own experience as a manager supports this view. Some of the best managers I ever had were ones who lacked credentials but whom I promoted based on ability. Many of these high achievers had been held back in today's business world due to not having college degrees or similar training. Brown and Geddes seem to have been most upset by Mike's lack of formal education. Owens' letters showed he was equally disturbed by their lawyer training instead of glass experience. Non-glass men were of no value to Mike. While Owens' letters reflected his power of description, his spelling was extremely poor. Mike did not care, feeling that the main function of a letter was to communicate thoughts, which his did extremely well. Owens asked, "Do you think it would be any clearer to him if all the words were spelled right?" Still, Brown and Geddes argued that his letters were a "poor reflection" of the company.

The results-oriented model of Toledo Glass seems to have been lost on other companies, as Ph.D.s started to run research and development centers. These centers of many large companies have become rigidly organized caste systems. Some years ago in the dying steel industry, a classic example of "modern" research and development could be found in the now-defunct National Steel Research Center. The organization had five layers of management. The cafeteria had three distinct eating sections based on management levels and credentials. These factors determined where you ate. Several times managers received a promotion in cafeteria level without any other reward. All higher levels of management were restricted to Ph.D.s. Projects with fuzzy goals were assigned to the lowest levels. Once research was completed, under heavy supervision by the upper levels, a draft report was issued with practical recommendations for the steelworks. The draft received another complete rewriting by the next level. It then moved to the next level for review of phraseology, and often changes were made on the changes. Finally, it moved to the next level, which reviewed the impact on organizational politics. Many times the originating engineer hardly recognized the finished report. The "customers" in the steelworks rarely found anything useful in these reports. This is exactly what Michael Owens feared fifty years earlier. Most large industries today have to downsize their research centers, since they contribute so little to the bottom line. However, in smaller, high-tech companies, a renaissance of Owens' research model is occurring.

Bottle Machine Development

The development of Owens' automated bottle machine gives a good a picture of that research model. It was a five-year effort with many setbacks. The story has a parallel in the development of Edison's incandescent light, requiring many small inventions and improvements in the supporting system. The development of the automated bottle machine must be viewed as an invention of a whole process. Corporate archives contain a 1925 description of the problem by Richard LaFrance, Owens' engineer:

> While we mention the "machine," it is a fact that the whole process of bottle manufacture, including such units as gas producers,

furnaces, mixing plants for materials into glassmaking, annealing ovens for the bottles, and machine shop equipment for making molds, was crude as can be imagined. All these things had to meet the demands of an automatic process. Pioneering work had to be done and equipment developed to automatically handle the bottles between the machine and the annealing oven. Such a thing had never been thought of before.

Even worse was that Owens had no support from the board, including Libbey. Owens was going to have to fight for his idea as he struggled to develop it. Without Owens, the automatic bottle machine was not five years away but thirty-five or more. In fact,

Glass workers at a furnace, 1902. (Owens-Illinois Glass Company Records, MSS-200, the Ward M. Canaday Center for Special Collections, University of Toledo)

Toledo Glass would have killed the project on the drawing board. When we look to criticize Owens for not giving enough credit for his technical support, remember that he stood alone in moving the idea forward. Invention is a complex mixture of the idea, creativity, development, and persistence. Many brilliant engineers lacked this combination needed to bring forth invention. This is where men like Owens stand apart.

The five-year development span might seem like a long time, but consider that Owens' machine was estimated by the industry newspaper, the *National Glass Budget,* to be an amazing eight to ten years ahead of the competition. Consider other inventors, such as Alexander Bell, who was a few hours ahead of the competition; Edison, who was a few days ahead of the competition; and Bessemer, who was actually a few months behind the competition. Furthermore, Bell, Edison, and Bessemer spent years studying previous patents and research, while Owens had nothing to study. Edison, for example, had a huge research library built at Menlo Park for this purpose. Owens, on the other hand, was pioneering his invention, with the possible exception of the suction device, which he may have borrowed.

Owens did have some competition spurred by the success of his semiautomatic glass-forming processes in the 1890s. Even earlier, Philip Arbogast, a Pittsburgh glass manufacturer, obtained a patent for a "press and blow" process to make jars and bottle. The problem was typical of so many Victorian inventions that were designed on paper without any practical testing. In England, two inventors, Ashley and Arnold, patented an impractical machine for jars. Still, Owens was always in a class by himself. His machines were working at the time their patents were issued.

Owens managed Toledo Glass the same way that Edison managed Menlo Park. Owens called his engineers together regularly to draw out his inventions and designs. As noted, his strength was his ability to envision spatial relationships, due to his vast experience in touching the tools and equipment. From this Owens was able to make spatial drawings in the tradition of Edison and Bell.

James Nasmyth, inventor of the steam hammer, believed that mental envisioning with "graphic language" was critical to engineering. Engineering historian Henry Petroski states, "All engineering starts with creative design, invariably accompanied by some kind of calculation in which the wisdom of giants is but part of the equation. It is in this realm that the engineer's mind works wonders, with or without a pencil and paper, and sometimes at what seem to be breakneck speed." It is in this realm that many engineers fall short today.

Owens was also similar to Edison in promoting the field of drafting. Owens' rough drawings had to be transformed into specification-based ones for mechanics and engineers. Mechanics need to know the specifications of each dimension in a single view. This is how Richard LaFrance came to Toledo Glass. LaFrance was a boy of seventeen who was studying mechanical drawing at Toledo Central High's Manual Training School. He would work for Owens for twenty-two years, becoming one of his oldest associates. LaFrance's engineering drawings helped transform Owens' ideas and rough drawings into "iron." LaFrance described Owens' genius:

> Owens was an inventor. He was no designer, but could direct engineers. He let them use their own designs usually without interference. He did not invent mechanisms. He decided on methods. He knew a good or bad design when he saw the machine and could see its faults in engineering and make suggestions when he saw a machine operate. I considered him to have an engineering mind and discussed problems with him and was glad to get decisions.

LaFrance's picture of Owens is reminiscent of a master craftsman managing journeymen and apprentices and certainly reflects Owens' paternal approach. Often in the glasshouse, a gaffer would rough out the drawing and work sequence of a new art piece for his gang to make.

Many today wonder why we have no Edison, Ford, Owens, Bell, etc. The standard answer is that the Victorian model of the lone inventor is dead. Actually, the concept of the lone Victorian inventor is in error. As we have seen, these inventive geniuses were supported by small armies of scientists, mechanics, craftsmen, and specialists. The problem more likely is that we ask too much of our graduate engineers. We expect them to be highly and equally endowed on both sides of the brain. Today's engineer is expected to be designer and mechanic, creator and practitioner, architect and builder. Men like Owens knew their strengths and weaknesses. Design has two parts. The first part Henry Petroski describes as "conceptualization that puts the idea on the back of an envelope." The second part is the process of building the idea. Conceptualization is a specialization in itself, consisting of a creative, mental phase and a sketching phase. Sketching or drawing is engineering and takes visualization. Toledo Glass was a company built around the creative conceptualizations of Michael Owens. In this respect, the whole concept of a master inventor working with his technical gang makes sense for the management of invention. It fits well with today's project-management approach to development work. With this approach, you have a project manager and a team of cross-disciplined technical experts. Owens in reality was the first to apply principles of project management to research and development. The only weakness was that Toledo Glass had only one project manager for all projects!

The wooden hand-held device of Owens that launched the development company of Toledo Glass was not much more than a bicycle pump and a cast-iron mold. It would have been a hard sell to investors. Mike and the company blacksmith had put the simple device together, while Mike had spent hours experimenting with it. Automation would require sound engineering. So the board approved the hiring of two engineering assistants to bring the machine to commercialization.

In the fall of 1899, Owens formally launched his dream to put an automatic bottle machine in iron. While he lacked support and encouragement from the board, he had two very able engineering assistants in Emil Bock and Bill Schwenzfeier. Bock had been hired by the board to be Owens' chief engineer, and in the end Bock would invent and even patent some key parts of the automatic bottle-making system. Bock was brilliant in demanding interchangeable parts for each arm and the overall machine. This early design requirement would make worldwide sales of future machines possible. Bock was born in Flat Rock, Michigan, and learned the machining trade at the Detroit company of Leland, Faulkner, and Norton. As a journeyman, Bock had worked at machine shops through out the Midwest. Before coming to Toledo Glass, he worked for Baker Brothers Foundry in Toledo, which was a supplier of machines to Macbeth-Evans. Bock was a skilled machinist capable of taking Owens' rough drawings and transforming them. The board hired him for $480 a year; Owens was under contract at the time for $2,000 a year. Both men were given stock bonuses as well. At the time Bock was taking a correspondence course in engineering, which Walbridge was paying for through Toledo Glass. Bock often used his basement to work on and construct Owens' ideas.

In later years, Bock invented the famous "tapered roller bearing" manufactured by Timken Roller Bearing Company. Bock was a great engineer, but he was, like Owens, a leader, not a follower. Bock went on to become a millionaire but lost it all on a final project to build a laundry machine that could both wash and dry. Like so many lieutenants of great inventors, Bock is lost to the pages of history.[3] Yet he was a great engineer in his own right with many inventions to his name. Besides his roller bearing, Bock pioneered the use of jigs and gauges in building the Owens machine. This advance allowed for standardized production of the machine for worldwide distribution. His use of gauge tools preceded the application of the principle by other great industrialists, such as Alfred Sloan of General Motors and Henry Ford. Bock must be considered an important part of Owens' success, but Owens would demonstrate that Bock could be replaced.

Owens' earlier semiautomatic machines to make bulbs and tumblers replaced the glassblower's lungs with compressed air, but the gathering of the molten glass remained a manual process. Inventors inspired by his earlier machines were making progress in the bottle industry. Products of the time consisted of wide-mouth jars and narrow-neck bottles. Progress on jars was well under way by 1896. These machines manually gathered glass to a "press and blow" mold. The jar or wide-mouth bottle was made in three steps. First, a gather was placed on a press mold and a plunger was pushed to form the mouth and neck. Second, a small "parson" (technical name for gob of glass) or beginning of a bottle was formed and transferred to a blow mold. Third, the blower completed the bottle by blowing into this second mold. Philip Arbogast of Pittsburgh anticipated the press and blow process in 1881. He never fully developed the machine, but some companies in West Virginia and Beaver Falls, Pennsylvania, were reporting its use by 1892. In 1893, Enterprise Glass was producing Vaseline jars using the press and blow machine. Charles Blue of Wheeling Mould and Foundry made a further improvement on the mold in 1893. Blue's machine would produce the forerunners of the Mason jars produced by the famous Hazel-Atlas Glass Company. In England, another patent of Howard Ashley further improved the press and mold process.

The press and mold process still was limited to wide-mouth jars, but the real challenge was the formation of a bottleneck. The press-and-blow method could not make a necked bottle. More limiting was the fact that press and mold was a semiautomatic process. The *National Glass Budget* spelled out those limitations in a July 21, 1900, article.

> That glass can be pressed and blown by machinery is a settled fact, and that it can be gathered and dropped into the molds by mechanical means is certainly a possibility, though in the present state of the art no pathfinder has yet appeared to blazon the way. . . . Eight and ten gatherings per minute is about all that mortal man can do for eight or ten hours without breaking down his constitution and by-laws, and machines going at such a speed cannot be properly called labor-savers—they are gatherer killers. A gathering machine is not only in order, it is an absolute requirement if further progress in glass working machinery is to be made. Who will lead the way?

Owens was now looking at a fully automated machine. Some stories exist that he started his earliest experiments at the Chicago world's fair, and conceptually there probably is some truth to them. But real engineering and equipment trials did not occur until 1898. Owens' first idea was that of using a type of bicycle pump or a hypodermic syringe to create a vacuum and pull molten glass out of the furnace and then inject it into a simple two-piece mold. This basic device, known as a "sucker-upper," had been experimented with over the years at Libbey Glass. A gatherer allegedly developed the simple "sucker-upper" for Libbey Glass, but no inventor was ever named or patent filed. Owens' improvement was handheld, so it could be dipped in a pot of molten glass. The lower end of the mold went into the molten glass as a piston handle was drawn back. The resulting vacuum sucked molten glass into the mold. A plunger at the top of the mold formed the bottle lip and neck. The holder then removed the mold and moved it to a finishing mold, where the piston was pushed forward, forcing air to form the bottle in the finishing mold.

This simple machine had been drawn by Owens and built in Bock's basement. Owens knew no boundaries—he respected no

The midnight shift at a glass factory, 1908. (Library of Congress)

corporate separations—so he would also slip into Libbey Glass to conduct experiments. Finally, Walbridge approved trials at the Macbeth-Evans plant on the midnight shift.

A Revolution Under Way

Owens had gotten his brother Tom a job at Libbey Glass. This was typical of the family nature of the glass business. Over the years, Libbey would also hire many of his own friends and family. Mike and Tom worked together on the midnight shift to fully develop the "sucker-upper," coupled with use of a mold. Tom was an extremely important part of these early experiments. He would become a supervisor in the Owens and Libbey organizations, but in those early days, he functioned as Mike's assistant. Tom was a good mechanic, and he was instrumental in the development of tooling.

One night, as usual, Tom was at Mike's side. Hours of failures finally resulted in a perfect four-ounce bottle by early morning. The "bottle" would probably be called a jar today! It had a wide mouth and was the type used for Vaseline at the time. Owens filed for a patent on this "machine number one" on December 26, 1899, and it was accepted on May 10, 1904. Several German patents claimed prior inventions, but the American patent went to Owens. Years later, once Owens was confident about commercialization, Toledo Glass bought up the rights to these German patents to avoid litigation. None of these German patents was ever demonstrated as practicable.

Still, that morning a revolution was under way. Walbridge was excited and suggested that Owens continue to improve on it but avoid involving any other employees. Bock was asked to develop an engineering drawing for another possible patent application, machine number two, and to contract a machine shop to build it. Walbridge and Libbey were now convinced that it might feasible to build an automatic machine, but Owens was still years away from a commercial machine. Machine number one could not have come close to competing with a skilled, manual bottle blower. Walbridge, however, had seen enough to believe in the future of Mike's process. Walbridge set up a drafting room for Bock at Toledo's Spitzer building to support the project. Walbridge's main concern became secrecy. Libbey set up a shed with a glass pot for all future experiments. Once Bock completed the engineering drawing, Walbridge and Bock hired a Detroit machine shop to build the second-generation model, while Owens worked on equipping the experimental "shed." This shed was on the Libbey property on Ash Street.

Machine number two was a more sophisticated version of number one. A wheeled frame supported it. A glass tank versus a pot was used for molten glass. It was hoped that the larger tank would be less affected by the chilling of dipping the bottle mold. At first, gathering still caused the chilling of molten glass in the tank. The dipped cast-iron mold drew heat out, chilling the molten glass. The repeated failure suggested the idea of a rotating furnace to keep the glass molten during dipping, which would be one of the keys to future success. Number two was far from automatic, requiring an operator and possibly one or two helpers. But it did, after many experiments, start to produce perfect bottles, at least in the first few draws. This trial-and-error approach to machine building was costly. There was a huge scrap pile outside the shed of stripped machines. The pile was becoming a sore point for Walbridge, who saw it as a mountain of money.

Machine number three was a major advance in the automated process. The project was now into the millions and anticipation was building. Libbey was adding personal funds at times to keep Toledo Glass in the black. It was now too late to turn back; Owens had to make a real leap in automation. Owens was far from a wealthy man, but his salary assured a high standard of living. He naturally turned to prayer and novenas to the Blessed Mother. Machine number three had five suction molds rotated by a motor. A larger glass tank was used, but the dipping of the cast mold continued to drop the temperature below where the glass could be worked. Experiments slowed and few advances could be found. It was frustrating, and furthermore, Owens' health was failing. He was overworking for a man in his forties. In the winter of 1900-1901, he was bedridden for some time. The failures of

Edward Libbey, 1900. (Owens-Illinois Glass Company Records, MSS-200, the Ward M. Canaday Center for Special Collections, University of Toledo)

Edward Libbey, 1904. (Owens-Illinois Glass Company Records, MSS-200, the Ward M. Canaday Center for Special Collections, University of Toledo)

number three in the summer of 1901 caused a similar exhaustion. Libbey was also feeling the pressure and was called "irritable" after three years of questionable success. Walbridge now had to become the standard bearer. However, that same summer brought Richard LaFrance into the organization. The young mechanic would inject a new energy into the project, plus the loyalty that Owens demanded.

These first three machines were complex even by today's standards. Owens had no electrical motors, gasoline power sources, or hydraulic control valves. He was designing a machine with almost all original, handmade parts. Even Henry Ford had major subcomponents, such as engines and gear transmissions, available for his inventive efforts. Owens had no major subassemblies. Lacking electric motors and controls, he had to use compressed air and mechanically leveraged hand and foot power. Control required individually designed cams and gears. Owens clearly needed much engineering help to make all the necessary parts and controls for the machine he envisioned, but only he could see the overall machine in his mind. At times, Owens designed like military jet designers today, moving ahead of the parts technology, which required development work of their own. This, however, was part of his inventive genius. Others would have given up because of the lack of developed subcomponents and parts. Owens' design methods of going beyond the available subtechnology are now utilized in our aircraft and military industries.

At some point, Owens started the development of a "revolving pot." This was the breakthrough that was needed, and it was another stroke of genius from Owens' mind. When breakthroughs were needed, great engineers are often at a loss because they are limited by paradigms of how it should be. This is where mechanics like Bock are stuck, because there is nothing yet to build. The project would require a creative turn supplied by Michael Owens. Owens was able to think outside of engineering paradigms, and that explains the source of his genius. A revolving pot even today seems like a strange idea. It is highly unlikely that a trained engineer would have considered such an odd solution. First, the revolving pot or circular pool was continuously fed from the furnace. The pot was then rotated, allowing the molten glass to be taken from a continuously moving surface, thus eliminating dipping into and chilling the glass. The revolving pot also allowed for sequential dipping to come from a different area of the pot. This avoided bubbles in the dipped area by moving to a new area of the pot. Owens applied for a patent, realizing the importance of the revolving pot. But like so many of his brilliant new concepts, the engineering proved difficult. The revolving pot was plagued by setbacks, but new help from LaFrance helped the team to persist.

The months of work on the revolving pot indicate the long, painful experimentation that was required. Owens needed to feed the revolving pot from the furnace on a continuous basis. A long furnace spout of clay was designed to allow a leisurely flow into the revolving pot, thus preventing bubbles in the molten glass. It was believed that this spout was a critical design requirement. For months the revolving pot broke off the spout, forcing redesigns of the machine. Owens was frustrated to the point of giving up on automatic gathering.[4] Finally, someone suggested just trying a short spout. The experiments actually showed it to be superior to the long one, and it did not produce bubbles. Another series of trials, taking weeks, were needed to identify the ideal spout position for feeding the revolving pot.

At this point, the proper formation of the neck of the bottle presented a sticking point. Freezing at the bottleneck deformed the overall bottle. Owens needed to resolve this problem.

Sucking up hotter molten glass allowed for more working of the product, but even this was not good enough for small necks. Machine number three had produced only wide-mouth bottles. The growth market was in long-neck beer and beverage bottles.

Machine number four would have that capability but at a cost. One unconfirmed story of number four claims that when Bock first showed it to Owens, it operated incorrectly. Owens allegedly attacked the machine with a sledgehammer, telling the "damn Dutchman" to "make it right!" Machine number four cost Toledo Glass an additional $500,000, but it solved the bottleneck problem.

Number four was rolled out in the fall of 1902. The early trials were major events attended by board members as well as the design team. That team consisted of Emil Bock (superintendent), Bill Schwenzfeier (his assistant), Richard LaFrance, and machinists Jim Cunningham, Win Rohr, Harry Brobst, Tom Feeney, Tom Mitchell, Lester Dull, Mac Linn, John Martinek, and Harry Spanier. Number four was designed to produce pint beer bottles and became known as "the machine of a thousand gears." Actually, number four had 9,576 parts, mostly manufactured by Toledo Glass. In its first test, number four produced eight pint-beer bottles a minute. This was done automatically with no dedicated operator. It was a major breakthrough, considering that a "shop" composed of three skilled men and three boys could only make at best five pint beer bottles a minute. It cost $1.25 per gross to handcraft beer bottles, while machine four could do it for eight to ten cents per gross. Finally, after four years of effort, this machine would revolutionize 2,000 years of glassmaking techniques. The first customer of the machine was Toledo's own brewery—Finlay Brewing. Corporate legend has William Walbridge taking the first bottles on his bicycle to the nearby brewery. Libbey, the salesman, now had something to work with. Within weeks he was in Pittsburgh selling the product and machinery to Pittsburgh Brewing as well as meeting with Adolphus Busch of St. Louis (Busch would become a stockholder of the company).

Owens described the process of inventing the automated bottle machine: "The basic ideas are mine. . . . That has thousands of separate parts . . . each representing someone who has had a hand in it." Owens produced none of those parts, but he envisioned what those parts working together would do. In fact, he lacked the ability to form those parts as much as those who could form them lacked the ability to envision the overall machine. It was Owens' fertile mind that would over and over again supply the needed creative breakthrough. Some of these broke critical "bottlenecks," such as the revolving pot that prevented chilling. Time after time, Owens' engineers and mechanics were stuck on solving a problem, requiring Owens to apply a totally different approach.

CHAPTER 10

Owens: The Revolutionary

The bottle machine trials of late 1902 were reminiscent of Edison's incandescent-light lab trials of 1879. In both cases, the observers realized that these inventions were part of a revolution. Within a few years of the 1902 Owens experiment, the world packaging industry would be forever changed.

The cheap production of bottles would allow for a new array of packaged products in pharmaceuticals, household cleaners, beverages, and food. The consumer could be guaranteed the consistency of weights and measures from a uniform manufactured bottle. The use of standardized manufacturing techniques and parts was an ancillary benefit of the production of automatic bottle machines. The uniformity of bottles would lead to automated filling in the packaging and food industries. Owens helped to design some of these filling machines. The crafts model of labor so loved by Libbey and Owens would be permanently changed to the industrial model. Along with that change would come the end of child labor in most of American industry, even though Owens had not set out to bring this about. In fact, he supported hiring boys in factories to start them on productive careers. The glass unions would also be forced from the crafts world into the cold reality of automation. Costs of production would drop dramatically with the elimination of high-priced blowers and gatherers, and output would increase. In addition, the bottle machine would create a demand for better melting technology and remove union blockage of its application. This technological revolution of

Owens would lead to an employment boom in glass and glass-related industries. Maybe his biggest contribution was the long-range commitment to research, development, and continuous improvement. It was in his drive to improve and invent that Owens was a revolutionary. On a personal level, the lives of Owens and his family would also be changed forever.

The Owens bottle revolution represents the first big engineering breakthrough of the American industrial era. He pioneered the concept of the bottle machine with almost no early experiments or science to fall back on. Edison's much-hailed incandescent lamp was more of a scientific breakthrough than an engineering one, compared to the almost ten thousand parts required to build the bottle machine with very few of those parts available on the market. Henry Ford's model T is a simple machine compared to the bottle machine. And in Ford's case, some of the critical components, such as the engine, were available from other manufacturers. Owens also required standardized parts to be made, so the machine could be reproduced rapidly. Machine-shop drawings were needed for components, since very few were off-the-shelf items. Owens, unlike Edison and Ford, was at least six to ten years ahead of his major competitors!

Rapid production of glass bottles would quickly lead to a need for additional automation. Continuous melting of raw materials and glass would be required to feed the enormous appetite of the bottle machine. This would further lead to a need for continuous handling of raw materials and mixing. Within ten years, Owens would pioneer continuous and automated glass production at the Charleston plant of Owens-Libbey Glass.

Owens was asked in later years to talk to his parish high school about the invention.

> We get the materials from which we make the machines from the earth. The earth also gives us the sand from which we make the glass. God put the iron and sand in the earth. He also gave some of us the talent for seeing those things in a certain way. The result is the Owens bottle machine—but all comes from God.[1]

Owens would always remember that fact, as he gave most of his financial rewards quietly back to the community and the poor.

In the summer of 1903, Libbey wrote a letter reporting that the big brewers were "thunderstruck with the machine." The wooden shed became the center of the glass industry as visitors streamed to see the new machine. The editor of the *National Glass Budget* reported, "It delivers the finished bottle automatically without the touch of the human hand, eliminates all skill and labor and puts the same amount of glass into every bottle, makes every bottle of the same length, finish, weight, and capacity, it wastes no glass, uses no pipes, snaps, finishing tools, glory holes, rosin, charcoal, and requires neither gatherer, mold boy, snap boy nor finisher and still makes better bottles, more of them than by any other process."[2] Another writer described it this way: "It feeds itself with a fiery fluid of molten glass; sucks it up methodically, clutches it with iron hands, blows its breath into it, releases its grasp, nonchalantly drops a finished bottle—and moves to another fiery gulp."[3]

A new revolution in the glass industry was under way. Experimental Bottle Machine Number Four was ready, but Owens planned for the final work on a commercial machine. The first sales prospectus claimed labor costs of eight to fifteen cents per gross as compared to $1.52 for hand production. It further highlighted the elimination of the two-month summer shutdown. In addition, no skilled operators would be needed. Hand blowers were earning around eighty cents an hour. The going rate for unskilled labor at the time was twenty cents an hour!

The union, the Bottle Blower's Association, was quick to realize the impact. In 1891, the union had forbade its members to work for any of Owens' development projects. The Bottle Blower's Association was still adjusting to the onset of semiautomatic machines when the bottle machine came to the market. Soon, however, the union took on a more cooperative strategy. Their response is an amazing model for unions today that are facing low global labor costs. The Bottle Blower's Association, far from becoming defensive Luddites, took a proactive approach, although a group of militant laborers did evolve in the Toledo area, which engaged in sabotage. The union suggested moving to three eight-hour shifts versus the normal two ten-hour shifts to

Machine number four, the first of the successful bottle machines. (Owens-Illinois Glass Company Records, MSS-200, the Ward M. Canaday Center for Special Collections, University of Toledo)

make hand production and semiautomatic production more competitiveagainst the continuous operation of the Owens machine. The union allowed for a reduction in the number of apprentices required per journeyman in hand-blowing operations, reducing costs. Finally, they recommended the purchase of semiautomatic bottle machines to prevent wide use of the Owens automatic. The union cooperated but resisted, as is common today, the reduction of wages. But in the end, it could not be avoided. The union, while working with manufacturers on costs, made progress on maintaining jurisdiction over the new unskilled labor force, thus assuring their role in the future industry. The union also worked with the manufacturers to move skilled gatherers into machine-operator positions, thus saving jobs. The union and Michael Owens even worked together to lessen the pain of converting to automation. In the end, neither the manufacturers, Owens, nor union could stop the revolution started by the Owens bottle machine.

In the long run, the union's cooperative strategy paid many dividends. First, the job-loss fears of the new Owens technology proved completely unfounded. In fact, the Owens Bottle Machine led to a boom in glass-industry employment. The increased availability of bottles had opened a huge pent-up demand. The reduced price of bottles spurred new applications and markets. The cheap and available bottles even stimulated employment in new industries, such as the bottled beverage and milk industry. Blower wages were reduced and blowers were eliminated, but skilled operator wages were above those of most industry workers. Union membership boomed as well with the new skilled and unskilled glass workers. This helped the glass industry avoid the labor strife so common in other industries of the time.

In 1903, Owens Bottle Machine Company[4] was formed, with the specific purpose to manufacture bottle machines and promote their sales. The owners were Owens, Libbey, Walbridge, Clarence Brown, and Fredrick Geddes. Brown and Geddes were from the same law firm used by Libbey. The company's charter mission was "to sell machines under license." Owens wanted the company to manufacture bottles as well, but Libbey and his other associates wanted to reap the shorter-term benefits. Owens argued for at least a small plant. The board, however, opposed any effort by Owens to enter bottle manufacture. Owens pushed for the need for an "experimental" plant to promote his machine and help machine sales. Under this initial guise, he got the approval for a plant. Construction was started immediately near the old shed on Libbey Street (known today as Wall Street).

Owens was working on the improvements for an "A" machine for use in the new plant. This was to be a standardized machine for sale to the world industry. The "A" machine would, however, require a great deal of standardized engineering by Emil Bock, and this of course was Bock's main strength. The "A" machine represented an astonishing breakthrough in bottle production and represented Owens' first commercial model. It held six

William Walbridge. (Owens-Illinois Glass Company Records, MSS-200, the Ward M. Canaday Center for Special Collections, University of Toledo)

molds of sizes between four to forty ounces. The "A" machine could manufacture twelve pint bottles per minute or 17,280 bottles in twenty-four hours. It was operated by two men and ran continuously. The best a hand-labor bottle glasshouse could be expected to produce was only 3,600 bottles in a twenty-four-hour period. The new experimental factory's conveyor annealing line was another step forward by Owens in continuous automation. Owens also added one of the first "continuous regenerative tanks" to continuously provide large quantities of molten glass. Initial production at the experimental factory of Owens Bottle was beer bottles, which quickly expanded to include milk and catsup bottles.

In October 1904, as a concession to him, Owens was permitted to make an arrangement where Owens Bottle built machines and Northwestern Ohio Bottle Company made bottles in the new factory. Owens' personal plan was to make the plant a major factor in bottle production. He hired his younger brother, Tom, as a shift supervisor. The plant maintained a two-shift operation using two bottle machines and fifty workers. Northwestern was given exclusive rights to manufacture wine and brandy bottles on the Owens Bottle Machine. The factory became a model glasshouse and a Mecca for glass-industry engineers to visit. Visitors were pouring in from all over the globe to see the world's most modern and automated glassmaking facility.

Mike Owens in front of machine number five, called "A." (Owens-Illinois Glass Company Records, MSS-200, the Ward M. Canaday Center for Special Collections, University of Toledo)

The board required that Northwestern's wares be sold through a special Libbey company—Ohio Bottle Company. This way, Libbey and the board effectively limited Mike Owens' plan to manufacture bottles. This complex network of companies in the "Toledo Faction" helped Libbey personally maintain control in the early days.

Glassmakers were slow to adopt Owens' first machines. This was due in part to their high cost and other required capital improvements to support them, such as larger furnaces and lehrs. Owens Bottle had decided upon its incorporation to sell licenses versus machines. Libbey, Geddes, and Brown felt that this strategy would give them complete market control without the need for horizontal mergers and buyouts. In this way, they helped build the mythical company of the "Toledo Faction." The "Toledo Faction" represents many companies that functioned as one entity and was controlled by interlocking directors. The arrangement would allow maximum profits for all of the Libbey companies. The "Toledo Faction" was initially headed by Libbey, Owens, Walbridge, Brown, and Geddes. Using licensing, they hoped to collect a royalty on every bottle sold. Initially, each license paid production royalties of 50 percent of the firm's estimated labor-cost reductions attributable to its use of the machine. In this respect, Owens Bottle was selling or renting out mechanical labor. That resulted in a royalty of forty cents per gross of milk bottles made.[5]

Baldwin-Travis and Thatcher Manufacturing took the first licenses in 1905 to produce milk bottles. Dr. Harvey D. Thatcher had "invented" the thick, square-sided glass milk bottle in 1900. Prior to that, milk was sold in unsealed containers from a milk wagon. Thatcher's initial efforts were expensive hand-blown bottles. Owens' invention was ideal for thick-walled milk bottles and gave Thatcher Manufacturing a commercial advantage. The Owens Bottle board was pleased (except Owens) that they gained profits without having to invest in physical plants and deal with the headaches of managing them. Owens wanted to manufacture, having no interest in stock arrangements, licenses, and interlocking boards.

License sales of the "A" machine came painfully slowly at first, but between 1906 and 1911, companies such as Ball Brothers, H. J. Heinz, Illinois Glass, Charles Bolt Company, and Hazel-Atlas (known for its Mason jars) became major licensees. By the end of 1911, 103 machines had been installed, producing 4 million gross of bottles annually. In the case of Thatcher, another expansion of the "Toledo Faction" occurred. To obtain the license, Thatcher gave Owens Bottle a major block of their stock. Eventually, the "Toledo Faction" had significant ownership in Charles Bolt Company and Hazel-Atlas as well. This strategy of licensing arrangements and stock trades gave the "Toledo Faction" an invisible monopoly of the bottle industry. This monopoly was amazing in its ability to generate money and control for the "Toledo Faction." For example, licenses were given to companies by product

The original workforce of Illinois Glass, 1876. (Owens-Illinois Glass Company Records, MSS-200, the Ward M. Canaday Center for Special Collections, University of Toledo)

type, allowing a single automated company to dominate that segment. Thatcher in milk bottles, Northwestern in brandy and wine bottles, Ohio Bottle in beer and soda bottles, Heinz in catsup bottles, Illinois Glass and Bolt in whiskey bottles, Ball Brothers in fruit jars, and Hazel-Atlas in general packaging bottles were examples of these segment licensees. The "Toledo Faction" usually took major stock positions in these profit-generating companies. It owned Northwestern and Ohio Bottle outright. Of course, all were dependent on Owens Bottle for the equipment to make bottles.

The royalty arrangement ultimately covered the cost of the machine. This unique royalty agreement can be credited to Libbey, Brown, and Geddes. Michael's interests were always in the machines and bottle making, not the financial arrangements, but he would play a key role in the success of the agreements. Owens Bottle and the bottle manufacturer, through the licensing arrangement, shared the labor-cost reduction. Bigger cost reductions resulted in higher royalties. The price of the bottles would actually be specified in the agreement. In fact, the Owens Bottle license agreement was price fixing. The "Toledo Faction" controlled prices until the implementation of the Sherman Antitrust Law in 1911. The union was at least pacified in that wages at the hand-blown manufacturers were maintained, thanks to the price control of the "Toledo Faction." It was a brilliant plan to maintain the price of bottles, increase bottle manufacturers' profits, create profits for Owens, and even hold hand-blowing wages level. In fact, when hand labor reduced its wages, it resulted in a lower royalty for Owens Bottle. This royalty system put the Owens Bottle Machine Company and the whole "Toledo Faction" in a position to control the bottle market. Owens Bottle was dictating the price of bottles as well as the wages paid throughout the industry.

The full control of the "Toledo Faction" was impressive, but most of it was below the eye of the public and government. Libbey also strategically kept banks out of the corporations, especially Eastern banks. This limited internal workings to a select handful of investors.

The directors of Owens Bottle, Libbey Glass, and Toledo Glass—all "closed" corporations—also owned stock in and served

on the boards of many related companies. Owens favored owner-
ship of raw material manufacture. For example, Toledo Glass subcontracted the actual building of the bottle machines to Kent
Machine Company of Toledo. While Toledo Glass did not own
Kent Machine, its major stockholders were Libbey, Owens,
Walbridge, and Geddes. The bottle machines required molds, so
the "Toledo Faction" formed the new company of Woodruff Glass
Mold Company. The amazing vertical and horizontal control of
the glass industry by the "Toledo Faction" could fill several books.
Until the 1920s, the government did not address these interlocking stock and board arrangements. There can be no doubt that
the "Toledo Faction" was a monopoly. Suppliers, customers, and
related industries were controlled through board and stock
arrangements. Libbey routinely brought out competing patents,
companies, and technology. Through their licensing agreements,
the "Toledo Faction" controlled wages in the American bottle
glass industry and by, the time of the deaths of Owens and Libbey,
the American glass industry as a whole.

Libbey and Owens were benevolent monopolists and paternal
industrialists; they did not reduce wages but actually maintained
them while increasing profits. They aggressively applied technology with as little pain to the worker as possible. The glass industry under their watch was free of major labor strife.

Libbey's European contacts inspired him to move just as quickly in Europe. The stockholders of Toledo Glass set up a new company to conquer Europe—Owens European Bottle Company.
Toledo Glass had suffered a setback in England in 1898 with its
semiautomatic tumbler machine. After Owens installed them, the
English were unable to use them and defaulted on payments.
Libbey needed to overcome this bad press to be successful with
the Owens automatic bottle machine.

Libbey launched a full campaign in 1906. First he applied for
patents internationally, and then he proceeded to build demonstration plants in England and Germany. Mike Owens was responsible
for the construction of both plants, but the team included Richard
LaFrance, Emil Bock, and Bill Schwenzfeier. The English plant was
erected on the Manchester estate of Sir Humphrey Trafford. Once

in place, the plant came under the supervision of William Boshart. Boshart owned the new Toledo apartment complex Owens lived in, and Owens brought him into the organization. Boshart at the time was also sales manager for the Cummings Glass Company in Pittsburgh. He represented an ideal choice, since Owens suggested him and he was an established financial swell. Boshart would become a significant shareholder as well as manager in Owens Bottle Company. The German plant was to supply a bottled water company—Apollinaris Company. Toledo Glass controlled the European company but additional blocks of stock went to Libbey, Owens, Adolphus Busch, William Boshart, and Julius Prince (managing director of Apollinaris). All this slowed improvements to the basic "A" machine back in Toledo, but Owens continued to make notes and work with Bock and LaFrance on new commercial machines.

The European industry initially had laughed at the idea of an automatic machine, believing it to be a Yankee sales trick. The two demonstration plants changed all that, with fear spreading throughout the continent that Owens would manufacture bottles. Apollinaris Company quickly lined up other mineral-water companies to form Rhein-Ahr licensing. A combination of other German companies started negotiations to counter that control. A London paper described the Apollinaris operation in mythical terms:

> Certainly, of all the evil looking machinery I have seen—and I have been privileged to see a good deal in my time—I have never seen any which so exactly reflected the appearance of an angry— even malignant—idol.
>
> I dare swear that if Arminius or any other of the old time gods of the Ahr Valley were to have seen it, they would have prostrated themselves before it as a worthy supplanter of their former gods, and within an hour or so would have been offering human sacrifices, too, in its honor.
>
> Probably the god whom of all mythology it must really suggest is Briareus, he had a hundred arms, for the first impression of the great mass of metal looming up over your head is that it is stretching out a hundred steel arms to clutch you by the throat. . . . The engineer in charge, . . . in his enthusiasm, said it is *so wonderful a piece of mechanism for the human brain to have invented.*

The result in 1907 was a European cartel known as *Europaischer Verband des Flaschenfabriken Gesellscahaft mit beschrankter Haftung* (Verband for short). Verband purchased the European rights for the Owens Bottle Machine for around 12 million in gold marks. Owens European Bottle Company agreed to stay out of bottle manufacture in Europe. With the Verband deal settled, the work and function of Owens European Bottle was over, allowing Owens, Bock, and LaFrance to return to development work in Toledo.

The Success of Owens Bottle Company

Libbey's European sales exemplified a new development that would come to be known as the "multinational corporation." Owens Bottle Company was the first American company to achieve the status of a multinational corporation. This unique status seemed to give it further protection from the American trustbusters of the time.

Owens as well as Libbey believed that continual development would be needed to stay on top of the market. This strategy had been at the heart of the formation of Toledo Glass and this was to continue. It would, however, depend on Owens' constant drive. Both Libbey and Owens were long-range thinkers, but Owens was the driving force behind the vision. He would continue to improve his machine until his death in 1923. The first improvement came in 1908, with the introduction of the "AC" machine. This version eliminated distortion from too rapid cooling of bottles and also improved the production rate up to twenty bottles per minute. The "AC" machine was reinforced and sturdier. One characteristic of Owens-designed machines was strength and durability, allowing many of them to be operated for over seventy years. After the "AC" version, Owens turned to a machine that could make a larger bottle, such as a gallon jug.

During this development period, in 1910, Bock left the company and LaFrance became chief engineer. This was a setback for the company, but Owens was happy to see Bock go. The Toledo Glass board argued to retain Bock, since they saw him as "critical" to the bottle machine. But Owens convinced Libbey to let him go.

Owens Bottle Machine and crew, 1910. (Owens-Illinois Glass Company Records, MSS-200, the Ward M. Canaday Center for Special Collections, University of Toledo)

Over the years, animosity had grown between Owens and Bock, with Bock feeling he never received the credit due him. No doubt Bock had a point, but the machine was never his idea nor did he fully envision its operation. Bock was a great machinist, draftsman, and engineer, but he was not essential to the organization or the developmental work on future machines. Bock did substantial work on the machine, but again that was the role he was hired for. He certainly deserves more credit for his implementation of standardized jigs and gauges. Bock made Owens Bottle Company into one of the first standardized-machine companies. He was named on a number of the patents and he was well paid in salary and stocks. Bock's engineering skills had gained him supporters in the company, and the board used him as a buffer for Owens. Bock's contributions to the bottle machine were many and significant, but in the end, there was no room for the egos of both Bock and

Owens. It was also clear that Owens would need a machinist
and/or engineer to help out, but that did not have to be Bock.
Bock no doubt participated in some of the damaging gossip that
went around about Owens' lack of mechanical ability. To his credit, Owens' own attacks were blunt but always direct, not behind
the back. The split ultimately proved beneficial for both men.

The bottle machine was Owens' idea, but credit for its full success goes to both Bock and Owens. LaFrance would say years
later: "If you locked Mike inside a machine shop in 1890 and let
him out in 1920 he wouldn't have made a thing. If you had done
the same thing with Bock, he might have come out with a
machine, but it wouldn't have made bottles." This statement was
somewhat harsh on both men. It should also be said that if you
put Bock in a room for thirty years, he would never have conceived of a bottle machine. The fact remains that many men of
great mechanical skill had worked in the glass industry and never
envisioned the possibility of an automatic bottle machine. Bock
was a great engineer, but he was incapable of envisioning the
complexity of a glassmaking machine. Bock's strength was always
in designing parts and subcomponents, not in envisioning an
automated process. He lacked the knowledge of the glass process,
the larger view, for which Owens was famous.

That larger and holistic view is considered the true touchstone
of great inventors. John Lienhard, inventor and author of *The
Engines of Our Ingenuity*, noted this ability:

> As inventors, we must see more than decomposed parts. We must
> also be able to put parts back into a whole. We must be able to find
> our way back to the thinking that once marked our childhood, but,
> once we have, the truest answer to the question of how a bicycle
> works is that we and the machine become a single thing. . . . The
> inventor must, at last, forget the wheels, chain, and sprocket of this
> wonderful device and, finally, sail down the road—riding the wind.

Lienhard, in effect, shows that there is a difference between an
engineer and an inventor. The inventor sees the machine and its
operation, while the engineer sees the parts needed to make it

function. While someone can be both, in this case, Owens is the inventor and Bock, the engineer. The project, however, was even bigger than Owens and Bock; it required many machinists and furnace men to help.

Owens himself understood the contribution of others in the development of the bottle machine. In an issue of *American Magazine*, he related the experience:

> It is a case of give and take all the time. How were my early experiments made possible? Because of Mr. Libbey's backing. How were the machines introduced? Because he furnished the capital we always have had engineers to help work out the mechanical problems. We have brought other men's ideas when they would be useful to us. The basic ideas are mine. The patents are in my name. But the achievement is like the machine itself. That has thousands of separate parts; it is not one piece of metal. And any big achievement has thousands of parts, each representing someone who has had a hand in it.

The view of many great Victorian inventors as lone mechanics or scientists does men like Owens a disservice. It is not a realistic view, but more the style of Victorian biographers. It was a time that loved heroes, and inventors were made to fit this view. Even Henry Ford, who was a fair mechanic, let others do a great deal of the handwork. Detail and handwork slow down the creativity and overall view that make men like Ford great inventors. Douglas Brinkley, a current biographer of Ford, noted, "Even though he could work with his hands, he almost never did, except in teaching others." Furthermore, Brinkley attributes Ford's success to "envisioning the product that would take the first and best advantage of that market." In this way, Ford and Owens share the same success factors. They invented by envisioning products and processes. In both cases these visions were so vivid and powerful, they dominated their companies long after their deaths. Those visions were bigger than the development of the individual parts. The story with Edison is similar; he hired mechanics to do his building and mathematicians to do his calculations.

Owens was more than just an inventor; he was the heart of the

"Toledo Faction." He was a one-man consulting firm to all the Libbey plants. In 1905, Walbridge wrote the president of Thatcher about Owens: "Bear in mind this: Owens is brusque in many ways, but as a factory manager he has few equals and his advice is sought by a great many and as example he is consulting superintendent of the Libbey Glass Company, employing some thousand hands, and through his advice their factory end is in most excellent shape. He may suggest radical changes but I should heed all he says and I believe he can get you out of the hole."

Owens in reality was chief engineer and vice-president of the "Toledo Faction" of Libbey assets. In fact, Owens himself was one of the major assets of the "Toledo Faction." He was the only true glassmaker of the group.

Owens quickly teamed up with Richard LaFrance, whom he made chief engineer. They made for a better technical team. Owens had the senior position and LaFrance's loyalty. The result was another series of improved machines. They eventually produced the "AN," which was a totally new design. The earlier machines dipped all the molds at the same time. This constant dipping caused excessive vibration and wear of the machine. The excessive vibration limited the production as well. This restriction had kept Owens out of the prescription-bottle market, which required higher production speeds. The new model featured individually dipped suction molds controlled by a cam system. In 1912, cam-driven control was itself a major engineering step. The "AN" became known as the "Diphead." It had ten arms and was able to make bottles weighing a fraction of an ounce. Even more amazing, the machine allowed for the first time for ten different (but similar) bottle types to be made at once. This was more than just a new generation of machine; it was a new invention and demonstrated that Owens could work his magic with another engineer. Owens and LaFrance would produce improved versions of the "Diphead"-type machine until 1921. Even the skeptical board realized that Owens was the man behind the bottle machine. The idea that Bock was key to Owens' success was put to bed with the advance of the "Diphead." Owens would now move into developing other processes.

Owens bottle plant, 1912. (Owens-Illinois Glass Company Records, MSS-200, the Ward M. Canaday Center for Special Collections, University of Toledo)

In 1907, the "Toledo Faction" had just launched its aggressive bottle machine sales and was starting to look to new areas. Libbey Glass had all along been developing as a major incandescent-bulb producer. Toledo Glass, with rights to Owens' semiautomatic bulb machine and automatic bottle machine, seemed like a natural to look at taking up automated bulb production. Owens mentally had been working on the bulb-making machine for years as he developed the bottle machine. Certainly, he had the answer in some blend of the two machines. Libbey, however, hated to dilute focus by having mixed projects in a single company. On November 6, 1907, Libbey incorporated Westlake Machine Company to focus on the development of an automatic bulb machine. Westlake's directors were Libbey, Walbridge, and Donovan, with other major stockholders being Richardson,

Robinson, and Owens. Viewed in terms of today's corporate organizations, Westlake Machine was a joint venture of Libbey Glass. Royalty arrangements, licenses, and patent agreements varied over the years, but for the most part Libbey Glass controlled these. Very likely, the formation of Westlake Machine was a concession to Richardson, president of Libbey Glass, to keep Owens from controlling bulb production.

Richardson, the hero of the Findlay bulb plant 1892, had always felt he owned bulb production. Libbey felt he owed this to Richardson for his help in the turnaround of Libbey Glass with bulb production. One personal characteristic of Libbey and Owens was that they never forgot, whether good or bad. This would be the last time for many years that Libbey would allow Richardson, Robinson, and Donovan to invest in a developmental project. Libbey and Owens always remembered the resistance to the world's fair and the development of the bottle machine.

The bulb machine lagged behind the work on the Owens Bottle Machine, but by 1914 he had a commercial machine. While Libbey Glass was the first to commercially use the machine, Libbey and the Westlake board moved into constructing machines for license agreements. The Westlake machines were rented at 10 percent of the construction cost. In addition, a royalty of one dollar per 1,000 merchantable bulbs was charged. The license was still a very good deal. The semiautomatic bulb process costs were around sixteen dollars per 1,000, compared to eleven dollars per 1,000 for the automatic machine. The license agreement emphasized the reliability of the machine and the quality of its product. Libbey Glass in 1911 controlled about 42 percent of the bulb market (about equal to that of Corning Glass). Libbey Glass was making some bulbs at Toledo and had a dedicated bulb plant in Sandusky, Ohio. Libbey Glass and Westlake would effectively sell the business to General Electric in 1918.

Where Owens was always straightforward with both enemy and friend, Libbey preferred to manipulate people indirectly. Libbey seemed to have designed the four companies of the "Toledo Faction"—Libbey Glass, Toledo Glass, Owens Bottle, and Westlake Machine—around the egos of his managers. Libbey was the key connection, but Owens had a free hand for years. Besides Libbey, Owens was the only one to move freely across corporate boundaries. Libbey would reward and punish by the amount of investment he allowed in his companies. Westlake was an example of this philosophy. Libbey was rewarding Richardson for helping turn around Libbey Glass, while at the same time trying to reduce friction by slowing Owens down. Westlake built an experimental plant in Toledo, with its main objective being to develop the automatic bulb machine and license its use to other producers. It would in the end take ten years to reach that objective. Owens remained consumed to a large degree with improving the bottle machine and expanding bottle production. Owens put little personal energy into the automated bulb machine probably because of Richardson's control of resulting profits through Libbey Glass. There is no doubt that had Owens taken on the bulb project personally, it would have seen commercialization in well under ten years.

Through 1905 to 1917 Owens focused on bottle production and machine reliability improvements. The team that aided him and LaFrance is sometimes forgotten. One of the unforeseen advantages of the Toledo location was the local machining expertise. Toledo had a major sewing-machine company, a bicycle company, and a pin factory, all requiring expert machinists. The bottle machine was an assembly of over seven thousand machined parts requiring expert machinists constantly working on the project. This pool of talent allowed Owens to build a mechanical team that was up to the challenge.

The team consisted of Tom Owens, Mike's brother; Jim Cunningham, a mechanic from Toledo Glass; eight additional machinists; and two glass furnace men. Walbridge was also part of the team, functioning as the purchasing agent. All referred to Owens as "the boss," a title he was particularly fond of. The team helped him make major improvements, in particular the production rates of his machine. Owens also modified and customized his machines to better service specific industries. After Bock's resignation, work continued on a new machine to be known as "AE." It was able to produce larger bottles and was released in 1911.

The "AE" could produce at 24 bottles per minute. The next big step, which might be considered a true new bottle machine, was "AN," as we have seen. The "AN" or "Diphead" model had ten arms and could produce bottles at a top rate of 60 bottles per minute (a major production jump).[6] The range of sizes was also amazing. It could produce smaller prescription bottles (one to three ounces) up to sixty-four-ounce jugs. Later models tended to be more specialized for the beer and catsup markets. Owens' 1920 model, known as the "CA," could produce 320 bottles per minute. Most of this work was done at Owens Bottle's experimental glasshouse in Toledo. The last machine to be retired was in 1982 at Gas City, Indiana (a 1914 "AQ" Diphead), a testament to the design and reliability of Owens' machines. All the team members were rewarded with company stock, which made many wealthy in future years.

The biggest impact of the Owens Bottle Machine on society was guaranteed measures and weights of products. This allowed the government to establish standard product and packaging specifications. The law became known as the Pure Food and Drug Act of 1906. The glass unions and hand manufacturers had opposed its passage. The law, however, caused a surge in the use of Owens bottles, because hand-blown bottles were not consistent enough to meet its specifications. The consistency in bottle shape and size resulted from Owens' constant improvement in the machine's operation, from his dedication to quality production in his machines. A lesser inventor might have settled for lesser quality. Many times Owens scrapped a machine due to less than perfect production. Owens maintained that an automated bottle machine had to also be an automated craftsman. His machines, like his approach to management, were integrated, bringing quality and production to an equal footing.

The effect on labor was also revolutionary. The original strategic plan of Owens Bottle Machine Company was to leave both wages and prices unaffected. However, in actuality, Owens Bottle and its licensees behaved as a cartel controlling prices. It would be illegal today, but the beauty of it was that Owens Bottle, the manufacturers (hand, semiautomatic, and automatic), and the union won! Even the consumer saw a steady price. Michael Owens, in particular, lobbied the union to keep wages high, since cost reductions due to automation would increase royalties. The pressure for the hand and semiautomatic industry, however, was to cut wages to remain competitive in the long run. The union realized that short-term wage control was a temporary reprieve, and the "Toledo Faction" would own its future.

This manufacturing utopia of the "Toledo Faction" depended on strong tariff protection, which the government supplied during most of the period. The glass industry was in all the major states; in effect, it was a national industry enjoying broad political support. It was a very functional monopoly, similar to the United States telephone companies of the 1950s and 1960s. However, control and balance of the glass industry were maintained not in Washington but Toledo.

Initially, the slow penetration of the automatic machines and the proactive approach of the union allowed both wages and prices to remain steady. In 1907 there were only twenty-three machines in operation. The license agreements with manufacturers included price-control clauses. Today, such clauses would be clearly illegal. Bottle demand was increasing, however, and that kept prices steady and wages high. In addition, the Owens licensees with 40 to 50 percent cost reductions were reaping huge profits. Actually, the bottle market almost doubled between 1899 and 1907, taking the pressure off all manufacturers. By 1909, the new machine models were selling well and the number of machines in operation had grown to fifty-two. Still, at the start of 1909, the price of a bottle was about the same as in 1899. Owens' continued machine improvements and license penetration began to worry the handcraft manufacturers and the Glass Bottle Blowers Association. The realization was coming that the "Toledo Faction" was in control and could at any time crush the hand blowers and semiautomatic producers. In addition, the Pure Food and Drug Act of 1906 was forcing businesses to convert to the automatic machines. As this happened, hand and semiautomatic producers started to lose market share, and with that the union lost jobs. As the market retracted in 1909 due to economic

The night shift at a New Jersey glass factory, 1909. (Library of Congress)

conditions, the hand and semiautomatic producers absorbed the decrease. If they and the union did nothing, they would steadily lose market share and jobs.

The "Toledo Faction"

Another part of the "Toledo Faction" control was the selling of exclusive rights to use the Owens Bottle Machine on a specific type of bottle. These exclusive rights not only required royalty payments but up-front cash payments. Thatcher paid $50,000 for these exclusive rights. Other companies, such as Hazel-Atlas, turned over $500,000 in capital stock. Once a company had exclusive rights for a kind of bottle, competitors were stuck using hand-blowing and semiautomatic processes.

The union correctly realized that something had to be done to offset the bottle production and machine sales by the "Toledo Faction." The union moved to cut the summer shutdown, allowing the semiautomatics to compete better with the Owens automatic machines. They followed with wage reductions of 20 percent in 1909 and again in 1912. The 1909 wage reduction helped the semiautomatic producers to cut prices to help regain lost market share. This price cutting ended the peace that had existed in the market. Owens Bottle started receiving reduced royalties. In 1910, the cut amounted to fifty cents per gross on the first million and twenty-five cents after that. This directly removed 30 to 50 percent from Owens Bottle's bottom line.

In 1911, the price war started in earnest, with American Bottle Company cutting the price of beer bottles from $3.75 per gross to $2.75 per gross. American Bottle was at the time the largest licensee of the Owens Bottle Machine. This, of course, immediately preceded the release of the high-production, second-generation machine, the "AN." As the union prepared to counter with another wage reduction, Michael Owens tried to intervene personally. He suggested avoiding making the wage cut, which would only continue the price war. Holding up price through cooperation seemed the only solution for all. The union went ahead in 1912 with the wage cut. Once the wage cuts started, it was a downward spiral. Not only were wages cut, but piece rates were reduced also. The union realized the power of the "Toledo Faction" and was not willing to be dependent on them.

Many have argued that Owens tried to help the union, but more likely he was only looking out for the interests of the "Toledo Faction." His attitude was always ambivalent towards the union. Owens often vacationed and golfed in Florida with Thomas Rowe, president of the American Flints, but he resisted unionization of his own plants. There were mixed feelings on both sides. Mike was a union man who had made good and was, therefore, the pride of many. He was a tough manager and businessman; yet, he was a compassionate man who gave much away.

Owens surely never wanted to see the union take wage cuts, but he realized automation could not be stopped. He honestly advised the union to come to terms with automation. His call for "cooperation" was best for all involved, with the exception, possibly, of the consumer. But again, even the consumer who paid the "higher" price reaped the benefits of higher employment.

The "Great Glassmaking Pax"—the period of peace among labor, unions, and companies from 1902 to 1915—maintained prices through the "Toledo Faction," while at the same time cost reductions spread throughout the process. These horizontal improvements in the process resulted from the crafts model transforming to the industrial model. For example, the crafts paradigm and the union had effectively blocked use of the highly efficient Siemens gas furnace and large melting tanks for

A 1913 Florida golf trip. Left to right: William Boshart, Mike Owens, Paul Welch. (Owens-Illinois Glass Company Records, MSS-200, the Ward M. Canaday Center for Special Collections, University of Toledo)

Owens enjoying a Florida vacation, 1914. (Owens-Illinois Glass Company Records, MSS-200, the Ward M. Canaday Center for Special Collections, University of Toledo)

Owens and Thomas Rowe, president of the American Flints, on vacation together in Florida, 1917. (Owens-Illinois Glass Company Records, MSS-200, the Ward M. Canaday Center for Special Collections, University of Toledo)

decades. The Siemens brothers patented the first continuous day tank coupled with a regenerative gas furnace in 1870. Continuous day tanks could hold up to three hundred tons, while the largest pot furnace held around twenty tons. The continuous tank technology could cut melting costs 50 to 70 percent, but it would have changed the crafts labor system. Continuous day tanks offered many advantages, such as less wear, longer life, higher fuel efficiency, better plant scheduling, less operating labor, and higher productivity. Because of its long hold times, lead was oxidized and this restricted its use in the flint-glass segment. In the flat glass segment, Local Assembly 300 had shut the door on any labor-reducing technology; even the bottle and container industry had been extremely slow in conversion (due to the crafts union). The Owens Bottle Machine required the use of day tanks, and therefore helped to significantly reduce melting costs and pushed everyone else towards implementing them. The rapid production and volume of the Owens Bottle Machine also drove up use of continuous annealing furnaces. These cost reductions would ultimately reduce prices as well.

The Great Glassmaking Pax had held prices steady for the most part until 1912. The pax, however, is hard to analyze. It was a time of rapid technology development and implementation. Tariff protection allowed the glassmakers to be very aggressive with investment. There was also a significant increase in demand for glass containers. The food industry, starting with milk, developed automatic filling machines. Michael Owens got more involved and developed an automatic catsup-filling machine in 1913. With the end of the peaceful cooperation, prices actually rocketed up, not down, in the long run. The price pax ended as demand for glass increased dramatically. The boom was driven by the electrical industry and construction. Raw material inflation started to rocket up as well. Also, glass exports increased after 1915, which moved domestic prices up.The decades of tariff protection on glassware came to a close with the Underwood Tariff of 1913. The economics of the period are still being debated today. Owens' interests never really changed, however, and from 1902 to 1915, he was the leader of the "Toledo Faction."

Owens differed from the others in the "Toledo Faction" in that they were content to license bottle machines as their main enterprise. They were not interested in development work or bottle production. Owens wanted Toledo Glass to remain a developmental company while having Owens Bottle Machine Company move more into bottle production.

Actually, the Owens Bottle experimental plant was already at capacity, making catsup bottles for local catsup makers. In 1909, Owens started campaigning the board to move from "experimental" production in Toledo to serious production out of state. The Owens Bottle board, including Libbey, Brown, Geddes, and Walbridge, opposed him. Brown and Geddes, in particular, favored financial projects over new operations. Owens argued that they were lawyers with little knowledge of glassmaking. They were conservative by nature and felt more comfortable managing licensees than manufacturing bottles. Libbey's interests were turning towards art collecting and trips to Europe. Many noted that he had become more conservative with age and more hesitant to invest in Owens' "wild" ideas. Walbridge tended to vote with Owens but he also lacked a passion for more bottle production. His hesitation was probablydue to his insight as an administrator that the company was losing focus. Walbridge realized that the company at that point lacked the managerial talent and structure to maintain a multi-state operation. On the other hand, Owens felt that the company was going down because of "the damn lawyers." Months of stormy battles ensued, but ultimately Libbey moved his support to Owens, as he had in the past.

Owens' victory resulted in an approval to build a bottle plant in Fairmont, West Virginia. Owens planned a state-of-the-art plant that would be a showcase for all of his process patents. It would also be a model of automation. Finished in 1910, the plant had three furnaces and two of the newest ten-arm bottle machines. It was hailed at the time as the "most modern glass plant ever built." The Fairmont plant offered Owens a chance to take automation to new heights. It pioneered automatic mixers, raw material conveyors, and automatic furnace feeders. This plant was to continuous glass manufacturing what Ford's first plant was to assembly production. It predated Ford's assembly operations as well. It could produce an amazing 600,000 bottles a year. Automation advances were Michael Owens' passion.

One of Owens' greatest achievements after the bottle machine was the automation of annealing furnaces. The bottle machine produced at rates never seen before. The stationary annealing furnaces with long heating cycles could not keep up in 1910. Owens installed his first automated lehr in the Massillon, Ohio, plant of a beer-bottle licensee, Reed Bottle Company. He pioneered this new technology at the Fairmont plant. Owens did not build the equipment but addressed overall process control. His annealing furnaces were the first to introduce pyrometers to measure temperature, bringing science into the annealing operation. He applied electric motors to control speed and movement. The combination of automated bottle production and automated annealing allowed for continuous production of bottles.

Smooth automation of the Fairmont plant required a great deal of Owens' personal supervision between 1909 and 1911. Fairmont had its share of problems, but it was a pioneering effort. Owens was not content with just one bottle plant, so he initiated a campaign of horizontal expansion against strong opposition by board members Brown and Geddes. Brown and Geddes believed they could maintain their monopolistic utopia indefinitely. Owens was a true industrialist, not interested in economic control but market control through manufacturing dominance. Owens, at the time, was at the peak of his career and completely uncontrollable by the board. In the end, he would prove to be right about horizontal expansion as a corporate strategy.

Being right had always been one of Owens' major problems. he never handled success well. He would become even harder to deal with, and the board would have to be reminded of him being right. Libbey usually stepped aside as Owens triumphed. He, like Owens, fed on power. It fueled them to pursue even bigger dreams. Owens' real business at times seemed to be the fulfilling of his dreams. Libbey, realizing that this was an asset to him and his companies, allowed Owens' bad corporate behavior.

Giving Owens a commercial success was like giving General Patton a headline; it only powered more drive to achieve. Mike could be extremely difficult to work with when he was on top. The board would feel the effects of Mike on a power drive. The board would wait for their own revenge.

The Fairmont plant's problems increased over its brief life of six years. The board documented all of these setbacks to use against Owens. Brown and Geddes were united in their move to limit him. These setbacks offered the first opportunity for the board to show weaknesses in Owens' engineering ability. The Fairmont plant struggled because of "layout" problems. It was built in a steep hill of a mountain valley, and wind currents were blamed for poor furnace operation. The plant also experienced a number of fires. The board capitalized on these problems. This finger pointing was unfair but successful. As is often the case in business, top management's search to place blame succeeded. The board's understanding and expertise, however, are what should be questioned. Walbridge started to side with Brown and Geddes, as Owens was often gone from Toledo on his many projects. Walbridge feared Owens' spending more than any managerial or technical shortcomings. He credited Owens as being a gifted inventor. Brown and Geddes saw Owens as a poor manager and attacked him often. More importantly, they had no interest in his developmental projects and production operations. Their documentation of Owens' failures continued for years and slowly eroded even Libbey's confidence in him.

Owens was battling the same group of "damn lawyers" on Toledo Glass's efforts as well. Toledo Glass remained the developmental arm of the "Toledo Faction." Owens was convinced that the automatic bottle machine required constant improvement to stay competitive. Again Brown and Geddes opposed this approach, feeling that the machine was good enough. Walbridge joined in the belief that "Owens' experimentation would bankrupt the company." Bankers had problems with extending credit for projects associated with Owens, not because they lacked confidence in the success of an Owens project but because they feared the cost of that success. Owens was considered unable to understand the "value of money." Actually, Owens' development work would have been a major problem for most corporations at the time, but Libbey enjoyed a great deal of autonomy from the bankers by limiting debt. Libbey had never forgotten the problems the bankers had caused him back in New England.

Owens' philosophy, however, was in agreement with that of many of the great Victorian industrialists, such as Carnegie, Schwab, Ford, Edison, Westinghouse, etc. The philosophy of ever applying the best and newest technology, regardless of cost, had propelled American industry into world leadership under the guidance of these men. Carnegie and Schwab had made the "scrap heap policy" famous. This policy involved applying new equipment and technology as soon as it was available, regardless of the "value" of the equipment in place. Today's accountants would be fearful of such a policy, but maybe that is where we have lost our manufacturing edge. Even Libbey, in his early days, was noted for saying, "To let well enough alone is slow commercial suicide." Owens felt that the competition was just a few steps behind at all times. Anything less than aggressive development would mean that someone would overtake them. Owens argued for continuous improvement to the moment of his death.

The boards of Owens Bottle and Toledo Glass generally were opposed to all of Owens' development and manufacturing philosophies. As usual, Owens was his own worst enemy. He pushed for another bottle factory to be built at Clarksburg, West Virginia. The board asked Owens to consider a more favorable location in New Jersey. After much hesitation, Owens set out with a number of board associates to look at an alternative site there. The group departed by automobile on a winter day in 1911. A snowstorm eventually prevented them from getting to the exact location, and they had to set out on foot for several miles. Owens' temper finally exploded and he yelled: "Hell, I'm cold, and I've already decided on Clarksburg anyway!" The group turned back and never did inspect the site. For the board, it was just another one of Mike's power statements. This type of bullying was, however, a weakness of his. Owens was feeling too much of his own success. Brown and Geddes would wait years, but they would cage this lion in the end. They did convince Libbey that the furnace and plant problems were related to Owens' choice of Fairmont and Clarksburg. The facts suggest that this was a case of Brown building a "file" on Owens. Libbey was quietly siding more and more with the conservative views of Brown and Geddes. He found more satisfaction in art collecting and he needed more cash-generating investments. Brown was adept at bringing Libbey back into the business as a defense against Owens.

The Glass Trust and Market Control

Owens not only pushed the Owens Bottle Company board on machine improvement, but he continued to fight for horizontal expansion in bottle manufacture. Libbey, for the most part, agreed with this strategy. American Bottle Company was a major competitor from 1903 to 1915. Actually, American Bottle did about double the production of bottles of Owens Bottle. American Bottle was the major bottler for the liquor and beer business. It was an early licensee of the Owens machine. American Bottle was the largest bottle producer, and even though it was under license, it was very independent minded. When American Bottle reduced its prices in 1911, Owens Bottle board saw the need to bring it into the fold. In 1915, Libbey led a takeover of American Bottle, bringing it into Owens Bottle. This brought in three bottle plants (two in Illinois and one in Ohio). Owens, of course, was overjoyed with the newfound direction of the board. The board was not only interested in maintaining profits from its licensees through monopolistic price control but was also looking to the day when the patents of the Owens machine would expire.

Owens Bottle plant, 1917. (Owens-Illinois Glass Company Records, MSS-200, the Ward M. Canaday Center for Special Collections, University of Toledo)

**First Owens Bottle Company factory
on Wall Street**

Michael J. Owens

**W. L. Libbey & Son Glass Company
(a.k.a.** *Libbey Glass*)

(Owens-Illinois Glass Company Records, MSS-200, the Ward M. Canaday
Center for Special Collections, University of Toledo)

Graham Glass of Indiana posed an even larger threat to Owens Bottle Company. Graham Glass was the largest soft-drink bottle manufacturer, having control of the Coca-Cola market. Even more threatening was Graham Glass's developmental work in semiautomatic and automatic bottle machines. Graham Glass actually had a semiautomatic bottle machine on the market in 1915. It was considered crude compared to the Owens machine, but it eliminated high-priced blowers, and the initial investment was a fraction of the cost of the Owens machine. The Graham machine only required skilled laborers—no craftsmen.

The Graham machine was Owens' first real competition, but it was marginally commercial. Still, the lower investment would allow smaller companies to automate, and that loomed as a serious threat to the Owens Bottle monopoly. Another unique and important advantage was that it could produce small orders more cheaply than the Owens machine. The ability to produce small runs of one bottle type would be attractive to the smaller and midsize companies. The Graham machine had also gained support in Europe, which was a major marketing threat.

Michael Owens informed the Owens Bottle board that while the Graham machine greatly reduced costs, the Owens machine still had a significant advantage in 1915. Owens was, however, impressed with their patented molten-glass feeder, which he believed could lead to the development of a superior automatic machine. The Graham machine was gravity fed versus the famous suction-fed process of the Owens machine.

Owens and Libbey were very concerned about the Graham machine's potential advantage with small orders and sizes. Libbey and the board again resorted to their monopolistic behavior and, in 1916, voted to purchase the Graham patents. On failing to get all the patents, Libbey bought the company in 1917. The purchase of Graham Glass ended the only serious threat to the control of the bottle business by the "Toledo Faction."

Interestingly, the Graham brothers would return after the deaths of Libbey and Owens to end the "Toledo Faction." The Graham brothers initially helped manage the factories after the Owens Bottle buyout but eventually moved into the auto industry.

In particular, they became directors of the Dodge Corporation. They never lost their interest in glassmaking and planned a return. In the 1920s, with the booming automotive market and the success of Libbey-Owens Glass in automatic sheet-glass production, they saw the opportunity. In 1928, working with a consortium of bankers, they took over Libbey-Owens Sheet Glass. So the Graham brothers would have their revenge in the future. Libbey and Owens did, however, treat them very fairly after the buyout, because Michael Owens wanted to know everything about their gravity-fed semiautomatic bottle process.

Owens and his engineers took Graham Glass's gravity feed patents and started to experiment with their application. A Graham machine was set up at Toledo Glass's Toledo plant for experimentation. The work was long and difficult, supporting Owens' observation that the machine was far from true commercialization. It was common at the time to patent inventions without testing to serve notice in the industry or to aid in future lawsuits.By 1921, Owens introduced the "AY" gravity-fed machine. While at the time it was considered a state-of-the-art machine, it did not sell well because of operating problems. Owens, therefore, was never able to realize any commercial value from the Graham patents. Still, Libbey and Owens had always applied a strategy of buying out the competition early before they commercialized equipment. This avoided long, drawn-out legal battles with other inventors. It also allowed Libbey to tie up competitors in legal fights when necessary to slow their development work. This is exactly what Libbey and Owens did to Beechnut Packing Company, which was working on a gravity-fed jar-making machine.

The purchase of Graham Glass and American Bottle was fortuitous. Owens had correctly foreseen a boom in the bottle market. Prohibition had hurt bottle sales, but the soft-drink and packaging markets exploded. Demand increased thirtyfold between 1919 and 1921 alone. The end of the Glass Pax in 1915 resulted in a price increase, which hurt Owens' licensees but greatly aided manufacturing profits. Owens Bottle, as the major bottle manufacturer, was able to reap the profits of that position, thanks to

Owens. However, he always believed that industry was about man-ufacturing, not financial agreements. Owens lamented the trend that moved American business from "captains of industry" to "captains of finance." He was vocal in his contempt for "the damn lawyers," "bean counters," and "pencil pushers." To him, great-ness resulted from success on the factory floor, not in the board-room. It should be noted that Owens' attacks on board members were not personal but part of the corporate battle that he envi-sioned. He could compromise, even eat humble pie if required (although not often), to achieve a goal. More importantly, Owens believed that profits resulted from risk. He was a natural gambler to the end, but Libbey lost that risk-taking approach with age and financial success.

Owens started to complain in public about Libbey's collecting trips and vacations. They were different people, and as time went on that difference became more pronounced. Owens lacked any real hobbies for most of his life, while Libbey was passionate about art and Egyptology and even had a telescope built on his roof to pursue his interest in astronomy. In 1901, Libbey opened a small museum in a rented building, and in 1903, he acquired an old mansion to house his museum. By 1912, he had built the core of what would become the Toledo Museum of Art. He and his wife became interested in its growth, and from 1913 on, Libbey's attention to aggressive business plans waned. Owens was left to battle the board on his own and had to better pick his fights, something he was never good at. Still, when Brown and others brought in Libbey, he sided with Owens. Libbey just could not say no directly to Mike. Libbey wanted a steady income to pursue his art and hobbies, and he was trying to move away from day-to-day management. Libbey's wife also wanted his involve-ment in the museum. Owens was more and more alone in his plans for aggressive growth. Without Owens, the "Toledo Faction" would have reverted to Libbey Glass after the bottle machinery patents expired.

The unusual bond between Libbey and Owens varied in strength. It dissolved for brief periods, but it never quite broke. Their somewhat strange arrangement allowed for a lot of internal

Toledo Museum of Art. (Owens-Illinois Glass Company Records, MSS-200, the Ward M. Canaday Center for Special Collections, University of Toledo)

politics. Libbey and the board often used "spies" to keep an eye on Owens. Brown acted as his enforcer so he could avoid direct conflict with Owens. Libbey often required his plant managers to write daily and weekly updates, particularly during his many trips to Europe and California. Owens in turn had his own group of "spies." He had a very strong network in the workers and front-line supervision. Internal politics is always a matter of information control. It was a game that Owens was extremely good at, when he did not let his pride get in the way.

Libbey also used Brown and Walbridge to confront Owens for him, and the conflicts between these men and Owens became more personal over the years. Owens realized this and knew when to go to Libbey. In all of his major inventions, he needed Libbey to overrule the board. Libbey often used the board to buy time for him to think things over that Owens suggested. Owens frequently chose to ignore the board, knowing that Libbey would at some time be drawn into the fight. The real struggle and ultimate decision involved Libbey and Owens.

Owens' dislike of the board increased with the years. He questioned the opinions of "the damn lawyers" and "a furniture salesman" more often. The board, on the other hand, saw Owens as an uneducated hillbilly.

The board used rumor and written character assassination as part of their internal politics. Unfortunately, these documents continue to take away from Owens' reputation as one of the premier inventors of the twentieth century. They belittle his achievements while highlighting his shortcomings.

The board floated rumors of Owens' lack of mechanical ability. From boyhood, he felt this deficiency. He hated to admit it and was ashamed to discuss it. Interestingly, when Owens had a portrait made of himself in 1918, he was shown with blueprints. The stories that he could not read a blueprint or use a screwdriver were exaggerations. Still, he often sent his engineers to make repairs at his home. What Owens did not realize was that two of the greatest inventors—Henry Ford and Thomas Edison—rarely worked with their hands. A *Harper's Magazine* article in 1932 noted: "Edison seldom worked with his hands. He had a mechanical man who did all the manipulating, while the master did the experimenting in his head." Edison never had to deal with enemies to the extent that Owens did. Edison and Ford always had strong positive publicity, and even their enemies built their legacies. The board's attacks on Owens were sardonic. These came from lesser, though educated, men, who left no lasting legacy to society. Owens was a genius. Without him, Brown and Geddes would have been good lawyers but forgotten within a few years after their deaths. Owens was a tough man, but he was proud of his achievements, so the attacks on his achievements hurt badly. Only after Owens' death did Libbey and the company start to purge the archives of these attacks. Many of the records reflecting discord were moved to secret vaults. In addition, corporate stories were culturally reinforced in the Libbey companies, such as the one about Owens' first job with Libbey. It is clear that

Libbey hoped to create a corporate legend out of his partnership with Owens, but his own untimely death prevented this.

Owens was not educated. He could not spell, but he probably read more books in a year than the board did in all their lifetimes. It is said he read more than five hundred books annually, which he housed in an extensive home library. Owens had been a reader of historical books and biographies since boyhood. He was an excellent historian and military expert. He was a student of the Civil War and spent many evenings studying campaigns and battles. It is said he once spent three days reconstructing the Battle of Gettysburg. He became an excellent speaker and debater through self-education as well. He was popular as a dinner speaker. His articles and talks were outstanding. But like so much of Owens' life, his private side is, to a large degree, lost to history.

Owens' family life was by his own request off limits for reporters. He avoided the local social circuit, preferring quiet evenings at home, reading and playing cards. He took no role in Libbey's art museum. In fact, Owens preferred cheap, realistic paintings for his home and office. He was a true workaholic, working late and on holidays when a major project was under way. As a workaholic, he managed to avoid a passion for drink. He traveled often for business, but when he was in Toledo, he ate at home with his family. In the summer, his wife and kids lived at a cottage on Clark Lake in the Irish Hills area of Michigan. The area was a favorite of Owens because of its Irish heritage. The little Toledo mission parish of St. Joseph's was dedicated to the Irish diaspora of the 1840s. His only close friends were a handful of priests and some of his West Virginia cronies. His involvement in fraternal organizations only included the Knights of Columbus and the Friends of Irish Freedom. He was basically an absentee father but was generous with his children to a fault. Owens represented the typical Irish family patriarch, a breadwinner and director. Rearing the kids would be the job of the mother, which was also common in that era. By the time his health slowed him down in 1918, his kids were grown.

CHAPTER 11

Owens: The Industrialist

Michael J. Owens filled the role of Victorian industrialist better than most. His was a rags-to-riches success story. Like Carnegie, Westinghouse, and others, he came from humble beginnings and maintained a simple lifestyle. Money came with success, but it was never a motivator. Achievement was the engine of his life. Manufacturing represented the core of his interests, and money represented the measure of manufacturing success.

By 1910, Owens and his associates in the "Toledo Faction" were extremely wealthy. The group's assets were considerable. Owens' original 400 shares in Toledo Glass were worth $440,000 in 1910 alone and that was but a small part of his total assets in the "Toledo Faction" network. Toledo Glass was a private company, but stock prices were recorded. The price grew from $150 a share in 1903 to $14,000 a share in 1928. The dividend payout rate was said to be 300 percent at times. The "Toledo Faction," with its base companies of Toledo Glass and Owens Bottle, aggressively expanded both horizontally and vertically. Besides licensing to companies, it purchased fifteen bottle-manufacturing companies as well as becoming a major stockholder in many others. Vertically, the Faction purchased equipment, sand, gas, and clay companies. In 1919, Owens Bottle Company was the largest producer of bottles in the world. By Owens' death in 1923, 94 out of every 100 bottles were being produced on an Owens machine.

The "Toledo Faction," with its automatic machines and production methods, had a technological monopoly that had been unseen since that of the Venetians in the Middle Ages. The "Toledo Faction" dominance in the glass industry is hard to imagine in terms of today's industry. The best current analogy might be Microsoft. What is also amazing is the monopolistic price control of the "Toledo Faction." The robber barons of the age rarely approached the control of the "Toledo Faction" in the glass industry, yet the "Toledo Faction" always remained within the legal boundaries of the time. They were sensitive to any changes on the legal front. They adapted quickly to the 1911 Sherman Antitrust Law (the Sherman Act was actually passed in 1890 but was ambiguous in application). The law led to the negation of licensee price control in 1912, anticipating the passage of the Clayton Antitrust Act of 1914. The "Toledo Faction" still controlled the American, European, Japanese, and Chinese bottle-production markets through its license arrangements. In 1911, Michael Owens was to lead the "Toledo Faction" into the only part of the glass business it did not control—sheet glass.

The growth of the "Toledo Faction" without government intervention remains a mystery. Somehow, the "Toledo Faction" stayed under the radar of the government, which seemed transfixed with oil, railroads, and steel. Yet, the "Toledo Faction" had price control of their market that Rockefeller, Carnegie, and Vanderbilt could only dream of. What remains striking is the absence in recorded economic history of the "Toledo Faction." Even in historical works on big business of time, the glass industry and the "Toledo Faction" are rarely noted. One factor of this low profile was that Owens pushed the group towards horizontal expansion. The government seemed more fearful of vertical arrangements involving raw materials than horizontal arrangements for product distribution. Libbey had briefly pushed for vertical control in 1913, with the formation of Toledo-Owens Sand Company and Buckeye Clay Pot Company. He even considered vertically entering into the mining of coal and related fuels, but Libbey and Owens perfected the horizontal monopoly to a high degree of profitability. Libbey did move aggressively to control gas sources because of his previous experience with fuel shortages.

Some of the Faction's success in avoiding antitrust action was due to the complexity of the companies' stock arrangements. In addition, these were closed corporations with few financial reporting requirements. The Faction also maintained a very low profile in the press compared to other industries of the time. Some historians point to some internal policing, but these efforts were minimal. In 1911, the directors of Owens Bottle Company did eliminate price-control clauses in their licenses, but the antitrustlaws required such action anyway. The use of licenses to control prices is cartel behavior at its worst, yet the "Toledo Faction" persisted on this path for years. What was different was that the glass cartel actually held prices and wages steady by its control of the market. When the cartel voluntarily took price controls out of the license agreements, glass prices started to rise!

The location of the "Toledo Faction" base kept it somewhat protected from the New York press and financial interests. Libbey financed internally and locally, keeping New York bankers out of the mix. Owens' aggressive manufacturing investments were atypical of a monopoly. Owens himself was branded as an inventor like Edison, not an industrialist. Libbey also had the nonthreatening image of an art collector. Because the Faction's companies were nontraded, private firms, its full financial strength is hard to calculate, but Owens Bottle was extremely profitable. Owens actually sacrificed his huge ego in lawsuits to underplay his invention. Europe was more aggressive at times in pointing out the monopolistic control of Owens Bottle Company. Verband brought several antitrust suits against Owens Bottle. Monopolistic behavior in foreign markets, however, was actually hailed in the American press, while domestic steel and railroad companies faced endless press scrutiny. Another plus for the Faction was that the complex ownership relationship with the various companies hid profits from the public eye. Even with spending all that developmental money, Owens Bottle paid out over 14 million dollars to its stockholders from 1903 to 1920. One analysis suggested that if a fifty-dollar share was bought in 1904 and held, with dividends reinvested, it would have a value near six hundred dollars in 1920. Still, Owens Bottle was known for its aggressive investments in technology, which even the politicians saw as a plus.

During this period of great financial growth, Michael Owens' behavior frustrated other board members of Owens Bottle and Toledo Glass. Since he wanted cash, Owens sold stock with little regard to market trends or prices. He often gave shares to friends and those who worked for him, which infuriated the board. Likewise, Mike gave blocks of fifty shares to nieces and nephews as rewards for good grades. He loved good clothes and fast cars. He was clearly visible around town with his Detroit Electric, Pierce-Arrow, and twelve-cylinder Packard cars. On the surface Mike appeared materialistic, but after his death, the world would know of his generosity. His son, Raymond, lived in Hollywood and created a few fast-living headlines himself.

Owens disliked traveling except when necessary, although later, as his health deteriorated, he went to Palm Beach and California often to relax. He was a giving man but functioned more as a private community chest. The story is told that, when he was growing up in Wheeling, the family's weekly expenses were taken out of a tin can and anything remaining on Sunday was given to the church. The Owenses, like most Irish-Catholic families, often invited street people to Sunday dinner, remembering the days of struggle in Ireland to just eat. Mike gave large sums to the Catholic Church. One associate said he knew how to tell if Mike was in church: "If there were a couple of hundred-dollar bills in the plate when it came around to you, you could bet he was in there somewhere." These sums would represent a couple of thousand dollars today! He also gave generously to build major additions to a Catholic church near his summer home on Clark Lake, Michigan. Owens worked quietly with his parish priest to supply needy families in the winter. Information about the amazing amounts he gave surfaced only after his death. One man approached Mrs. Owens after Mike's funeral to tell of how Mike had given money to help with his son's illness. A contractor told of Owens seeing the poor condition of an orphanage and giving him $7,500 (a huge sum for the time) to repair it. Owens had a soft spot for orphanages, having worked with so many orphans in the glasshouses of West Virginia. He always talked of how blessed he was to have had the support of an Irish family.

When a nervous Father Dean came to Mike's door to ask for a donation for the future Rosary Cathedral in the Diocese of Toledo, he got $15,000 (about $200,000 in today's dollars) and a lifelong friend. A few years later, Owens made another pledge of $50,000. Father Dean used the money to build a main altar of beautiful Italian marble, which today draws the praise of many visitors. As is the case with all of his charity, there is no mention of Owens in the church archives or plaques to point out his donations. For Father Dean, however, Rosary Cathedral was the embodiment of Mike Owens' spirit of faith and giving. Owens was a patron of young men studying for the priesthood as well, giving thousands of dollars to support years of study. Owens was never an investor or a public donator, and this mystified board members. Many felt he managed his assets poorly. Owens lived on cash and gave privately, true to his Irish immigrant roots. Considering the millions of dollars that passed through his hands, his estate of $1.5 million at his death might be considered disappointing. In business and in his personal life, Owens looked at money for what it could do, not what it could earn. He never saw his legacy in terms of money but in terms of invention, industry, and his relationship with God.

Owens was just as generous with his children and extended family. Ray Owens, in particular, was allowed to spend money liberally. Ray Owens in his latter years lived fast in Beverly Hills, California. Mike never really approved of this lifestyle, but he could not say no to his son.

It was Owens' attitude towards money that most differentiated him from the other board members. In business, he believed that money should be used for development and new equipment, not to earn interest. Owens sounded much like the other Victorian industrialists, Andrew Carnegie and Henry Ford. Ford put it this way:

> Money is not worth a particular amount. As money it is not worth anything, for it will do nothing of itself. The only use of money is to buy tools to work with or the product of tools.[1]

These Victorian industrialists were operating managers who poured money back into the businesses. They made their huge profits in this manner. All of them feared the interference of bankers, lawyers, and the new breed of managers who saw money in terms of interest earned. Toledo Glass's board fell in the latter category. Raw-material investment made more sense to them than manufacturing assets. To Brown and Geddes, the conservative approach was slow, vertical expansion into raw materials and licensing agreements. They further believed that no more "risky" and expensive developmental work should be pursued. Owens Bottle controlled the bottle and container market, so merely cutting costs through vertical integration could increase profits. Why manufacture when you can lease and get royalties? To Owens, manufacturing was the only justification for a company to exist.

Owens pioneered the idea of design for manufacturing. Owens, like Ford, was a pure operations man. He envied Ford's marketing strategy of one color, which meant considerable additional speed in his assembly lines. The automobile, of course, was a product of the industrial age, while the bottle was a remnant of the crafts era. Each bottle was unique in size, shape, and color. This was a major cost factor for the bottle manufacturer, who had to maintain countless bottle molds and endure endless downtime for mold changes. Owens believed that even product design should be based on manufacturing parameters. He argued that huge savings could be made by standardization, using the label to distinguish and market. In a speech of May 1922 to bottle producers, he laid out his argument for standardization:

> The manufacturer should have the co-operation of the users to simplify and standardize the articles they demand. As an example of needless expense and waste, our Company alone, apart from its subsidiaries, has spent $900,000 for molds in the last five years. We estimate that this year we will spend $300,000 for new molds. It is clear that if this cost is felt so heavily in the case of a single company, it must bear down in still greater proportion upon the other glass manufacturers. Eventually, of course, all this expense goes into the cost of bottles and is absorbed by the users.[2]

Owens also realized that automation favored product standardization, which allowed some competition by the hand and semiautomatic producers in the unusual sizes and odd shapes. In fact, in small lots, the Owens machine lost its economic advantage. Automation has its power in high volume and low variety. Unfortunately, this usually is opposed to market customization. This desire of users to have special sizes allowed the hand and semiautomatic processes to serve a substantial part of the market. In 1917, Owens machines controlled 50 percent of the market. By Owens' death in 1923, his machines had 80 percent of the market, with the balance held by semiautomatics. Still, his last improvements focused on more product flexibility of his machines, so as to better compete with the semiautomatics.

Owens and Libbey Move into Flat Glass

Owens Bottle Company and the Owens glass machine dominated the packaging market with automation and technology for the first decade of the century, but window and flat glass remained in the Dark Ages. Window glass was still produced by the cylinder or crown method. The cylinder, as we have seen, was a manpower-intensive process, requiring highly skilled laborers. Another inventor, Irving Wightman Colburn, had started to do in 1906 for flat glass what Owens had done for bottle glass. Colburn looked to develop a glass-casting method for flat glass. He had a tough struggle. In 1906, the national press had claimed him to be the next Michael Owens, but failures plagued him. By 1911, he and his struggling Pennsylvania Company were nearly bankrupt. Colburn had also spent his health. The project needed a champion, and Mike Owens was to be that champion.

As late as 1915, the cylinder process made all window glass. Window glass blowers and their apprentices had a very tight "guild." A select group who passed down membership by family ties controlled entrance into the profession. The National Window Glass Union had its roots in the original Local Assembly 300, one of the most powerful locals in the Industrial Revolution. In 1904, a window cylinder blower earned double that of bottle blowers and flint-glass gaffers. This segment of the glass industry stood as a walled fortress against automation. Union bylaws restricted workers from employment in automated shops.

Many had envisioned a more direct route to producing flat

glass. The idea of drawing or rolling flat glass was not new. C. Boynton had suggested in a *Scientific American* article of 1869 that glass might be drawn into a thin sheet. A British glassmaker replied that he had tried twenty years earlier but failed. In the 1880s several inventors applied for and were granted patents for the continuous drawing of glass. In a related field, Henry Bessemer had suggested that liquid steel could be drawn into a sheet. He also received a patent. Yet none of these inventors ever developed a practical process. Meanwhile, John Lubbers was working on automation in the cylinder process. In 1896, he introduced a machine that could blow cylinders twenty-five to thirty feet long versus six feet for a hand blower. The Lubbers cylinder diameters reached twenty-four inches versus fourteen inches for hand blowers. The cylinder size, of course, was the determining factor in the end size of flat glass windows. Demand was growing from retailing and department stores for large plate windows. The Lubbers process expanded sizes and market.

The Lubbers process allowed for the elimination of skilled blowers and gatherers as well. The National Window Glass Workers changed the number of cylinders allowed to be produced, so that hand-blowing shops could compete better with Lubbers plants. The Bureau of Labor Statistics estimated that the Lubbers process increased productivity 133 percent and reduced labor costs 57 percent. Still, the Lubbers process is an example of how short-term thinking can inhibit long-range improvement. The semiautomatic blowing of large cylinders had cut production costs, but it was far from a direct, efficient process. A cast-drawing process could offer even greater savings. The union, however, had dug in. The Lubbers process still allowed for some skilled workers. The success of the Lubbers process slowed most flat-drawing experimentation, except for that of Colburn. The Lubbers process did also have some inherent quality problems from waves and wrinkles commonly found in the initial cylinders.

Colburn was trying to break into the most highly controlled segment of the glass industry—flat glass. The Knights of Labor and its power base, Local Assembly 300, had helped control wages, output, labor availability, and technology from 1870 to

1900. The manufacturers had formed an association as a reaction to the power of union. The American Window Glass Manufacturers Association was formed in 1879. It represented over 90 percent of the industry. The association soon learned to cooperate with the union to form an industrial-labor monopoly. The government started to investigate the flat-glass industry as early as 1882 because of its monopolistic behavior. The industry then tried to move to a more politically correct structure. Under this guise, the American Glass Company was formed in Pittsburgh in 1895. It started as a loosely organized group controlling 85 percent of the flat-glass factories. In 1899, it became a formal corporation with fifty-three glasshouses. The company quickly formed an alliance with Local Assembly 300 to assure labor, but at a controlled price and with a restricted apprentice program. With monopolistic price control, the manufacturers and union kept technology that would eliminate jobs out of the industry. This anti-technological block impeded Colburn's progress.

Even the independents in the flat-glass industry learned to cooperate on blocking new technology. They controlled only 20 to 25 percent of the market but soon understood the advantages of monopolistic behavior. The monopoly also had strong political support due to its high-cost, low-tech production methods. Tariffs were in place to protect the industry on the East Coast from cheaper European flat glass. A tariff commission actually showed that American labor costs for flat glass were double those for Belgian glass. Most of this difference was attributable to the rejection of any technology advances. This could be seen in the continued use of pot furnaces versus day tanks in the flat-glass industry. The day tanks offered huge cost reductions, but with price control, the motivation to reduce costs is diminished. The melting costs could be halved with day tanks, but the amount of molten glass would push the blowers to produce more, which neither the union nor manufacturer was interested in. Colburn's process required day tanks, but he was already an outsider. The industrial-labor flat-glass monopoly strengthened its resistance to Colburn's experimentation.

James Colburn was a natural inventor, like so many Victorians.

Born in 1861, he had invented a foot-pedal-driven dynamo just out of high school. He installed the first telephones in Massachusetts in the early 1880s as well as the first electric light. He went on to form a machining and manufacturing company in Fitchburg, Massachusetts. It manufactured a variety of electrical devices. He had come from a long line of machinists and inventors. His brother and sister had moved to Toledo and were actually working for Mike Owens. On a visit to Toledo, Colburn met Owens and became interested in glass. Like Thomas Edison, Colburn looked to an area where experiments might offer great rewards. Flat-glass production had that potential. He launched a tour of American glass factories to explore and study processes. Colburn sketched a number of rough ideas on this tour.

In 1901, Colburn started some experiments in Franklin, Pennsylvania. His first thrust was to improve the cylinder process. Colburn found some success in automated blowing of cylinders and the cutting of cylinders. He continued to improve his process mechanically, but by the time it was ready, the Lubbers process had secured the market. He scrapped the machine he had spent over four years on and started to look at sheet-drawing processes. His first crude experiments showed hope that a uniform sheet could be drawn, but quality was another matter. The sheet produced had many imperfections, such as air bubbles. In addition, it was extremely brittle. By 1905, Colburn had a machine that was at least patentable, which he proceeded to do. The Colburn machine pulled a sheet vertically from molten-glass baths. By 1906, Colburn was attracting press coverage and new investors. Even the *Toledo Blade* claimed in a headline that the invention "Rivals Owens Machine." Colburn was far from commercialization in 1907, but he continued to tear down and rebuild machines to gain minor improvements. His patents continued to be hailed in the press. The *New York Herald* reported in 1908 the comments of one glassmaker: "Give me this machine and a man and two boys and I can do more and better work than 13 skilled laborers under the old process." However, it was not until 1909 that Colburn convinced a company to install his process.

Colburn was not alone in 1901 with his experiments in producing flat glass. The Czechoslovakians were casting and drawing flat glass horizontally around 1890, but their process was not commercial quality. Emile Fourcault in Belgium was working on a vertical drawing method. Colburn also vertically pulled the sheet but then pulled it over a horizontal roll. The Fourcault process in Europe advanced at the same rate as the Colburn process.

Colburn convinced Star Glass Company of Reynoldsville, Pennsylvania to install the first machine. The installation was problematic and the machine never functioned well. The actual casting of the sheet turned out to be the least of his problems. Colburn's sheet had internal defects and the annealing furnace could not keep up. The poorly annealed glass could not be cut because of its brittleness. The machine also produced a wavy product, requiring more flattening. Colburn Machine purchased the machine back under a clause that required successful operation within ninety days. The machine required all the personal funds and borrowing Colburn could amass. By 1910, it was producing some usable glass but not consistently. Owens visited the plant in 1910 and believed that the machine could work, but it was a single opinion. Twenty-three glass companies had turned the idea down.

Colburn continued to make improvements and progress, but the development work was costly and investors scarce. He and his personal friends infused the development with all the free cash they had to keep it going. Stockholder and board fights over the development were mounting also. Patent defenses were pulling money out of the project as well. Eighteen court battles had drained much-needed funds, and Colburn still faced more legal battles in 1910. It was estimated he would need $125,000 to keep development going. Pennsylvania oilmen were getting cold feet over the investment. Colburn hoped that Owens might get the needed cash.

Owens first brought the idea to Toledo Glass's board in 1911. Colburn's ten years of failure, the rejections of other glass companies, and a lack of a working, consistent machine left the board cold. It was these very reasons that attracted Owens to the project. He felt that his legacy would be in his ability to achieve the impossible. From that standpoint, this was a project made in heaven for Mike. The board, however, looked at it from a cold business perspective. The history of rejections by twenty-three companies seems to support the decision of the board. Libbey, Walbridge, Brown, and Geddes saw no reason to go into experimentation on a new machine. Brown and Geddes wanted to stay the profitable business course they were pursuing. Walbridge had learned to fear Owens' propensity to spend money on experimental equipment and was aligning himself with Brown and Geddes more often. Libbey had long ago lost his tendency to gamble. Owens' approach was strong headed as usual, which gained him little support. So it was that Owens lost the first round with the board.

The carrot for Owens was the potential that the Colburn process might cut flat-glass production costs by as much as 80 percent. This would be accomplished by eliminating skilled workers, such as cappers, splitters, and flatteners. In addition, product handling could significantly reduced. The Lubbers process quality was subpar, requiring a lot of in-process inspection and resulting in high scrap rates. Of course, the development challenge of the Colburn machine was formidable and costly. Owens also lacked experience in flat glass.

In fairness it must be stated that Owens lost the first round with good reason. Even the powerful "Toledo Faction" was not in a position to take on the flat-glass industry. It had no relevant plants to form a base, and it lacked experience. Colburn had failed to gain any financial support without Pittsburgh Plate Glass, which controlled price and distribution of flat glass. Owens alone believed that, with a technological breakthrough, you could break Pittsburgh Plate's market, but it would require developmental work and capital. This challenge offered him the size and difficulty that, if he succeeded, would assure his legacy. As usual, Owens would start the process with slow moves, asking for only $15,000. How could they refuse such a relatively small sum?

Colburn was getting close to a commercial machine. His machine at Reynoldsville, Pennsylvania had made some impressive advances. The plant had a 700-ton continuously fed melting furnace fired by natural gas. Colburn had developed a continuous anneal as well. Even with defects and annealing problems, he had produced marketable window glass and had shipped it. The machine, however, lacked consistency. Owens had seen enough and was extremely confident that he could make the process work. The flat glass industry, headed by Pittsburgh Plate Glass, made a huge mistake in believing that the project had died. It was a mistake that Owens and Libbey would have never made; in fact, they had made a policy of buying up competing technology in bottle manufacture. Owens sensed early on that the Colburn process could hold the key to control of the flat-glass market. The possible labor savings were enormous. Using the hand process, it took 5 man hours to make fifty square feet of window glass; with the Colburn machine it would be possible to do it in .6 man hours.[3]

Owens brought Colburn to Toledo without any commitment from the board. As always, Owens seemed sure of his ultimate success. Owens and Colburn both believed in Mike's ability to win over the board. While they waited during the summer and fall of 1911, Colburn introduced Owens to golf. They started to spend a lot of time at Inverness Country Club, discussing the project. Owens quickly became an enthusiastic golfer, joining Inverness and Sylvania country clubs and later Lancaster Country Club, plus several Florida clubs. The two became very good friends, their unique bond probably forged in the rejection both experienced. Colburn's respect for Owens can be seen in a letter to his brother at the time:

Since I have been in Toledo I have gotten very close to Mike Owens and I find him to be a most remarkable man. He has an extraordinary amount of real ability. I believe that there is none of his friends that know him better than I. He is rough shod at times and sometimes difficult for others to understand. He knows how to get results better than any man that I ever knew. He knows men thoroughly and is a wonderful judge of mankind. I find him fair to all at all times. He is a man of his word. In fact it is rather hard to give more credit than is his due. He has enemies plenty and a host of friends. . . . I have been much with him playing golf and taking trips around the country. . . . What he wants is results. Excuses will not count. He has no use for a man that has excuses. Nothing but results count with him in the least. He is a pusher under a high pressure all the time. I am most delighted that I succeeded in landing him.

Owens in Florida, 1917. (Owens-Illinois Glass Company Records, MSS-200, the Ward M. Canaday Center for Special Collections, University of Toledo)

Colburn's description of Owens' nature is very insightful. Colburn was a brilliant inventor, but he lacked two essential elements of the great commercial inventors—breakthrough creativity and determination. Owens was exactly what Colburn needed, and he realized it. Owens was confident he could get his organization to make Colburn's machine work. First Owens had watched Colburn's machine in operation, and he was able to make one evaluation on the spot. He was sure the machine needed strengthening. The process was simple, unlike bottle making. This time Owens had the advantage of prior developmental work, which he had lacked for his own bottle machine. The board of directors may have doubted his ability to make the Colburn machine work, but the *National Glass Budget*, the industry newspaper, hailed Owens' entry as the keystone for its success.[4]

Mike was sure he had found two technical problems with the machine. For one thing, he noted that the vertical pull was too long. When the glass was bent horizontally over the roller, it was too cold and brittle. Owens suggested that experiments look at the time elapsed from melting pot to roller. His understanding of glass gave him this insight, which a non-glassmaker like Colburn could not see. The other problem Mike saw was that the machine was not sturdy enough to withstand the weight, strain, and heat of glassmaking. The lack of sturdiness caused vibrations, and those translated into glass faults. Owens felt he and his team could eventually resolve both problems.

Owens was sure of himself and his organization. He told Libbey, as he had twenty-three years earlier, that he would go it alone if necessary. This time it was not a bluff; Owens had the money to back it up. The board still stood firmly against getting involved with the Colburn machine. Walbridge, in particular, was sure Owens would "experiment us to death." Libbey, however, wavered because of Mike's determination. Later, a friend of Libbey noted, "He was astonished at his friend's determination and apparent faith in the window glass machine." Owens had good reason to be confident. The Colburn machine and process were much simpler than the bulb and bottle machines Owens had built. Brown and Geddes, hoping to stop any investment, argued that a legal review had shown thirty instances in which Colburn's patents infringed upon others in the glass industry. They were ready to let Owens go it alone, but Libbey was not. Ultimately, in 1912, the Toledo Glass board gave Owens $15,000 to buy Colburn's machine, which was being sold at a sheriff's auction. Toledo Glass used an agent, but Pittsburgh Plate Glass was not even there to bid.

Amazingly, while the Toledo Glass board, Pittsburgh Plate, and the flat-glass union saw this as a wild idea of Mike's, the industry news held great respect for him and his organization. The *National Glass Budget* paid this tribute upon the purchase of the failed machine: "The reputation of the 'Toledo People' for carrying to successful conclusion whatever they undertake is pretty generally understood, and it may be taken for granted that they would not now be backing the sheet drawing patents if they were not convinced of ultimate success."[5] This was a huge vote of confidence in the ability of Owens.

The movement of Owens and the "Toledo Faction" into flat-glass technology caused a movement of investors as well. As the *Budget* pointed out, the "Toledo Faction" had a reputation for success. The flat glass industry also feared Owens' entry into the market, which had functioned for decades as a true monopoly. However, some industry members were starting to feel the pressure of cheaper flat-glass imports. The political power of the Knights of Labor had declined, causing tariff reductions. The union had also softened its stance against technology.

Some initial experiments began at the Toledo plant of Buckeye Clay Pot Company. In November 1913 Owens moved the "CX" machine (Colburn Experimental Machine) to a new experimental plant in Toledo at the intersection of Castle Boulevard and the New York Central tracks. The board had allotted an additional $125,000 for development work. The initial costs, including the building, were actually $252,819. Walbridge noted that Owens again had sucked the board into a larger investment. However Walbridge and the board had no choice once Libbey had given his support. Owens shifted some of his best engineers, including LaFrance, to the project. A newly hired engineer from the University of Michigan, Arthur Fowle, joined the group. Fowle was a cousin of Libbey. In addition, the board brought in William Boshart, who in 1914 would rise to board member. Boshart had been originally hired on Owens' suggestion and had successfully followed Owens as manager of the Manchester, England experimental plant. Boshart would add some support to Owens' struggle with the board. Owens also added some new expertise to his staff. He "borrowed" (never to return) Joseph Crowley from Libbey Glass. Owens also brought in his friend William Jacobs. He added a full-time draftsman, James Angus, to support the Colburn project. This was the old Michael Owens in charge of the "Toledo Faction" and all its assets. As usual, he drew resources from any of Libbey's operations. Still, this campaign was a real tribute to Michael Owens as a project manager. He had learned how to build the human resources to get the job done.

Commercial Success

Experiments started poorly at the new plant on Thanksgiving of 1913. Owens was out of town, but Colburn was not willing to delay for the holiday. The team was in a difficult position: the machine had a long record of failure. The machine actually started to come apart, as Owens had foreseen, because of the light construction. Bolts and casting supports literally flew off after several hours of operation. Working hot glass at 2,000 degrees can cause the strongest construction to twist and bend. Owens' suggestions had made some improvement, but much more was needed. In fact, that Thanksgiving, Colburn seemed farther than ever from success. Casting liquid material vertically and rolling it horizontally was exactly the process the great steel engineer, Henry Bessemer, had patented for steel in the 1860s. It took the steel industry a hundred years to make Bessemer's idea commercial. The Owens team would do it in three years with liquid glass! Even if you add in eight years of preliminary work by Colburn, you still have a true engineering coup. The commercial development of the CX machine is almost unrivalled in the history of engineering for the magnitude of breakthrough. Owens' team solved problem after problem at record pace.

After that Thanksgiving, Colburn had become depressed. Owens, however, returned with his drive and enthusiasm. The first thing Owens addressed was the construction. Another problem was the bending rolls and guides, which continued to mark the glass sheet. The first Toledo machine used clay rolls with a sodium silicate coating. This caused a type of "sticking" on the sheet. Applying a new alloy of copper and nickel, Monel, helped resolve this problem, but it chilled the glass too quickly for bending. The timing that Owens had first identified as a problem had to be adjusted to allow maximum flexibility. Then he applied an even newer nickel alloy, Nichrome, which worked better, but months of timing adjustments were needed. As the team resolved one problem, another would appear. Flattening of the cast sheet had always been a problem in the Colburn process. The process to correct the flattening was a slow one, requiring costly teardowns of the machine.

Owens' role in the development of a successful machine is confirmed by most of the team members. Colburn was the team leader, but Owens dropped in often and made significant improvements. More importantly, Owens had evolved from an inventor into a developmental manager. The resolution of the flattening problem was an example of his input. John Drake, one of the team, described this input as the key to success.

The solution of the flattening was typical of Owens' step-by-step approach to individual problems. The struggle cost millions, and the board questioned both Libbey and Owens' sanity on this project. Hope outside the organization also fell as the project dragged on for years.

Clyde Belden, another member of the team, confirmed the importance of Owens in the development of the machine:

> Mike Owens helped immeasurably in the final perfecting of the machine. A frequent visitor to the experimental plant, Owens was keenly interested in the machine's progress. Time and time again he demonstrated his thorough knowledge of the work with helpful suggestions. When the machine was not operating correctly or the quality of the glass was poor, Mike seemed to be able to put his finger right on the source of trouble which Colburn's crew might have spent hours trying to track down.[6]

The testimonies of Drake and Belden came after Owens' death and clearly support his true genius. In many ways, the development of the Colburn machine proved Owens' inventive brilliance.

Owens' perseverance, genius, and creativity brought the Colburn machine into exsistence. Owens had matured as a manager, leaving the headlines to his underlings and Colburn. The ultimate success of the Colburn development would be Owens' revenge against the board. It would also end their efforts to belittle Owens' inventive importance in the organization.

Owens had developed into a true research and development executive and an excellent project manager. As hard as it was for him, he learned to delegate as well, not because he wanted to, but because he saw it as a way to extend his work on a wide number of projects. Another key reason for Owens' ability to delegate was his trust in the team. He had hand picked the team and it had no spies from the board. The project team, including Colburn, was extremely loyal to Owens; it was a luxury that Owens had rarely known. He completely trusted Colburn. This team success showed that Owens could manage a number of teams if he was free to build them. Too many times in the past, he was battling technical problems and internal politics on projects.

Owens, Toledo Glass, and Owens Bottle were involved in a number of other development projects from 1913 to 1915. His attention remained mostly focused on his bottle machine, which he continued relentlessly to improve throughout the period. He was able to triple the production rate of the average bottle. In addition, Owens was working on a new machine known as the "AT" or "Carboy." The Carboy represented the largest of the automatic glassmaking machines. It was fifty feet high and thirty feet in diameter and weighed over one hundred tons. The Carboy could produce fifteen-gallon containers and was introduced in 1915. It represented the biggest advance in automation since Owens' original machine.

From 1914 to 1915, the painful trial-and-error development of the Colburn machine moved slowly forward. Some of this slow progress was due to Owens' drive for perfection and quality. As with the bottle machine, he would not go to market until he had a dependable machine. Owens had learned this lesson from his earliest inventions in paste molds. His Colburn equipment was now well built and proven, but final testing took months. It was not until May 1915 that Toledo Glass shipped usable, high-quality product. Eight thousand boxes of window glass were shipped to Smith & Wyman Sash & Door. The company wrote Toledo Glass to praise the quality of the shipment. Still, much work was required to improve the yield of quality product. By the fall of 1915, Owens told the Toledo Glass board that success was imminent. The board voted to start the search for a production plant. Arthur Fowle was assigned this task. Libbey started to look at the formation of yet another company.

Owens was victorious, gaining revenge through accomplishment. Success was a strength that would become a weakness. Owens now envisioned a rapid entry into the flat-glass market. The Toledo Glass board faced the problem of moderating Owens while using his expertise.

On May 17, 1916, Libbey-Owens Sheet Glass was formed. It would own the patents while Toledo Glass was the major stockholder. The original experimental plant was sold to Wills-Overland Automobile Company. A new plant was to be built in Charleston, West Virginia. Libbey and Owens planned to use a similar business model to that of their bottle-making-machine business. They hoped to license the Colburn process worldwide. Libbey-Owens Sheet would control that foreign effort without any additional corporations being formed. The directors of the new company, besides Libbey and Owens, were Clarence Brown, vice-president of Owens Bottle Company; Arthur Fowle, the newly named vice-president of Toledo Glass; William Walbridge, treasurer of Toledo Glass; Fred Geddes, secretary of Toledo Glass; and Charles Schmettau, of Brown and Geddes's law firm. Again we see the "Toledo Faction" of Geddes, Brown, Walbridge, Libbey, and Owens in control of three companies—Toledo Glass, Owens Bottle Company, and Libbey-Owens Sheet—as well as indirectly controlling Libbey Glass.

However, there had been much debate behind the scenes on what role Owens might play in the future of Libbey-Owens Sheet. Brown claimed that Owens was in an administrative position, and there is some evidence that New York and Toledo bankers did not want to see that be the case. Mike's risk taking had always made investors nervous. Brown, as usual, wanted Owens' duties controlled with "proper restrictions, properly prescribed." Geddes, Fowle, and Walbridge supported no role for Mike at an administrative level. Walbridge had now become determined to limit Owens' role. A letter to Libbey in Brown's private files sums up the problem:

> Concerning the temporary organization of the Libbey-Owens Company, the situation is this. It had been suggested that I should be named President and Fowle vice-president, while Owens was not even to be made a director. It occurred to me that this would not be wise and certainly not be agreeable to Owens. There seemed to be no sufficient reason why Fowle or I should be put, even in temporary authority over Owens, nor any justification for not putting Owens on the Board of Directors, in interest in the future of the company. . . . I think Owens' cooperation in the enterprise is very important and have no doubt, when it comes to a permanent organization, you will agree with me that he should be placed in a position of authority.

This shows the behind-the-scenes operations of the "Toledo Faction," which by 1916 had three factions itself—Libbey, Owens, and the board. Still, thanks to Libbey's control, the "Toledo Faction" functioned externally as a united entity. It was now involved in all segments of glass production and equipment manufacture. Though the "Toledo Faction" operated below the government's radar for trusts, Wall Street understood the group's power. Owens Bottle stock, for example, rose from $50 a share in 1903 to $1,200 a share in 1916! The stock of the newly formed Libbey-Owens Sheet doubled in 1917 from $25 a share to $50 a share in a few months. Michael Owens had become one of the wealthiest men in America. He and Libbey, however, had set 12 percent of the stock aside for the lesser-known men on the development team. This included clerks and draftsmen. This represents the generosity and management style of these two great innovators.

Owens was not formally listed as an officer of Libbey-Owens, but as always he was the force behind the scenes. Owens realized he was not an administrator, and he was happier running the operations. The other directors and officers were clearly picked by Libbey, with Brown's input. Owens was not happy with the addition of a third lawyer to the group, particularly one from Brown and Geddes's firm. Owens, however, had the real task of building and running what would become the largest glasshouse in the world. It was to be the challenge of his career and the very thing that Mike loved. Owens was also at the height of his personal power. He had shown his ability to create and develop. Even the "lawyers" had to concede the point in 1917 by taking out an insurance policy on Michael Owens. It was Owens' creativity that had been behind the Libbey empire of companies. However, the problem soon became Mike himself, more difficult to deal with than ever. Brown, Geddes, and Schmettau continued to build their stock-ownership base, which required Owens to deal with them. Owens as usual bullied the board, with the implicit support of Libbey. Meanwhile, Colburn's health continued to deteriorate and he died in the spring of 1917, prior to seeing the reality of full production.

The board had accepted Arthur Fowle's suggestion to build a sheet-glass plant at Kanawha City, a suburb of Charleston, West Virginia. Owens, struggling with health problems himself, recommended that William Jacobs manage the new project. Jacobs had functioned as Colburn's assistant on the development of the CX machine and was a loyal friend of Owens. In addition, Owens asked for a large amount of cash and stock for his development of the Colburn machine. Mike's plan was to stay free of direct operating responsibilities, instead doing what he did best, create. The board saw it differently, and Brown was asked to negotiate a deal with Owens. Brown offered him around $50,000 of stock, but more importantly, they wanted Owens to become general manager of the Charleston plant. The board, while not happy about it, would allow Jacobs to be plant manager. This would serve two purposes. First, Owens was the best operations man in the company and knew plant startup problems. Second, and probably just as important to Brown and the board, it would keep Owens busy, not free to wander around dabbling in his own interests.

In fairness to the board, this was the right job for Owens. The Colburn machine still required much development work, and plant startups called for perseverance and tenacity. Owens had in the past demonstrated that the research and development does not end with a new process or machine. The final phase is bringing a process to full commercialization. This part of corporate development is often forgotten even today, as R&D departments turn a process over to plant operations to implement. Mike only hesitated because of his health and a desire to expand his legacy in other areas.In particular, he was interested in developing machines for automobile and optical glass as well as improving his bottle machine for larger and more specialized applications. Owens was given a salary of $30,000 a year (almost a half-million a year in today's value) to oversee the plant's building and operation. Jacobs would be the plant manager, receiving a salary of $4,800 a year. Jacobs was also awarded $75,000 in stock for his part in the development of the Colburn machine. Ideally, Jacobs' role was to manage the day-to-day issues. Arthur Fowle was also assigned to oversee the construction of the plant.

The arrangement of management responsibilities seemed to focus on bringing the Charleston plant up. The board once again figured they had Owens contained. Owens, however, quickly pulled himself into the development of a model glass plant. The Charleston plant would achieve his dream of a fully automated process. Some might say it was the fulfillment of the dream that started with his many visits to Chicago slaughterhouses in 1893. Owens would become the Henry Ford of continuous batch processes. The company's annual report of 1917 hailed the new plant as one where "raw materials and finished glass are untouched by hand from the time material is received from the railroad up to the point of the finished glass delivered at the end of the lehr ready for cutters." Libbey described it as "the most modern factory in the country with respect to advanced ideas and labor-saving devices." The *Toledo Bee* prophetically noted that the product would "revolutionize the window glass market." However, the vision of continuous automation would bring many problems. The plant construction went smoothly, with two Toledo companies leading the way, Dervore-McGormley and American Bridge. Startup was a different story. Brown was upset also that Owens remained in Toledo, making visits to West

Virginia instead of moving there. Owens refused to be tied down to one project, regardless of its size. He was working on a new generation of bottle machine at Owens Bottle Company and was spread very thin. With Libbey's tacit support of him, however, there was nothing the board could do. Furthermore, Owens fully trusted his man Jacobs at the Charleston plant.

The actual installation of the Colburn process progressed smoothly. Owens in this case used the experience of his development team. The operating problems varied, but most were related to the overall automation and continuous processing. The plant was designed to have six furnaces and six Colburn machines. The process would produce a seventy-two-inch-wide sheet, which would be annealed in a 200-foot lehr. The initial product was free of the waves that had plagued Owens and Colburn at the experimental plant in Toledo, but it was annealed poorly. The continuous operation of the plant required a type of balancing that early continuous-operations pioneers such as Henry Ford had discovered. This involves a trial-and-error approach that is slow and costly. The "damn lawyers" did not understand this, but they did understand that the slow progress frustrated Edward Libbey. Brown and the board would use these difficulties to finally tame Owens.

Owens' use of the term "damn lawyers" did not represent a dislike for lawyers themselves but rather of their participation in glass-company management. Actually, Mike's trusted friend J. H. McNerney was a lawyer from the firm of Brown and Geddes. Mike was simply passionate that glasswork be managed by glassmakers.

Ultimately, the Libbey-Owens Colburn machine would produce 5 square feet of flat glass per minute or 7,200 square feet of flat glass every twenty-four hours. The Owens process would be the first truly continuous process ever used. This would make window glass available at extremely low prices. Eventually, plate-glass producers, such as Pittsburgh Plate Glass and Ford Glass, were forced to buy the Colburn machine. Artists for stained-glass and colored-glass windows would still produce cylinder-blown and crown glass. The distortions break the light in a way reminiscent of the Middle Ages.

The year 1917 represented another key year for the "Toledo Faction." Libbey started to dream the dreams of young men again, but those dreams were not of glassmaking. He wanted to create a major art museum for Toledo. Libbey's art interests required the support of huge profits from his businesses. He looked to more horizontal expansion in bottle making to achieve this. This of course was a bit different from Owens' ambition to expand and control the flat-glass market. Libbey expressed his expansion goals to Clarence Brown in a letter dated August 7, 1917:

> Our most favorable channel through which to expand is, in my opinion, the acquisition of the large U.S. companies. These if secured upon a fair basis . . . would give our company not only supreme control of all branches of the bottle trade, but to its stockholders, a total of 6 to 7 million dollars earnings, which if proven true would exceed my previous year's estimate of $5,000,000 net profit in all branches of the bottle business under the controlling influence of the great and wonderful invention of ours. I hope to see this a fact soon and I shall then feel that it was worth living for—to be one part of the mechanism that gives its stockholders, its original inventors, and promoters a keen satisfaction in its success physically and financially and, greater than all, to be instrumental in giving to the world cheaper bottles when the time may come.

The "large U.S. companies" to which Libbey referred were Ball Brothers, the major producer of fruit jars (the famous Mason jars); Hazel-Atlas, producer of packaging (and major supplier to J. H. Heinz); and Illinois Glass, a major producer of prescription, specialty, and whiskey bottles. Libbey owned stock in both Ball Brothers and Hazel-Atlas. His interest was driven by the cash required for his art-collecting trips. To Libbey, horizontal bottle-industry expansion was the safest and quickest means to raise cash. Again, this vision would put him in conflict with the dreams of the risk-taking Owens.

CHAPTER 12

The Taming of the Lion

Owens would hear nothing of retirement. He talked of dying "in the harness." Truly, Owens never lost his enthusiasm for work or invention. Doctors slowed him down, but he never quit. Vacations increased and most afternoons he was at Inverness Golf Club, but he was still every bit in charge at work. He tried hobbies with little success. His reading of history did increase with age, but work remained the core of his existence and nothing could replace it. Work was a war of campaigns for this history buff, and there was always a new campaign. Owens had a passion for achievement that few have known.

Henry Ford, when looking back at the early success of Ford Motor, noted the following basic principle: "Thinking first of money instead of work brings the fear of failure and fear blocks every avenue of business—it makes a man afraid of competition, of changing his methods, or of doing anything which might change his condition." Owens never knew that fear, but like most organizations, the "Toledo Faction" did lose its fire and drive. The board turned to building a financial empire that could give them and Libbey a good return. When Libbey's passion became art collecting, Owens alone remained fearless in his outlook. Libbey noted in a 1917 letter: "For some years my attention and energies have been devoted, and purpose increasingly devoting them, to activities which I deem even more useful than those primarily concerned with business profits." Owens, however, did not slide gradually into retirement but continued to drive at new projects. A year before his death, he was actually trying to convince the board to implement a new ten-arm machine! Libbey clearly saw art as his gift and legacy to the community, while Owens looked to industrial development and jobs as his legacy.

The raw statistics seem to bear out Owens' belief that technology and automation created jobs. In 1899, bottle and jar production was 7.8 million gross, worth $2.5 million. In 1925, it reached 26 million gross, worth $100 million. In 1899, 52,818 were employed in the bottle industry; by 1925, 69,371 were employed. The average annual wage in the bottle industry in 1899 was $512.78, while in 1925 it was $1,250.32. The window-glass iustry showed similar increases, with a total gain of 10,000 jobs during that period. A shop with an Owens machine had thirty times the productivity of a hand shop. The American glass industry's output and costs so improved that cheap foreign product was locked out of the market. The last part of the technology cycle was the increase in market. As Owens reduced the costs of glass containers, new applications were found.

Owens demonstrated that tenacity of purpose is part of the research and development function. More important, research and development were to be focused and pragmatic. Organizationally, Owens believed that research and development were a function of operations, not a separate department as in most companies today. Development was a function of process improvement, technology application, and cost reduction. Owens firmly believed that reducing production costs and increasing markets and profits were a natural consequence of development. He preached this his whole life to both the union and executive management. In the end, it was the executives who refused to listen. Owens' simple approach was revolutionary for an industry that separated science and engineering. He made research and development a profit center for corporations.

Owens also became a promoter of corporate research methodology. He approached research and development as a series of interlinked steps. The first step was a survey of technological knowledge. This was to be followed by experimental work and machine models. Finally, a small-scale experimental operation would be set up to perfect the invention.

Owens, 1919. (Owens-Illinois Glass Company Records, MSS-200, the Ward M. Canaday Center for Special Collections, University of Toledo)

Most historians agree that after 1920, the developmental and pioneering work of the "Toledo Faction" was at an end. The very size of the Faction's network had gone beyond the span of control of Owens and Libbey. Libbey's enthusiasm and drive had certainly peaked, and he found more interest in art. His wife also wanted him to retire from the stress of the business and join her in developing the art museum. Even Owens, worried over his

Owens, 1920. (Owens-Illinois Glass Company Records, MSS-200, the Ward M. Canaday Center for Special Collections, University of Toledo)

health problems, had developed an interest in sports cars, golfing, and trips to Florida. Michael knew he needed to relax, but he did not know how. His hobbies and vacations tended to be activity based, and work was never out of his mind. Business in general was changing as well. One glass historian described the change in the Faction: "The new crop of associates initiated into the group after 1916 were definitely 'captains of business and finance' and not technical innovators. This was true throughout America as the Carnegies and Edisons had retired, turning over their organizations. Owens bucked this new institutionalized approach to business of a new breed of managers known as the 'Industrial Edwardians.'"[1] Owens could not function well in these new, highly structured organizations.

Board members, such as Clarence Brown, started to question Owens' future role in the growing company. Michael Owens had to some degree made himself irreplaceable in the organization, but he had no real box in the organizational chart. Libbey had long ago decided that Owens could never be an administrator, yet he was still capable of striking project oil. Owens also was the best startup manager they had. Brown, as a seasoned administrator, realized that no organization should be dependent on any one individual. He appears to have resented Owens' success and managerial power to some degree, but as intense as the feuds seemed, they were more on a business level than personal. Owens was always a lightning rod for criticism from a board with financial authority. Brown, of course, could count on support from board membersGeddes and Schmettau (Libbey-Owens Sheet) in trying to tame Owens. Walbridge also had problems with Owens' free-spending ways. By 1916, it appears that Walbridge was leading the opposition to Owens. Owens had always treated Walbridge gingerly because of his family ties to Libbey, but Walbridge became a force in his own right as things changed. Mike would often use sarcastic humor to embarrass Walbridge. Owens resented Libbey's degreed cousin, metallurgist, and board member Arthur Fowle even more.

Owens was more and more isolated by the board made up of Libbey's relatives and the "damn lawyers" (Brown, Geddes, and

Schmettau). Libbey was the power behind Owens' freedom, but the board was determined to limit that power. Brown and Libbey agreed that they should groom someone to replace Owens if necessary. The man Brown recommended to Libbey would seem a strange pick, but in the end he would prove to be an able administrator and part of the desirable new breed of operations manager— James Blair. Blair was a Brown loyalist, and the board trusted him.

The Golden Age

The golden age of the "Toledo Faction" had been 1903 to 1917. In this period the partnership of Owens and Libbey dominated a large group of companies. Libbey and Owens acted with daring and aggressiveness in the pursuit of technology. Brown and Geddes lent legal advice and administrative skills, as well as acted to moderate Owens. Walbridge watched daily expenditures and specifically Owens' propensity to spend. Operations were king in this loose-knit group of Toledo companies because of Owens' relentless drive. He was the power behind the throne. Libbey stayed focused on marketing and finance while allowing Owens a free hand. Money was flowing back into equipment and development work. The "Toledo Faction" revolutionized the industry, and the experimental plants and sheds of Toledo attracted all of the glass industry. Most importantly, Owens' creativity was left unrestricted. The "Toledo Faction" depended not only on that but also on his middle-management role. Fiery and explosive, Owens was still able to bond and fraternize with the workers, who considered him one of their own.

The year 1917 might be considered the peak of the "Toledo Faction." After that, Libbey pursued a strategy of conservative investment, and developmental work ebbed, other than bringing the Charleston plant online. Slowly, he started to allow outside ownership in many of the companies. Up until 1917, Libbey, Richardson, Robinson, and Donovan effectively owned Libbey Glass, with only three other minor stockholders, such as Owens. By 1919, Libbey Glass had seventeen stockholders. Libbey Glass's somewhat unique ownership allowed it to sometimes be called the "Libbey Glass Faction," a schism from the "Toledo Faction." The split widened with a lawsuit between Libbey Glass and Owens Bottle over some applications of the Owens automatic machine (and Libbey Glass design variations) in the container field. It was a bitter fight that continued throughout the 1920s.

The roots of the fight went back to the refusal of Richardson, Robinson, and Donovan to support Libbey's world fair proposal and, in 1895, Owens' developmental program. Owens Bottle Company, in fact, treated Libbey Glass as just another licensee. Libbey seemed to have remembered the rebuff of 1893 and remained "neutral," which effectively allowed the schism to widen. Libbey sold off the profitable bulb business and sales of tableware were declining, eroding the bottom line and cash flow. Libbey Glass went into a glass-tubing development program, which upset the Owens Bottle board. Edward Danner of Libbey Glass developed an automated glass-tubing machine in 1919. The Danner Machine was sold to a number of companies. Owens Bottle brought suit against them in 1921, arguing they were making a form of container in the production of test tubes and vials. Libbey Glass won, but by 1922 the two boards were not on speaking terms. Owens was in the middle of this. He saw lawsuits as a waste of time. Mike felt that issues should be dealt with in a direct way. It is said that at courthouse lunches during the suit, the two boards sat apart, and Owens sat alone.

The Westlake Machine Company was caught in the middle of this as well. Westlake had been formed in 1907 to build the Owens automatic bulb machine and parts. Westlake built the machines for sale and did no development work. Libbey, Owens, Richardson, Robinson, Donovan, and Walbridge controlled the Westlake. Westlake had always functioned as a joint enterprise between Libbey Glass and Owens Bottle Company. Westlake was the only tie with Richardson, Robinson, and Donovan, whom Libbey prohibited from purchasing shares in Owens Bottle and Toledo Glass. In 1916, Libbey relented and allowed them to buy some shares of Libbey-Owens Sheet Glass.

The real sign of the "Toledo Faction"'s decline was the deterioration of Toledo Glass. Its great development work had included the semiautomatic tumbler machine, the semiautomatic lamp-chimney machine, the fully automated bottle machine, and the Colburn sheet-glass machine. Toledo Glass had always functioned as the developmental arm of the "Toledo Faction." It had few employees, preferring to apply project management to specific development projects. It also functioned as a licensing agency. But more importantly, it was the heart and soul of the "Toledo Faction." It embodied Owens' aggressive developmental views. Toledo Glass started its decline with the resignation of Owens in 1917, followed by the death of Clarence Brown in 1918. Geddes resigned in 1918 as well. The developmental work (really process implementation) passed to Owens Bottle and Libbey-Owens Sheet Glass. Toledo Glass slowly dissolved, leaving licensing as its remaining function.

Owens lived daily with internal politics, but he seemed to thrive on them. He would often storm out of board meetings when Libbey was not present. Mike and the boards were business adversaries most of time. Members of all of the Faction's boards noted his every blunder. In later years, board members Brown, Geddes, Walbridge, Schmettau, and Fowle opposed him as a bloc. Owens achieved in spite of these political attacks. With all his faults, he was still a master corporate politician. His perseverance in experimentation was mirrored by his resilience to political setbacks. Just when he seemed weakest, he mounted his most successful power drives. Owens never achieved over internal politics but used internal politics to achieve. This was a strange characteristic of his. He was power driven and temperamental but could turn on his charm to disarm an antagonist. He had a great sense of humor that he could bring to bear in a tough situation. He also fostered a loyalty in his staff and workers that made him a difficult opponent to defeat. He had a core of close and faithful friends throughout the corporation and industry and maintained a good relationship with local and national union leaders. His support of Irish issues strengthened his union ties as well, since the Irish remained a majority segment of the workforce.

Final Frustrations

Owens' problems had truly begun in 1917, as Libbey's interests moved into collecting and Walbridge's into administration. When Libbey selected Brown to replace Owens as head of the Owens Bottle board, Owens gave up his total control. The board increased from seven to seventeen members. These were brought in from companies Owens Bottle owned or controlled. Owens, Brown, Libbey, Walbridge, Schmettau, William Boshart, and John Biggers now ran the "Toledo Faction." Boshart and Biggers represented the second generation. All of these changes, plus the aging of the group, started the decline of the "Toledo Faction" as a developmental force.

Owens was out of his element on the newly formed Libbey-Owens board as well. Owens could never have functioned in the top administrative position of a major company. Still, no one could tell him he could not. To this end, when Libbey asked him to step down as president of the Libbey-Owens board, it opened up a struggle for the position. Libbey had to support Brown for president because of the need for an administrator. Owens wanted power and resented the loss of it. He was named general manager over all manufacturing. Through a number of internal concessions, Owens remained on both boards and was general manager of both companies. Still, with Brown in charge of the boards, Owens would be heavily scrutinized. Owens' ego was enormous, and to be less than the top man in his "own" company would have been difficult. It would normally have been an explosive situation for Owens and the board, but shortly afterwards, Owens learned that he suffered from heart disease. This knowledge certainly had an impact on Owens, but he remained closely involved, even with the additional vacations.

The boards of Toledo Glass, Owens Bottle Company, and Libbey-Owens Sheet Glass were controlled by members who opposed, resented, or hated Owens, or some combination of these. Owens' relationship with Libbey's brother-in-law, Walbridge, had been deteriorating for years, as they both wanted to be Libbey's right hand. Walbridge remained an admirer of Michael Owens throughout his life but, like his brother-in-law Libbey, felt that Owens required close control on investment matters. Walbridge in later years became a sort of folk historian of

Owens and Libbey. Many of Walbridge's reviews do show a bias against Owens, while exaggerating his role in Owens' inventions. Walbridge had always considered himself to be "a harmonizing influence on three dominating personalities," referring to Owens, Libbey, and Brown.

Then there was the group from Brown's law firm, Brown, Geddes, and Schmettau. Boshart and Biggers tended to be neutral about Owens. Libbey remained the kingpin of the organization. By 1916, most things boiled down to a fight between the board and Owens, to be decided by Libbey. Owens almost never compromised; it was not in his nature. Brown was always the lawyer, and no matter how wide the difference, he could compromise. Brown also realized that Owens was almost always successful. Even Robinson and Richardson regretted having opposed Owens in 1895 and asked to be allowed to buy stock in Libbey-Owens Sheet.

The problems of the commercialization of the Charleston window-glass plant became the board's weapon against Owens. Startup problems mounted, from glass formula mixing to annealing. Arthur Fowle, with the construction completed, moved into sales, leaving Owens and Jacobs with the problems and responsibility. The board supported this, because with Fowle out of the situation, they could blame the lack of progress just on Owens and Jacobs. Jacobs, as plant manager, was the first and primary target, but Owens quickly came to his defense. Owens realized that startup was a process of problem solving.

Cost overruns began to pressure the finances of Libbey-Owens Sheet Glass. Libbey, with his art collection and museum, was becoming impatient for return on investment. Owens in the meantime was using sheet machine number six to start work on optical-glass experiments. While these could be managed in the framework of the startup, the board played it as Owens off experimenting and losing focus. These experiments did start to draw Owens away from his administrative duties as general manager, which was easy to do. Owens never wanted, nor was he prepared, to be an administrator.

Setbacks were now being reported to Libbey daily. The very

thing that Owens had requested years ago with the first Toledo plant—the nailing shut of Libbey's factory door—was now a common occurrence. The board and Libbey were now in agreement. The board asked Owens to replace Jacobs with an experienced sheet expert. Owens, as was typical, resisted. First, Jacobs was his man, and second, Owens did not want any outsiders in his operation. Owens had resisted all of the board's suggestions to hire sheet-glass professionals as well as a glass chemist. One historian put it this way: "Owens never curbed his pride to the point where he could cheerfully support any subordinate who seemed to know more than he or who attracted much public attention." Owens rejected even the smallest request for improvement from the board. The board found another ally in Harry Bamford, sales manager at Toledo Plate Glass, a customer of the new plant. He had Toledo ties to Brown, Libbey, and the rest of the board. With the encouragement of the board, Bamford started to visit the Charleston plant and make "informal" reports to them and Libbey. His sheet experience gave weight to his opinions. Bamford's reports of problems drew Libbey into the issue. Owens was now fighting on two fronts to bring the Charleston plant online. This played to his tendency to resist any suggestions.

With Libbey's backing eroding, and with a board of administrators and lawyers, Owens was finally tamed from an administration standpoint. Brown brought in a young understudy in 1917, James Blair. He was the son of industrialist Alfred Blair, who had been president of the Wheeling and Lake Erie Railroad and owner of a mining company. James Blair was a dentist with an 1897 degree from the University of Michigan. A native of Toledo, he practiced dentistry in the city for a year, then, bored with dentistry, he accepted a position at Owens Bottle. Brown looked to bring in Blair as another control over Owens. Blair was a Brown loyalist and had his full trust. Blair, however, was also a "Libbey man" and stayed close to Libbey on all decisions. His aristocratic background fit what Libbey and the board favored in corporate managers. Blair excelled early on in administration, setting up an employee stock plan. He was an able enough administrator but never adapted to plant management. The plant and operations managers of Owens Bottle referred to him as "that dentist" or "that pencil pusher." Owens developed a liking for Blair, who always showed great respect for him. Owens was caught up in other battles, which allowed Blair time to develop as Brown had hoped. Blair often brought in "efficiency" experts to study the performance of seasoned managers. It was not surprising that after the death of Libbey and Owens, Blair took over the helm of Libbey-Owens. For years, he would share Owens' strong belief in research and development.

Bamford's reports, however, continued to cause Owens problems. Bamford had the ear of Libbey and the board. He felt that the furnaces were suited for bottle rather than sheet production. Bamford in particular found fault with Jacobs as the plant manager. Bamford felt that Jacobs was using "bottle glass formulas," which he believed would never make good sheet glass. He had a point, and Owens would have recognized that if he had not been so hardheaded. Owens was angered by these formula suggestions and continued to defend Jacobs. Bamford suggested that Owens was overextended with his responsibility and that Jacobs lacked glass-sheet expertise. Eventually, Bamford recommended that Jacobs be replaced, suggesting Seth B. Henshaw, a veteran sheet-glass producer. Henshaw was very similar to Owens, demonstrating a constancy of purpose, a hard-driving work ethic, and a fiery temper. Libbey, now convinced, moved quickly to replace Jacobs with Henshaw. Owens soon resigned as general manager, agreeing that he was overextended and also remaining loyal to Jacobs.

The board appointed Libbey to take over as general manager. He and Henshaw were to have full responsibility for the Charleston plant, with the exception of machine number six, which was to be an experimental operation under Owens. This management shift hurt Owens, who felt that Libbey had let him down. Owens brought his friend Jacobs into the developmental work on machine number six. Mike could not be held down. He grieved the setback, but he mounted a new drive for things he could control. Mike's interests were in two new development areas—automobile glass and optical. The sheet-glass experience had also sparked his interest in the only part of the glass process that remained a hand operation—that of cutting and polishing. New dreams of automation and invention soon diverted Owens' anger and energy. This surprised the board, who half-expected Owens to retire.

Weaknesses Highlighted

The failure to get the Charleston plant running smoothly highlighted Owens' major weaknesses. His hardheadedness had prevented him from hiring the expertise he needed to do the job right. The board had baited Owens into a battle he could not win, but pride blinded him. He was loyal to Jacobs to a fault. Loyalty was a virtue highly prized by the immigrant Irish. Jacobs was typical of an Owens subordinate—he was loyal, his expertise did not threaten Owens, and he looked to Owens for all major decisions. Sadly, as with many of the great industrialists of the time, Owens' lack of formal education made him feel insecure. This kept him from hiring the expertise in chemistry and sheet glass he needed to run the plant. Of course, on the surface there was no sign of insecurity, but it clouded his selection of good subordinates in operating positions. Surprisingly, in his developmental projects, he had always brought in the expertise he needed. Of course, Owens defined expertise in terms of glass experience, not formal education.

Henshaw was just as obstinate and opinionated as Owens, but he was a sheet-glass expert. Yet it was not Henshaw's expertise that made the difference. Henshaw built a strong and expert organization. He immediately brought in sheet-glass men to fill the key positions. This had been one of Owens' hardheaded mistakes. Owens never wanted a lot of experts other than him running around. Henshaw also hired Oliver Brown, who held a degree in chemistry from Cornell University. Oliver Brown had also worked for the Ball Brothers. Henshaw, with Oliver Brown, moved to correct the formulas, which had been the source of many problems. Owens' own stubbornness had prevented him from resolving these issues earlier. He had shown brilliance in creating, perseverance in developing processes, and even at times genius in starting up plant. Owens, however, was not an organization man, and once a plant or company had reached that level of development, he could become a roadblock to smooth operations. This is typical of the careers of Edison, Ford, and many other creative inventors. They needed the freedom to create and experiment in order to function at their best.

Owens' managerial approach is difficult to evaluate fairly. Internal records of the Libbey/Owens companies are biased against Owens because of the board's campaign against him. He was a Victorian manager at the end of the Industrial Revolution, which also colors his approach. Owens was no different from Libbey—both were paternal Victorian managers. They believed in a highly centralized "military command" structure. Owens was a student of military history and found that type of organization best suited for industry as well. He had also grown up with the hierarchical structure of the glasshouse craftsmen. Like most Victorian managers and entrepreneurs, Owens believed in pyramiding control and responsibility using loyal lieutenants. These Victorians were more drivers than leaders. Victorians who found success with this approach usually had people skills and earned respect in their field. As the organization and network under the control of the "Toledo Faction" grew, this hierarchical structure became more difficult to maintain. It has been argued that Owens became a dinosaur in the large organization, but this perception comes from the bias in the corporate records of the time. Owens actually had learned and adapted to the larger organization. He would always be the general, but his poor health had forced him to delegate more. In fact, Owens did not have a problem delegating, assuming he had loyal and obedient managers in place.

Owens could be a difficult boss to work for; he demanded long hours and dedication to the job. He pushed hard and had a famous temper. He required punctuality. He liked being called "boss." He grew up in an industrial town where plant superintendents were considered gods, which defined his style to a degree. He was not afraid to yell or even kick someone in the butt. Stories exist of Mike using his fists in the early days of Libbey Glass. He managed with a physical presence not often seen today but common in the Industrial Revolution. William Fairfield noted, "There is no room in the boat for passengers; everyone rows or they find themselves swimming." Mike was not afraid to fire someone who could not meet his performance standards. Owens also demanded employee loyalty and a chain of command. Of course, he was overly sensitive here because of the strange network of "spies" in his organizations. Yet, if you could meet his requirements and demands, you were assured a powerful and lifelong ally.

Owens' hardheadedness had cost him in the area of glass chemistry. One of the major problems that dogged the Charleston plant was crizzling of the glass. Owens adjusted annealing and glass formulas but was ignorant of the technical problem. His constant adjusting of glass formulas made the problem worse. Owens just would not give up his "right" to control the glass melt mix. That stubbornness cost both the company and Owens. George Ravenscroft had first noted the chemistry problem of crizzling in the 1600s. Adjusting potash and lead could have helped. A degreed glass chemist could have saved Owens years of technical and personal problems. A chemist would have made the difference in his battle with the board. His pride was always his Achilles' heel.

Henshaw for months basked in the turnaround of the Charleston plant. It contributed to an amazing 1920 manufacturing profit of $4.2 million for Libbey-Owens. This allowed Libbey to announce plans for even more expansion. Henshaw's ego was even bigger than Owens', but Henshaw lacked his "Irish charm." Henshaw tried to follow Owens as a type of corporate emperor, but the board would have none of it. In particular, newly named Vice-Pres. James Blair would have no part of it. Henshaw had become drunk with success, feeling he *was* the "Faction." He believed he had replaced Owens on the throne. But Mike Owens was one of a kind, and Henshaw was no Mike Owens. Blair had been a Libbey and board man, but he revered Owens. Henshaw battled Blair openly. He refused his phone calls and told him to stay out of the operations. Blair hired a group of efficiency experts, Stevenson & Harrison & Jordan, to review the organization at Charleston. Blair was also a brilliant administrator and had hired Thomas McKinley, a window-glass expert, to back up Henshaw. Henshaw flatly refused to cooperate with or even talk to the efficiency experts. Blair called Henshaw and McKinley to an emergency board meeting on July 27, 1921. At the meeting, Blair presented Henshaw with a letter of dismissal and promoted McKinley to plant manager.

Owens would move back to his role as developmental manager for the companies of the "Toledo Faction." Again, however, the board and the other administrators had a different view of corporate research than did Owens. They saw it as a well-defined function, with university-trained engineers and scientists. Owens had refused to add such a chemist. He felt that glass chemistry should be learned from experience. Unfortunately, both sides were at extremes, when a more moderate approach could have helped. Ultimately, the board hired Elbert Fisher, a Cornell University trained chemist. A merger of twentieth-century science and pragmatic Victorian engineering would not be possible. Research became more disciplined and expert, but it lacked fire and drive. Owens' "drive" produced a model for R&D that integrated operations and profitability. There seems to be some evidence that fire and drive were significant factors in the advance of technology. Charles Murray, in his exhaustive, statistical study of scientific developments over the last thousand years, shows a decline since about 1890.[2] This came as the twentieth century saw large growth in a rigid corporate R&D model. This beaucratic R&D function tends to be too removed from operations and the bottom line.

Technology sales were just starting for Libbey-Owens Sheet in 1919. The Colburn process threatened the whole makeup of the sheet industry. The Belgian Fourcault process was able to compete, but the Lubbers cylinder glass was made obsolete. Early on in 1919, the Japanese had visited the Charleston plant and were sold on the Colburn process. Machine manufacture was subcontracted with Kent-Owens Machine Company. This became the first of many foreign sales and license agreements. Libbey, with Schmettau, took personal charge of European sales. In 1920, Libbey-Owens reported its profit of $4.2 million, as the Colburn machine started to pay the dividends Owens had foreseen years earlier. Many had forgotten that it was Owens who had saved the Colburn machine from the scrap heap in 1912.

Now free of administrative duties, Owens returned to dreaming and creating. Automobile applications had taken hold of his imagination. The Colburn process had eliminated most of the distortion of cylinder-produced glass. Owens already had one of the six Colburn machines at Charleston tied up in optical development, but he won Libbey's support to dedicate machine number three to automobile work. Owens again had his finger on the pulse of the market. The automobile market was rapidly overtaking windows as the key glass segment. Owens was a few steps ahead of Henry Ford, who also saw the huge potential of Colburn process glass. Owens developed a thinner double-strength product than did his competitors. Henry Ford followed Owens' work closely in continuously producing automobile sheet glass and would ultimately move into the glass business. By 1929, auto glass made up 50 percent of sheet-glass production. Owens had seen the market potential. The Libbey-Owens board, however, wanted only to become the premier producer of window glass.

The Colburn machine made excellent glass for autos compared to the cylinder process, but it was far from perfect. As automobile speeds improved, however, a new problem arose. The surface of Colburn glass had microscopic glazing. As long as you were looking directly into the glass without any motion, you could not notice the glazing. When the automobile was in motion, these slight waves on the glass created a distortion. Prolonged driving caused eye fatigue. One solution was to grind and polish the sheets, but this added costs. Most grind-and-polish operations, like those being done at Edward Ford Plate Glass, across the river from Owens' office, were hand driven. Owens wanted to develop machines to do the polishing, seeing this as another opportunity for automation. At first the Libbey-Owens board balked at the idea. They reminded Mike of the problems that resulted from him jumping into a new area at Charleston—in particular, how he had used bottle-furnace design for sheet glass and how a sheet expert was needed to straighten out the problem.

Once again, the board suggested Owens hire a man with

experience in polishing to investigate the idea. But this was Mike's idea, and he was not going to pass on developmental work. Owens relentlessly hammered Libbey with his ideas and the potential in the automotive market. Like so many times in the past, Libbey finally gave Owens permission to start an experimental operation. Libbey, as usual, hoped that Owens' passion would sideline him for some time. It was a decision that years later would lead Libbey-Owens Sheet into the safety-glass market. It would also result in ties with local sheet-glass maker Edward Ford, who joined the Libbey-Owens board. This would ultimately lead to the formation of Libbey-Owens-Ford Glass through the merger of the two Toledo companies.[3]

The year before his death, Owens had taken an interest in the manufacture of safety glass. He prophesied its future in a July 1922 article of *American Magazine*. Owens hit a piece of safety glass for the reporter, noting its application for an auto windshield. Mike pointed out:

> Suppose you were sitting in the front seat of any motor car with the glass windshield in front of you. Scores of persons have been terribly cut by broken glass under such circumstances. It is not an uncommon thing for a person to be thrown against one of the windows with a force enough to break it, and receive cuts around the face and head. But this glass does not shatter to pieces.

In 1910 a laminated sandwich of glass plates (known as Triplex) was being produced in Europe for automotive applications. Both Henry Ford and Michael Owens had followed the European development, realizing the potential of the product. The discovery of a shatterproof glass had been one of serendipity in 1903. French chemist Edouard Benedictus had accidentally dropped a flask coated with celluloid and was amazed at its shatter resistance. Years later he developed a shatterproof glass consisting of a piece of celluloid sandwiched between two sheets of glass using gelatin as a bonding agent. Before Benedictus's successful product emerged, an English chemist in 1906 patented a similar product with Canadian balsam as a bonding agent. Both products had manufacturing problems, high costs, and product imperfections. World War I saw some less-demanding, non-automotive applications, such as goggles, gas-mask lenses, and airplane windshields. By 1920 Henry Ford was demanding its use in his Model T, citing the fact that over half the injuries in the Model T were related to shattered glass. Still, safety glass distorted vision because of the poor processing, and the cost was over $250 to equip a car. It was the perfect technical challenge to attract Michael Owens.

Owens was actively involved in the basic research of the problem as early as 1919. He had convinced his young protégé and Libbey-Owens vice-president James Blair to start a survey of the available technology. The Owens R&D method then called for the formulation of a developmental and experimental strategy and then for the setting up of a small experimental operation. Blair would institutionalize the Owens approach.

The administrative approach of men like Blair was very much in vogue. Owens' hardheaded manner was becoming a problem for Libbey. Libbey wanted to retire to museum work, with a stable organization running his business. He tired of the costs of Owens' impulsive decisions, unwillingness to compromise, and combative business approach. Not only was Libbey defending Owens internally, but often externally as well. The *National Glass Budget* had written of Owens' "extravagant egotism and intellectual arrogance" since 1909. Even the *Budget* had to honor his success, however, writing in a 1910 article: "Having thus advanced himself from a position in the trade of no greater comparative importance than a pimple on a pickle to that of being the admitted greatest glasshouse manager this country has ever produced, he is entitled to unstinted credit, not an iota of which would the *Budget* deny him."

Libbey was growing less tolerant of Owens by 1917. Libbey liked to function quietly in business, with little press or fanfare. Owens' financial adventures were also an embarrassment to Libbey and the "Todelo Faction." Libbey would have preferred Mike's charity to be more community oriented and public. Mike focused his charity at the church and personal level. Libbey was not a churchgoer and disliked formal religion.

Even Mike's political views were becoming a liability. By 1917 Owens had joined the Friends of Irish Freedom, a U.S.-Irish organization founded to support the IRA. Owens was president of the Toledo chapter (Wolfe Tone Branch). Owens from his boyhood was interested in and closely followed the Irish freedom movement. The Friends of Irish Freedom were considered hardliners and opposed a divided Ireland. No records exist, but Owens' financial support appears to have been substantial. When Eamon De Valera, future president of the Irish Republic, visited Toledo and Cleveland in March of 1919, Toledo donated $150,000 to the cause while Cleveland gave only $50,000. The difference can be attributed to donations by Michael Owens. With America's entry into World War I, the U.S. government moved to restrict the Friends. Woodrow Wilson ordered Secret Service agents to examine their finances. It has since been confirmed that the organization was a front for Clan na Gael, a secret Irish society, which Owens belonged to from about 1910. Even his family members knew little of his involvement. Clan na Gael funneled American money to the Irish revolution. The extent of the federal investigation of Owens is not known, but Owens played a key role in both the Friends and Clan na Gael. Libbey found these types of political and religious affiliations distasteful, and the boards of Owens Bottle and Libbey-Owens Sheet found them dangerous. With its monopolistic behavior, the last thing Owens Bottle wanted was any type of government investigation.

The Final Years

Another dramatic change in the "Toledo Faction" occurred with the death of Clarence Brown, in July of 1918. Brown, who had dominated the boards of Owens Bottle, Toledo Glass, and Libbey-Owens Sheet, left his legacy in the makeup of the boards. He had brought in Geddes, Fowle, Schmettau, Boshart, and Blair. He had been Owens' biggest adversary on those boards. In many ways Brown and Owens were diametrical opposites in their approach to business. Libbey often used Brown to play "bad cop" to mute Owens. Owens called Brown a "damn lawyer." Brown resented Owens' importance in the organization and always felt he needed to be restrained. Brown had little interest in how the money was made, and he often rejected the expansion of glass-making operations, preferring licensing and machine rentals. Owens always aggressively supported glassmaking ventures and horizontal expansion. Brown was a lawyer with no roots in the manufacture of glass. He kept the most extensive files and records of the "Toledo Faction," and these form a major part of the Owens-Illinois early archives. Brown's views have therefore been given heavy weight in history. Both Owens and Brown were tough political fighters, but both were generous in their own way. Upon Brown's death, he left a large portion of his estate to charity. Family challenged the estate, which resulted in Toledo's greatest court fight. It was settled twenty-two years after the death of his wife. Ultimately, his estate went to charities such as Toledo, St. Vincent's, Flower, and Mercy hospitals and the YMCA. Other than Edward Libbey, Brown remains the greatest philanthropist in Toledo's history.

The Libbey-Owens Sheet board changed the most after Brown's death. Members would be Owens, Geddes, Libbey, Schmettau, Henshaw, Blair, Fowle, and Boshart. The officers of the company defined the power structure: Libbey, president; Owens, vice-president; Blair, vice-president and general manager; Fowle, treasurer; Schmettau, secretary; and Henshaw, assistant general manager. Blair was the big winner, being on the board and general manager of both Libbey-Owens Sheet and Owens Bottle. Another rising star was John D. Biggers, who was vice-president and assistant general manager at Owens Bottle. Both Blair and Biggers had the support of both Libbey and Owens. They would be the future of the "Toledo Faction."

In 1919, Blair was named general manager of both Owens Bottle and Libbey-Owens. Owens remained vice-president of Libbey-Owens. Libbey, as usual, worked behind the scenes to maintain balance and calm Owens. Libbey is said to have told Owens he should never overrule or give orders contrary to Blair's and to have told Blair to discuss all matters with Owens. Blair would later say that Owens was the power behind his throne.

Owens, 1921. (Owens-Illinois Glass Company Records, MSS-200, the Ward M. Canaday Center for Special Collections, University of Toledo)

Owens with Owens Bottle and Owens-Illinois sales force, 1921. (Owens-Illinois Glass Company Records, MSS-200, the Ward M. Canaday Center for Special Collections, University of Toledo)

Blair seemed to avoid Owens' resentment because Owens rightly blamed Libbey for his steady decrease in power, and Owens had come to like Blair. Owens also gave Blair tacit approval. Owens was even talking about the transfer of power to the "younger generation." Some of this was due to Owens focusing more on advancing his legacy through his projects. He realized he did not have the time for endless administration battles.

The transfer of operating control did come about, and it went smoothly, because Blair had the utmost respect for Owens. Blair had shown his toughness with the firing of Henshaw, an action

Owens probably applauded. Owens and Blair seemed to function well together.

Owens took the step down in power better than in earlier times because of his health. As we have seen, he tried to adjust his lifestyle, but he could not pull away from work entirely. Even with more leisure activities and Florida trips, he kept working full time.

Golf, in particular, became an outside passion. Although Mike had his own "winter rules," he saw no difference between putting a ball on a tuft of grass and teeing it up with a mound of sand. So at Inverness Golf Club, his caddy always carried sand for Owens to tee up with. Golf, however, really did not provide much relaxation. At times, Owens responded to his poor shots by throwing his club. He was a competitor even at play. He refused to play with "slow" players. By his death, Owens was considered a fair golfer and used it for business. He gave memberships to many Libbey-Owens managers so he could have his afternoon foursomes. Still, it was more relaxing for him to do business in the fresh air.

In his later years, Owens pursued his boyhood passions for reading and history. In particular, he continued to build an outstanding library on Napoleonic and Civil War battles. He spent most of his evenings reading. In his last five years alone, Owens spent $30,000 on books (equivalent to about a half-million dollars today!).[4] He loved cars to the end of his life as well.

The period from 1917 to Owens' death in 1923 was one of tremendous growth for Libbey-Owens Sheet Glass. Sheet glass was experiencing a huge boom, driven by the general economy and the increasing automotive market. Libbey-Owens took over United States Sheet & Window Glass Company and built a large sheet plant in Shreveport, Louisiana. In addition, it acquired controlling shares in West Virginia and Louisiana gas companies. Libbey-Owens also developed and improved on wider sheet machines. It incorporated Fairfield Glass Company in Lancaster, Ohio. Mike Owens led the installation of some new wide machines there and joined the Lancaster Golf Club to pass the time and do business. Libbey-Owens also expanded operations and machine sales in Belgium, France, Switzerland, and Germany. It established its headquarters on the twelfth floor of the new Nicholas Building (later renamed the National Bank Building) on Toledo's Madison Avenue. Profits of the company continued to climb, making everyone in the "Toledo Faction" extremely wealthy.

Owens' personal assets were also growing at a fast pace. He was a millionaire many times over, even with his constant giving and spending. As with other areas of his life, Mike left few records dealing with finances. He was what the Irish of the time called "fruit-on-the-table Irish," meaning wealthy Irish who did not forget their origins (as opposed to "lace-curtain Irish"). Mike gave large amounts of cash to help various Irish national organizations as well as Catholic churches in Ohio.

Meanwhile, Mike's son, Ray, was involved in prolonged and very public divorce proceedings in Beverly Hills. Owens started to move cash directly to his son, in case of his death, so that his soon-to-be-ex-wife could not make claims on the estate. The amount Mike gave to his son was significant but has never been accounted for. Mike seemed to be well aware of his failing health, since it was not typical for him to do such advanced financial planning. A lawsuit over the transfer continued for years after his death. His will actually "cut" Ray out of the formal estate distribution so that his ex-wife could not get any money. Mike's preparation can be attributed to his trusted friend and lawyer, J. H. McNerney.

While sheet glass was booming, Owens never lost his interest in bottle production and Owens Bottle Company. From 1917 to 1923, Owens constantly struggled to improve the automatic bottle machine while developing the Colburn machine. The board was content to maximize short-term profits by neglecting developmental expenses for bottle manufacture. They merely wanted to ride out the patent-advantage time, even though industry experts believed that Owens was a full ten years ahead of the competition at the start. Again, the board, led by Brown and Geddes, preferred to buy out competitive patents. This strategy was their alternative to the aggressive development work that Owens felt was necessary. Still, Owens continued to push development until his death. His first machine could produce 13,000 two-ounce bottles per day; his last machine built shortly before his death could do 300,000 two-ounces bottles a day. His greatest machine was released soon after his death by LaFrance. It could make over a million prescription bottles a day, requiring plants to slow production so as not to flood the marketplace. Owens knew the technology of the industry better than the board did. He also knew business better than they thought he did. High profits, royalties, and market control tend to inspire further invention. Owens correctly realized that, in the long run, manufacturing dominance resulted from technology and process dominance.

In 1912, a consortium called Hartford, consisting of Beechnut Packing Company, the Monongah Glass Company, and a group of Hartford engineers, formed to produce an improved bottle machine for Beechnut. It took years, but they succeeded. They improved on the feeder systems, which greatly improved the quality of the bottles produced. Owens Bottle felt that it had purchased the feeder patents and unsuccessfully tried to stop Hartford-Empire (the company name changed in 1922). Owens argued that legal competition was no substitution for product development. He had realized that the weakness in his machine lay in the feeder system, and he was constantly experimenting in this area. The Hartford-Empire machine development exploited this one weakness. By 1922, Hartford-Empire machines were competing successfully with the Owens machine for the production of one-pint and one-quart whiskey and milk bottles. In 1924, after Owens' death, Owens Bottle came to a legal compromise with Hartford-Empire. It was a shared royalty and licensing agreement.

The last day of Owens' life was typical of his whole life. He never gave up his inventive drive. He called a board meeting of Owens Bottle Company to explore new ideas in bottle making. Owens was sixty-four and silver haired by December of 1923. He was well aware of his failing health, but so many times in his life he had worked to exhaustion, requiring hospitalization. December 27, 1923, was a cold and raw day, but as usual Mike was focused on a new project. He wanted to present a plan for development work at the Charleston plant of Libbey-Owens Sheet. The company directors, Libbey, Blair, Boshart, Biggers, and William Ford, had assembled at the company offices in the Nicholas Building. The meeting had been going for an hour when Mike rose and said, "Excuse me for a moment, gentlemen." He staggered down the hall to a couch in Biggers' office. Biggers had followed him, sensing a problem.

Biggers found him struggling for air and asked what the trouble was. Mike replied that he was ill and asked that Father Dean of Rosary Cathedral be called. Mike's first concern was for his soul, which was typical of his strong faith. Biggers called Father Dean and the doctors. Father Dean arrived and gave Mike the last sacraments of his faith. A peace came over him as the doctors tried to save him. He died shortly after. Libbey was visually shaken and cried as Mike's body was removed. Libbey needed the help of associates to get home. Michael's wife was called at their Collingwood Avenue home (formerly the house of Bishop Schrembs).[5]

Owens' grave in Toledo. (Owens-Illinois Glass Company Records, MSS-200, the Ward M. Canaday Center for Special Collections, University of Toledo)

His death stunned the city of Toledo. The day of his funeral, schoolchildren were given the day off. The funeral mass was held at Rosary Cathedral. Father Dean was the celebrant, and Fr. George Johnson delivered the sermon. Dr. Johnson had been one of the priests whose education Mike had sponsored. He would go on to become a monsignor and director of Catholic Welfare. In addition, many other priest friends of Mike were present, including Bishop Stritch of Toledo (a future cardinal) and Bishop O'Connell of New York. Mike had left his mark on the Catholic diocese of Toledo but with no markers or plaques, at his own request. His greatest legacy, however, was not the buildings but the young priests he helped educate. Among the pallbearers were J. H. McNerney, his trusted friend and executor; William Clarke and Tom Rowe, national labor leaders for the glass industry; and Sam Cochrane, who had come up with Owens from West Virginia.

The whole city mourned as a procession of limousines stretched for blocks on the way to Calvary Cemetery. Probably his greatest admirers were the unknown thousands watching from the sidewalks to whom Mike had given financial help and personal encouragement.

CHAPTER 13

The Owens Legacy

The real tribute to Michael Owens' vision was that, at his death, 94 out of every 100 bottles were produced on Owens Bottle Machines. Honors continued long after his death. In 1959, to honor the 100th birthday of Michael Owens, an unusual ritual took place. Plaques honoring Michael Owens were hung simultaneously at thirty-four Owens-Illinois Glass Company plants in thirty-three U.S. cities. This honor seems only fitting, since he had been awarded the Franklin Institute's Elliott Cresson Award for advances in the mechanical arts. Michael Owens took a handcraft industry into full automation with machines that produced bottles, light bulbs, and plate glass. His inventions were critical to electric lighting, reduction of child labor, packaging, food preservation, beer and milk distribution, advanced optics, and automotive safety. Other than Edison's light bulb, no other invention rivals the glass-bottle machine as to its impact on society. The glass-bottle-making machine was the most complex machine of its time. In 1982, the American Society of Mechanical Engineers declared the Owens Bottle Machine an International Engineering Landmark.

Owens belongs in the pantheon of the world's greatest inventors. He had forty-nine patents. We have seen many similarities and differences between the styles of Owens and other inventors. But at his core, he shared with them that spark of creative energy that all inventors have. He found happiness in the thrill of creation and the joy of achievement. He loved the mountainous challenge of going into a new area of technical exploration. The thrill was in his mind not his hands. While he had many short-comings as a manager, he excelled in what we call today project management. Owens deserves the title of father of project management for his work from 1910 to 1923. The machines he brought into being represented the most complex and cutting edge of the age. Spin-off technologies included standardization, gauge control, and automated control.

Owens remains the avatar of focused invention. While he dom-inated his industry, he found inventive interests in other areas as well, which is typical of men such as Owens, Edison, Westinghouse, and Ford. His brother Tom noted that, at one time, Owens was experimenting with making gas from oil. He was also interested in folding streetcar doors and steps, but nothing came of it. Near the end of his life, Owens had begun to study the production of safety glass for automobile windows. He did make significant contributions to the equipment for automatic filling of bottles. He invented a catsup-filling machine and worked on milk-filling machines. Owens designed a number of special rail-road cars to handle raw materials.

Owens pioneered the concept of project management as an approach to corporate research and development. He would have excelled in any industry, but serendipity did play a role in his finding a backer such as Edward Libbey. In the end, the team of Libbey-Owens would set the model for all corporate research and its management. It was the perfect blend of risk taking, mar-ket analysis, and finance.

Still, with all the honors, Michael J. Owens has not been given his proper place in the pantheon of inventors. This can be seen in the continued failure of Owens to gain entrance into the Inventors Hall of Fame in Akron, Ohio. This failure seems relat-ed to the industrial nature of his inventions as well as the lack of biographical records. Owens had avoided the press his whole life, and Libbey kept his inventions below the government's radar because of their monopolistic implications. Even more amazing is that Owens' machines failed to make Charles Murray's list of critical and significant inventions. One reason is that the various automated glass-making machines were not consumer inventions, such as the telephone, automobile, electric light, and computer. Few people today can name the key inventors of the business computer, but almost everyone can point to Steve Jobs' and Bill Gates' roles in developing the personal computer. Owens never had a corporate propaganda machine the way Ford, Edison, and Westinghouse did. This was an indirect result of the campaigns against Owens by "Toledo Faction" board members. Libbey also downplayed the organization's success in order to stay out of the sight of government regulators. Another factor is that Owens always remained in the shadow of his boss—Edward Libbey. Biographers have ignored both men because of a lack of personal records; the focus has been on the corporate histories of the companies they founded. There has also been a tendency to reduce the Owens legacy to a series of mythical stories repeated over the years. Walbridge and LaFrance, in particular, seem to have revised the historical facts.

Mike had an unusual poem hanging on his wall that many in the press had noted over the years.

IT CAN BE DONE

Somebody said that it couldn't be done
    But he, with a chuckle, replied:
That "maybe it couldn't," but he would be one
    Who wouldn't say so till he'd tried.
So he buckled right in, with a trace of a grin
    On his face. If he worried, he hid it.
He started to sing as he tackled the thing
    That couldn't be done and he did it.
Somebody scoffed: "Oh, you'll never do that;
    At least no one ever had done it."
But he took off his coat and he took off his hat.
    And the first thing we knew he'd begun it.
With the nod of his chin, and a bit of a grin,
    Without any doubting or quiddit,
He started to sing as he tackled the thing
    That couldn't be done, and he did it.

There are thousands to tell you it cannot be done.
    There are thousands to prophesy failure.
There are thousands to point to you, one by one,
    The dangers that await to assail you.
But just buckle in, with a bit of a grin,
    Then take off your coat and go to it;
Just start in to sing as you tackle the thing
    That "cannot be done," and you'll do it.

The poem, while simple and somewhat self-serving, does capture Owens' strong drive to succeed at a difficult task. Even the press often seemed to believe in his ability to make things work. It was Mike's revenge on the board to be successful. He embodied the Irish tradition of not hurting or humiliating his opposition but surpassing it in the glory of success. When Owens was put down or attacked, his response was to reach higher achievements. He used the energy of the resentment to produce something positive.

The editorial of the *Toledo Blade* upon his death put it this way.

> Mr. Owens was a genius—a successful genius. He maintained an unwavering faith in his work and was undaunted by the scoffing and skepticism of glassblowers and mechanics older and more experienced than himself. He possessed the power of perseverance, the ability to concentrate and withal a sense of humor.

The *Toledo Times* editorial of the same day mimicked the *Blade:*

> In the early days of his work of an inventor, when he possessed only a general idea of the bottle machine that was to bring him fame and wealth, he was told that the plan was "impractical." Experts sought to discourage him; offered him no hope, told him that he would surely fail. But Owens smiled and went back to his workshop.

Edward Libbey echoed all this in his eulogy of Michael Owens: "His creative mind, his resourcefulness, his method of investigation, his great vision, his indomitable will in surmounting all difficulties, his simplicity, and his faith in his fellow man, class him in my estimation as an unusually great man." And finally came this tribute by the president of the Flint Union: "It has been stated that he revolutionized the glass industry of the world, and this is no exaggeration. He accomplished things in the way of producing glassware by automatic machinery that astounded those not familiar with the progress he had made step by step, even those well informed frequently stood in amazement at his achievements."

The 1959 plaque ceremony took place on September 3. It also marked the fifty-sixth anniversary of the founding of Owens Bottle Company. The plaques were multicolored glass, bearing a representation of Mike Owens and his bottle machine. The inscription read: "Developer and inventor of automatic glass-forming machines that helped eliminate child labor and benefited his fellow man by bringing mass production methods to the industry he served. His name lives in the corporate titles of the three leading companies that continue to make glass an increasingly useful servant of mankind." The three companies referred to at the time (1959) were Owens-Illinois, formed in 1929 with the merger of Owens Bottle and Illinois Glass; Libbey-Owens-Ford Glass, formed in 1930 with the merger of Libbey-Owens and Ford Plate Glass; and Owens-Corning Fiberglass. John Biggers, then chairman of Libbey-Owens-Ford Glass, made the Toledo presentation.

The industrial recognition of Michael Owens continued while his public recognition faded. In 1971, Westinghouse Electric hailed the great inventions of Owens in its calendar: "It was a revolutionary idea that was totally foreign to the thinking of the glass industry and one man who was willing to entertain the idea of change was Edward Drummond Libbey, the owner of the New England concern. Mr. Libbey saw the soundness of Owens's ideas and let him go ahead, encouraging him when he ran into difficulties. Thanks to Mike Owens and his contemporaries, they made glass a commodity rather than a luxury and glass is now an important part of our environment." The making of a commodity, like the elimination of child labor, was a consequence, not goal, of Owens' effort. Mike had achieved his own goal to become

Edward Libbey, 1923. (Owens-Illinois Glass Company Records, MSS-200, the Ward M. Canaday Center for Special Collections, University of Toledo)

the Napoleon of Industry. His greatest contribution to his fellow-men could be found in the thousands he helped with his anonymous giving. In 1982, Owens Technical Institute was established in northwest Ohio to honor him. Today Owens Community College is one of the largest technical community colleges in the United States.

At the 1900 Universal Exposition in Paris, it was prophesied: "Steel and glass are without a doubt the two substances that will characterize the 20th century and give it their names." Certainly, the name of Owens dominated the twentieth century.

Notes

Chapter 1

1. Actually, with Edward Libbey's propensity for forming companies in various states and countries, the Owens name was found in well over twenty companies, such as Pacific Libbey-Owens Sheet and Canadian Libbey-Owens.

2. Macfarlane, Alan, "Modern World Has Heart of Glass," *New Scientist* 11 (September 2004): 14.

3. Apsely Pellatt, *Curiosities of Glass Making* (London, 1849), 23.

4. Warren Scoville, *Revolution in Glassmaking* (Cambridge: Harvard University Press, 1949), 32.

5. Ibid., 33.

6. Ernie Pyle, *The Journal of Ernie Pyle, 1900-1945* (Toledo: Libbey Glass, 1941), 101.

7. Pearce Davis, *The Development of the American Glass Industry* (New York: Russell & Russell, 1949), 126.

Chapter 2

1. Carl Bridenbaugh, *The Colonial Craftsman* (New York: Dover, 1990), 44.

2. Lura Woodside Watkins, *American Glass and Glassmaking* (London: Max Parrish, 1950), 28.

3. Deming Jarves, *Reminiscences of Glass,* 2nd ed. (New York: Beatrice Weinstock, 1969), 48.

4. Scoville, 33.

Chapter 3

1. Keene Sumner, "Don't Try to Carry the Whole World on Your Shoulders," *American Magazine* (July 1922).

2. "The Owens Story," *Columbia Magazine* (June 1959).

3. E. William Fairfield, *Fire and Sand* (Cleveland: Lezius-Hiles, 1960), 6.

4. *Wheeling Daily Intelligencer,* September 14, 1886.

5. *Toledo News Bee,* November 13, 1930.

6. Ohio's minimum age was mostly ignored by the state's glasshouses.

7. Jack Paquette, *Blowpipes: Northwest Ohio Glassmaking in the Gas Boom of the 1880s* (Xlibris: 2002), 477.

8. Sumner.

9. Ibid.

10. Paquette, appendix B.

Chapter 4

1. Jim Mollenkopf, *The Great Black Swamp* (Toledo: Cat, 2000), 18.

2. Toledo Business Association, *The Industrial Advantages of Toledo, Ohio* (Toledo: James McKinney, 1892), 15.

3. *Toledo Blade,* May 5, 1888.

4. Allen Sanders, "Genius of the Bottle," *Toledo News Bee,* November 30, 1934.

5. *Toledo Blade,* May 5, 1888.

Chapter 5

1. Randolph Downes, *Industrial Beginnings* (Toledo: The Historical Society of Northwestern Ohio, 1954), 14.

2. Toledo Business Association, 27.

3. *Toledo Bee,* February 17, 1901.

4. Scoville, 80.

5. Paquette, 332.

6. Businessmen Association publication (1888), 23.

7. Downes, 75.

8. Fairfield, 25.

9. Ibid.

Chapter 6

1. Paquette, 324.

2. Fairfield, 31.

3. Edward Meigh, "The Development of the Automatic Glass Bottle Machine," *Glass Technology* 4 (February 1960). See also Fairfield.

4. Ralph W. Heller, "Edward Drummond Libbey: Gentleman, Citizen, Pioneer Glassmaker" (thesis, University of Toledo, 1948).

5. Scoville, 277.

6. Fairfield, 38.

7. "Plaques honor Mike Owens," *Toledo Catholic Chronicle,* September 11, 1959.

8. Fairfield, 25.

9. Heller, 27.

Chapter 7

1. John Winthrop, *Men and Volts* (New York: Lippincott, 1941).

2. Paquette, 97.

3. American Society of Mechanical Engineers, Corning Glass Dedication Program (1983).

4. Ben Pope, internal memo, Owens-Illinois (September 1959).

5. Scoville, 94.

6. *National Glass Budget,* June 25, 1898.

Chapter 8

1. Fairfield, 46.
2. *National Glass Budget,* July 29, 1899.

Chapter 9

1. Scoville, 291.
2. Marshall Dimock, *The Executive in Action* (New York: Harper and Brothers, 1949), 252.
3. Bock is best remembered in Toledo for his donation of the bronze statue of naturalist John Burroughs at the Toledo Museum. In addition, he left a beautiful mansion and gardens in Rossford.
4. Scoville, 325.

Chapter 10

1. *Toledo Bee,* October 10, 1924.
2. *National Glass Budget,* November 23, 1903.
3. Davis, 28.
4. This was the intial incorporated name. In 1919, the board voted to change it to Owens Bottle Company.
5. Paquette, 361.
6. Meigh, 32.

Chapter 11

1. Henry Ford, *My Life and Work* (New York: Doubleday, 1922), 39.
2. Address of M. J. Owens before the Proprietary Association, Hotel Astor, New York, May 7, 1922.
3. C. Philips, *Glass: The Miracle Maker* (New York: Pitman, 1941), 202.
4. *National Glass Budget,* August 17, 1912.
5. Ibid.
6. Paquette, 48.

Chapter 12

1. Quentin Skrabec, *The Boys of Braddock* (Heritage, 2004).

2. Charles Murray, *Human Accomplishments* (New York: HarperCollins, 2003).

3. Ford Plate Glass and Libbey-Owens merged in 1930 to form Libbey-Owens-Ford Glass.

4. "The Batch," Libbey-Owens-Ford newsletter, January 1941.

5. The house at 2345 Collingwood Avenue in Toledo's West End was demolished in 1959. Mary Owens had long before sold the house, moving into an apartment in the Commodore Perry Hotel. Mary Owens died March 18, 1948.

Bibliography

Aiken, E. William. *The Roots Grow Deep*. Cleveland: Lezius-Hiles, 1957.

American Society of Mechanical Engineers. "International Landmark Award." Toledo: 1983.

Broderick, John. *Forty Years with General Electric*. Albany: Orange, 1929.

Clark, V. S. *History of Manufacturers in the United States*. Washington: Carnegie Institute, 1916.

Diamond, Freda. *The Story of Glass*. New York: Harcourt, Brace & World, 1953.

Fairfield, E. William. *Fire & Sand*. Cleveland: Lezius-Hiles, 1960.

Fauster, Carl. *Libbey Glass, Since 1818*. Toledo: Len Beach, 1979.

Fowle, Arthur. *Flat Glass*. Toledo: Libbey-Owens Glass, 1924.

Hallenbeck, Thomas. Papers, interviews, and research on the glass industry. Lucas County Library, History Room, Toledo.

Harrington, J. *Glassmaking at Jamestown*. Richmond: Dietz, 1952.

Heller, Ralph. "Edward Drummond Libbey: Gentleman, Citizen, Pioneer Glassmaker." Thesis. University of Toledo, 1948.

Jarves, Deming. *Reminiscences of Glass Making*. New York: Houghton, 1965.

Lezius, W. "The Glass Industry in Toledo and Environs." Thesis. University of Toledo, 1937.

Paquette, Jack. *Blowpipes*. Xlibris, 2002.

———. Papers. University of Toledo Archives.

———. *The Glassmakers*. Toledo: Trumpeting Angel, 1994.

Phillips, C. *Glass, the Miracle Maker.* London: Pitman & Sons, 1948.

Scoville, Warren. *Revolution in Glassmaking.* Cambridge, Mass.: Harvard University Press, 1949.

Skrabec, Quentin. *The Boys of Braddock.* Westminster, Md.: Heritage, 2004.

Spillman, Jane. *Glassmaking: America's First Industry.* Corning, N.Y.: Corning Museum, 1976.

Walbridge, William. *American Bottles.* Toledo: Caslon, 1920.

Wilson, Kenneth. *American Glass.* New York: Hudson Hills, 1994.

Index